THE BOOK OF
LLANGAIN
From Farming Community to Residential Village

HAYDN WILLIAMS

HALSGROVE

First published in Great Britain in 2007

British Library Cataloguing-in-Publication Data.
A CIP record for this title is available from the British Library.

ISBN 978 1 84114 636 2

HALSGROVE

Halsgrove House
Bagley Road, Wellington
Somerset TA21 9PZ
T: 01823 653777
F: 01823 216796
Email: sales@halsgrove.com
Website: www.halsgrove.com

Frontispiece photograph: *On their way to milk by hand at Gilfach, 1930.*
Left to right: *Sarah the maid, Mollie Evans.*
Left to right: *Irene Jones (Minyrafon), Dilys John (Islwyn), Mollie Evans (Gilfach).*

Printed and bound in Great Britain by CPI Antony Rowe Ltd, Wiltshire

Foreword

BY J. TOWYN JONES

PRESIDENT OF THE CARMARTHENSHIRE ANTIQUARIAN SOCIETY

"Hold hard, these ancient minutes..." so said a renowned poet who held these acres dear and immortalised Fernhill in his famous poem of that title. Dylan Thomas' close association with the area certainly ensured that Llangain achieved international fame through his work. The admirable and definitive study by David N.Thomas, the prime authority on the poet, *Dylan Remembered* Volume One 1914-1934, published by Seren, 2003, is based on interviews of local characters, Dylan's family and friends by Colin Edwards in the 1960s. His connections with the district are thus exhaustively examined and so many of those names, faces and places appear in the pages of this delightful present volume.

Places like Lletyrneuadd, where I well recall old Mrs Lewis speaking of Dylan as a babe in arms. Llangain has a profusion of such particularly lyrical place names, full of historical significance and I fervently hope that these ancient Welsh names will prevail and that the culture they represent will be understood, respected and loved.

Surely such a magnificent publication as this will not only play an effective role in that capacity, it will also enrich the lives of those who have made Llangain their home and promote awareness of the colourful heritage they have adopted by doing so.

Natives will derive immeasurable enjoyment from it. One of the most delectable volumes of Welsh memoirs must be *Give Me Yesterday* by James Williams, published by Gomer, 1971. The author took his title from a play 'The Silver King': "Oh God! Put back Thy universe and give me yesterday". One might consider that a futile wish, yet when the Times Literary Supplement, no less, reviewed that publication, it was with the memorable praise that obtaining a copy was like finding a forgotten bottle of a treasured vintage in some dark recess of the wine cellar! I can well imagine many crying out on turning the following pages in the same vein as old Scrooge did when conducted back to his past:"Why, it's old Fezziwig! Bless his heart; it's Fezziwig alive again!"

As President of the Carmarthenshire Antiquarian Society (founded in 1905), a society very highly respected throughout the Principality and beyond for its invaluable contribution to the study of the history of the county, I welcome this work with profound appreciation and admiration. Thanks to the diligent research and untiring effort of Haydn Williams, his worthy chronicle of Llangain can now be treasured by us all and by the generations to come. Pob llwyddiant i'r gyfrol.

The famous Land's End landmark with 'Llangain' signposted at 340 miles away! Unfortunately, the names of those visiting from Llangain are unknown.

Preface

L ocal history is the study of the history of a relatively small geographic area; typically a specific settlement, parish or county and the events of the past that impact that area; the story of what has happened before in that small area.

The subject came to the fore with the antiquarians of the nineteenth century and the legacy of local topographical writing - the secondary published sources with which virtually all research begins. Primary sources are records of events as they are first described, without any interpretation or commentary e.g. original manuscripts and documents, minute books and school log books. Secondary sources, on the other hand, offer an analysis or a restatement of primary sources e.g. printed material such as articles, books and journals. They often attempt to describe or explain primary sources.

The modern growth of interest in local history has brought with it an upsurge in publication, ranging from substantial academic monographs through the mass of books and pamphlets published by individual local historians or societies, to the ephemeral newsletters of such groups, as well as the more scholarly annual volumes of the older antiquarian societies.

I have been conscious of the fact that there was a need for a history of Llangain ever since my schooldays but none more so while studying at Trinity College, Carmarthen. There I received excellent guidance and encouragement from my mentor, the Very Revd. Gordon MacWilliam, Head of Religious Studies. Also thanks to Mr Malcolm Jones and Mr Cyril Jones, Senior Lecturers in History who developed my skills in recovering the human experience behind the prosaic facts contained in deeds, legal documents, and indeed within ruins.

The Book of Llangain is written for anyone who has an interest in or a connection with Llangain. Its primary intention, however, is to offer an historical record of the development of the parish to local people. It will also be informative to those who have come to live here and to show how a close knit farming community changed into a residential village.

Glascoed, Llangain, 2007

DEDICATION

*To my parents, to whom
I owe so much.*

Introduction

Llangain lies near the banks of the River Tywi, four miles from the county and market town of Carmarthen in south-west Wales. The parish extends from near Johnstown to Llansteffan in one direction and from Llangynog to the river in another. It consists of very pleasant countryside with gentle hills reaching 350ft, and stretches of woodland. The parish encloses an area of almost 3,000 acres.

Samuel Lewis in his *Topographical Dictionary of Wales*, 1838 described the parish of Llangain as 'the smallest parish in this Shire, in the higher division of the hundred of Derilys Union and County of Carmarthen. The parish is beautifully situated on the north bank of the River Towy which is here navigable for ships of large burden and comprises a large extent of good arable and pasture land, which is enclosed and in a good state of cultivation. The soil is extremely favourable to the growth of corn of which great quantities are raised of a quality not surpassed by that of any part of the principality. The surrounding scenery is richly diversified, the views comprehending a portion of the beautiful vale of Towy, with the ivy-mantled ruins of Greencastle overhanging the river and other picturesque and pleasing features.'

The prehistoric cromlech at Meini Llwydion (greystones) was once covered by a mound of earth and stone, all trace of which has vanished. It was a communal burial place for family groups dating back to the very earliest farms and settlements in the area.

The stones at Dolaumeinion (meadows of the stones) form part of a cromlech dating back to Neolithic times (c.3000BC). Centuries later they became linked to Merlin, a figure of Celtic myth and legend. He was so powerful a magician that such great stones were his quoits or playthings! The site is part of an ancient drover's road from Narberth to Carmarthen.

From the late Middle Ages until the present, Green Castle has been owned by the families of Reed, Browne, Vaughan, Brett, Bludworth, Morris, Stubbs, Wyke and Robinson. The first section of Chapter 1 offers a brief history. The second section on farming within the Estate is work the author researched while at Trinity College The resulting study of the map-book 'of the Estate of Fred Bludworth, Esq in the County of Carmarthen, 1779' includes plans of properties and names of fields, their statutory acres and their use.

Welsh field names offer the reader interesting information. Among the farm names are those of Waun (field or meadow) Meini Llwydion and Llwyn Llech Leah both of which by today have been curtailed to give Meini and Llwyn respectively. "Waun Llangain", for example can be connected with the observation made by Leland back in the sixteenth century about how ships used to be at anchor below Greencastle. No country is able to boast of more beautiful place names than Wales and to the visitor to our country they are a sign that he or she is in a land which has a language and culture different from any other.

Churches and chapels of all sects deserve a guide, for they symbolise the highest aspirations of individuals, groups and whole communities over many centuries. Chapter 2 contains the history of both St Cain's church and Smyrna chapel. The former part on the parish church is the guide written by the author in 1989 which was dedicated to the memory of his maternal grandmother - mamgu Pantydderwen. The latter part tells how the congregational chapel, a well known landmark came to be built on a hill half way between Carmarthen and the seaside at Llansteffan.

Chapter 3 recounts the history of Llangain Board School set up in 1875 after the passing of Forster's Education Act in 1870 which made primary schooling compulsory. The new school opened after the centenary celebrations. Numerous quotations which appear throughout the chapter are taken directly from the logs, thus making the text a living reminder of the past.

No history of a house can be considered complete without a knowledge of the families who lived there, their way of life and contribution to their times. Some families have lived in the same house for many generations; others were transient so that over a period, a house might have had several owners. Chapter 4 takes a trip around the historic buildings within or on the parish boundary. It is important to remember that they were all built as homes for families. Within each home were living characters and figures. Undoubtedly, the most familiar name to be associated with one of these residences is the world famous poet, Dylan Thomas and his well known poem called Fernhill. If his maternal grandmother, Anna Williams had not moved to Swansea after marrying, where Florence, Dylan's mother was born, he might very well have been a Llangain boy!

Parish councils which were formed as a result of the Local Government Act,1894 were to become Community Councils in Wales in 1974. The penultimate chapter traces the development of local government within the parish and the council minute books again bring the past alive.

Photos are in more abundance in the last chapter and the captions play a significant role intelling the story of the last forty years. A new era began with the building of the Memorial hall in the1960s and all the bustling activities that such a modern hall brought to the local community. This coupled with the gradual residential development of the 1960s and 1970s and more so in the 1980s and 1990s saw the gradual change from a close knit farming community into a residential village.

Acknowledgements

First and foremost my gratitude goes to Halsgrove for wanting to publish a history of Llangain. They have built an excellent reputation in recent years for producing Community Histories, and this title is amongst the first in Wales in this award-winning series.

My sincere thanks to the Revd J. Towyn Jones FRSA for agreeing to write the Foreword. He is the president of the Carmarthenshire Antiquarian Society and was my parents' minister from 1976.

Professor Keith Watson of Reading and D.T. Rees MBE of Llangain have been extremely kind in commenting on and proof-reading the manuscript and offering invaluable suggestions along the way. I can't thank them both enough for their time, effort and encouragement.

A special thanks to Annette Thomas of Oaklands Office Services, Cross Hands, for her secretarial assistance, efficiency and reliability, but above all for her patience. Also my appreciation goes to Philip Williams, my nephew, for creating the charts used in the book, and to the staff of both the Carmarthen Library and Carmarthen Record Office for their assistance at all times.

My appreciation is also extended to those who were willing to be interviewed (the majority did so in Welsh, their native tongue) after reminiscing, namely, 'Mamgu Pantydderwen' – the late Mrs Sarah Jane Davies, Pantydderwen, and the late Mrs Annie Lewis, Lletyrneuadd, both of whom were interviewed 30 years ago; Mr Tom Thomas and the late Mollie Thomas, Gwynfan (formerly of the Gilfach); Mr Roy Davies, Canada (formerly of Old Castle), Alcwyn Rogers, Canada (formerly of Minyrafon) and Louie Mellows, Port Talbot. A particular appreciation to the oldest parishioner, namely Miss Maggie Howells, Arfryn (formerly of Danlanfach), aged 97, for her co-operation with the interview and for being available in person or even by telephone whenever a query arose requiring a memory call!

Above all, however, I am immensely appreciative and grateful to all those who have provided photographs, which are invaluable in producing a book such as this.

They are: Carl Atkins, Val Bowen, Erica Buckley, Angie Davies, Cledwyn Davies, Diane Davies, Enor Davies, Geraint Davies, Gwen Deakin, Gwynfor Davies (Nathan's poetry), Helen Davies, Jean Davies, Jill Davies, Marilyn Davies, Gillian Edwards, Becky Evans, Dan Evans, Glanmor Davies-Evans, Wyn Evans, Wyn Gruffydd, Nest Harries, Margaret Heath, Nesta Hobbs, Jim Hopkins, Margaret Jenkins, Peter Jenkins, Marilyn John, Phyllis John, Allan Wynne Jones, Angharad Jones, Beti Jones, Dilwyn Jones, Eiry Jones, Elvira Jones, Gwen Jones, Howard Jones, Mair Jones, Myra Jones, Rhys Jones, Wendy Jones, Dora Lewis, Glenys Lewis, Mair Lewis, John Lloyd, D.J. Marks, Louie Mellows, Heulwen Morris, John Parry, Merril Parry, Cynthia Phillips, Gethin Robinson, Alcwyn Rogers, Gwilym Thomas, Margaret Thomas, Mollie Thomas, Nia Thomas, Linda Weaver and Philip Williams (graphs).

Aerial view of the village, 2003.

CONTENTS

Trig point at Heol Smyrna.

The first motor service from Llansteffan to Carmarthen, 1 May 1909.

The view from the back road up towards Smyrna of the Brook area of Llangain in the 1930s. Note Ty Isaf in the foreground, Belmont (formerly known as Siop Newydd), Ty Newydd, Penybont, Glyn Lodge, Brook Forge, Minyrafon (Post Office), Meurig, Glyn, Ty Canol, Waunfort, Pilroath Lodge (Pilroath is just out of sight), Morfa Bach, Clifton, Llety and Pantyrathro.

✦ CHAPTER 1 ✦

Green Castle Estate

At the beginning of the nineteenth century almost every farm within the parish was part of the Green Castle Estate. According to Kelly, in his *Directory of Monmouthshire and South Wales, 1906*, the chief crops were wheat, barley and oats. The whole parish covered an area of 2,695 acres of land, 63 of tidal water and 68 of foreshore. There was no village as such. It is only at the turn of the twentieth century that one sees a concentration of houses arising in the area called 'The Brook' and 'Morfa Bach'. In the main, the parish consisted of farms and cottages scattered in and amongst the hills.

The following is a description from the sale catalogue of 1819 regarding the estate of Green Castle.

The manor of Llangain is co-extensive with the parish of Llangain, which is supposed to contain upwards of... acres. The picturesque ruins of Greencastle House, fine thriving woods, varied with hill and dale, views of the Tywi, Carmarthen Bay, Llansteffan Castle, and rich scenery on the banks of the Tywi, which with the respectability and compactness of the estate, together with the perpetual right of presentation to the living of Llangain, renders the whole not only desirable for residence, but also an object for investing a considerable capital to advantage.

Green Castle stands on a steep bluff some 200ft (62m) above the Tywi, three miles to the south of Carmarthen and one mile from Llangain village centre. There is a precipitous drop to the river, with a wood called Allt Castell Moel, below which is Pwll Du (Black Pool), said to be haunted by strange phantoms. In former days the entrance to the farm led through a lane or 'drive' off the hillside road below the house and not via the present entrance, which is of a later date.

The name 'moel' is the Welsh word for bald, bare, and it is not unlikely that the eminence was once bereft of vegetation. That once a small earthwork did occupy the site or very close to it is not unlikely. On a knoll about 600 yards (554m) south of the present structure possibly stood a motte and bailey structure. This would explain the meaning of the name Old Castle given to the nearby farm.

William Camden, an English antiquarian and historian, wrote in the sixteenth century: '... it is also called Castell Moel and supposed to be the Humphreys Castle of Dr Powell and built by Uchtred Prince of Meironeth A D 1138', to which John E. Lloyd, in his *History of Carmarthenshire*, adds:

... note the wonderful situation of Greencastle at a point

The west view of Green Castle by Samuel and Nathaniel Buck, 1740.

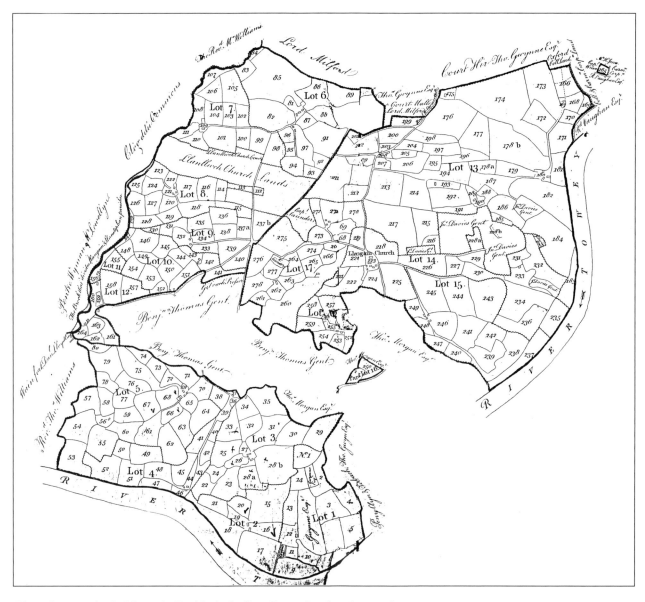

Plan of properties in Llangain Parish, including Green Castle, nineteenth century.

where after some miles of cross country the road from the sea emerges to touch the estuary of the Towy. Greencastle might well have been built by Alfred, son of his lordship Anschetil Druie, whose son lay in the neighbourhood of Llangain.

As the surrounding district was amply protected by two powerful stone-built castles, Carmarthen and Llansteffan, the Normans would hardly have found it necessary to fortify this outpost. The earliest record of this house occurs in 1435–36, when the authorities at Carmarthen paid 18d. for the boatage of Gascon wines from Green Castle to Carmarthen quay. So it is apparent that, even as early as the 1430s, certain vessels could not get up to the town quay, but offloaded their cargoes to be transported by lighter. An additional reminder of the existence of an important anchorage below Green Castle derives from field names in an eighteenth-century mapbook. One is called 'West Indies field', which recalls the exotic

destination, or port of origin, of some shipping that anchored close by at Black Pool.

By the middle of the fourteenth century Carmarthen's port gained a monopoly in the principality for the export of wool, which gave it a considerable advantage over other West Wales ports. Carmarthen's trading links were further afield than the English Channel. Excavations at Greyfriars, Carmarthen, recovered pottery from countries such as Portugal, Spain, France, Italy and Germany.

In around 1480 Lewis Glyn Cothi wrote this song of praise, which tells of wines and other wares being landed at a quay below Green Castle:

High o'er Tywi's banks and fertile vale
Stands the Plâs of Nicholas Reed so hale,
Manor of the men of Maenor Gain
Where the bard is hailed with rippling wine
At Castell Moel above the river's flow
The tall green tower greets the craft below,

Painting of Green Castle farmhouse by Frank Evans.

Whose holds provide abundant fare
To cheer the soul and banish care.

Towards the end of the 1530s John Leland noted that: 'about four miles above Llanstufan on the same ripe is a place or clif caulled Grene Castel, where the shippes use to lye at ancre', but he found Green Castle already in ruins. This is very important because it shows that ships could not ascend to Carmarthen, but had to anchor at Black Pool (below Green Castle), where their cargoes were off-loaded and then transported three miles upriver to the quay.

It is clear that a number of people made a living by transporting goods from the large ships that could not get up as far as Carmarthen itself, and these were based near the lower reaches of the river. Black Pool was, therefore, a major point of disembarkation, and this was recognised by Leland, who called the pool the 'haven of Cairmardine'.

Although the importance of the wharf waned, it continued in use well into the nineteenth century, as indicated by an entry, dated 14 August 1847, in the diary of Grismon Philipps of Cwmgwili, who took his wife and young daughters in a carriage to 'a bend in the river below Green Castle, where the steamer stops', and, having boarded, sailed down the Tywi to the open sea and on to the joys of seaside Tenby.

From Leland's statement that 'only small tokens' of the edifice remained in 1538, it seems that it had become ruinous. As the owners continued to reside there during the sixteenth century, their dwelling was probably the adjacent house which developed into the farmhouse in use today. The original structure, built in the fifteenth century by the Reeds, had ceased to be their home by the close of Elizabeth I's reign (1533–1603), and it is singular that subsequent owners, all absentee landlords, enjoyed the consider-able estate for a further three and a half centuries.

Major Francis Jones, in his *Annals of an Old Manor House: Green Castle*, writes extensively and with authority on the families that have owned the property, and the following is a brief synopsis of his account at this stage in the history of Green Castle:

The Reed Family became owners of Green Castle which they held for some two centuries. Between 1419 and 1646 the family contributed seven mayors and nine bailiffs to the town of Carmarthen. With the death of Maud Reed in 1655 the last of the Reeds of Green Castle passes out of Carmarthenshire history.

The next owner of Green Castle was Humphrey Browne, a Bristol clothworker and merchant. He left the estate to his brother, Francis, who lived there periodically, and he in turn left it to his son, Humphrey, who married his cousin, Mary. Since their two sons died young, their only daughter, Mary, inherited the property. She married John, Lord Vaughan of Golden Grove, to whom she conveyed the Green Castle estate. Mary died childless at the age of 18, and in 1674 Vaughan sold 'the capital messuage or manor house and demesne lands' called Green Castle and Penycoed, the lordship or manor of Gaing, alias Llangaing, alias Green Castle (co-extensive with the parish), a water corn mill and 30 other messuages and lands, all in Llangain parish, for £2,800, to Richard Brett from London, but he never visited his Welsh possessions. So when he died in 1689 Green Castle lost a squire it never knew. He bequeathed Green Castle, the manor of Llangain and the Carmarthenshire properties to his daughter, Margaret, who, at the age of 16, married Charles Bludworth.

The Charles Bludworth who now enters the

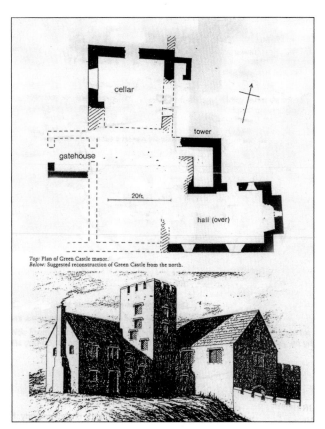

Top: Plan of Green Castle manor.
Below: Suggested reconstruction of Green Castle from the north.

A plan of Green Castle manor with a suggested reconstruction of Green Castle from the north.

chronicle of Green Castle is said to have been a younger son of Sir Thomas Bludworth, Lord Mayor of London in 1666. Hardly anything is known of him, apart for his marriage in 1696 to Margaret Brett, and that he had died by 1703. Margaret survived him. In 1704 she seems to have been in need of ready cash and mortgaged both the Green Castle and Whitland estates to the sum of £1,060. On his mother's death in 1715 Thomas Bludworth inherited the Green Castle and Whitland estates. When he died in 1772, his only son and heir, Frederick, was the last of the family to own the Welsh estates.

In 1812 Frederick Bludworth decided to sell Green Castle estate, but either the sale was stopped or the bidding did not reach the figure required by the vendor, for on 12 January 1819 the same properties were again offered for sale. How many of the properties were sold in 1819 is not known, but it is clear that Bludworth continued to own the capital messuage of Green Castle, and much, if not all, of the attached estate. By 1841, however, not an acre of land in Llangain remained in Bludworth hands.

In 1841 the estate consisted of Green Castle, Penycoed (above the woods), Church House (Tŷr Eglwys), Danyllyn (below the lake), Clomendy (dovecot), Coch y Barlis, Hendy (old house), Tŷ Hên, Cornel Cae, Lletty'r (an inn or lodging), Noyadd, Llwyn Llech Leah, Derwen Felen, Rhydlydan (wide ford), Meini Llwydon (grey stones), Llangain Mill and Dolau Meinion (meadows of the stones),

totalling over 1,266 acres, all (including Green Castle) occupied by tenants.

The mansion had been a total ruin for many generations and was replaced by the nearby farm-house. Landowners were not infrequently described as 'of ' the landed estate they owned, even when living elsewhere, as in the case of Thomas Morris, who lived at Carmarthen, Hastings and London. The grandson of David Morris, a Carmarthen busi-nessman, he opened a banking house in the town which developed into a successful and expanding enterprise, contributing notably to the commercial life of West Wales.

By 1878 the Green Castle estate was inherited by Emily and Ellen Bowers, nieces of Mrs Thomas Morris. Emily Bowers married William Stubbs, solic-itor, and settled in Hastings, where they occupied a highly respected position in local life.

The next reference brings the story back to Carmarthenshire. In *Kelly's Directory* for 1920 we read, under Llangain parish –'Mrs Stubbs' who is lady of the manor, and the Trustees of the late J. Morris Esq, are the principal landowners'. The vicar of Llangain, the Revd Evan Jones, Brynderi, acted as agent and collected the rents till his death in 1934.

Miss Gwyneth Davies of Waterloo Terrace, Carmarthen (formerly of Penycoed, Llangain), and her cousins, Mr Les Davies and Miss Olwen Davies, of Pwntan Bach, Llangain, whose forebears had long been tenants of Green Castle, recalled visits made by Mrs Stubbs in the 1920s. These three were also related to the author.

By 1950, with the passing of her other children, the only surviving trustee and heir of the Stubbs family was Mrs Zeal of St Leonards. In 1953 she sold Green Castle (224 acres), with all rights over the river Tywi and foreshore where it adjoined Green Castle land, to Mr and Mrs Douglas Wyke of Green Castle, where they had been tenant-farmers for several years. In 1970 the Wykes sold the property to the brothers Philip and Glyn Robinson of Somerset. The owner at the time of writing is Gethin Robinson, son of the late Glyn and Dawn Robinson.

Extracts from Shipping and the River Tywi: Problems of Navigation
By Terry James

It is generally accepted that from some time after AD60 or thereabouts there was a fleet of the Roman navy off the Welsh coast. Very soon, and for the first time, shipping capable of navigating the oceans of the known world was sailing into Carmarthen Bay and up the River Tywi. At what is now Carmarthen they established a fort about the year AD75, which became known as 'Moridunum'. This place-name is of considerable interest to us because, taken literally, it means 'sea fort', from the Celtic 'mor' for sea and 'dinas' for fort. Roman Carmarthen grew to become

Parish map, 1856.

the 'civitas', or regional capital, of the tribe that inhabited West Wales, so it must have become a bustling port.

What a splendid picture those single-masted Roman vessels must have made as they ascended the Tywi. But imagine for one moment the difficulties of navigating a vessel without all the modern aids used by present-day mariners. We know little of the charts, pilots or guides to pilotage, or the tools for position fixing so essential to safe passage-making, but with its phenomenal tidal range, there must have been an organised system of pilotage in operation in the Bristol Channel during the Roman period.

William Camden, writing over 400 years ago, states that the Tywi was navigable for ships of small burden, although there was 'a bed of sand before the mouth of it'. By James I's reign (1566–1625) the problem of river silting was clearly no better, for a survey stated that, whereas Carmarthen had been 'a convenient haven for ships', it was now 'sore pestered with sands and shelfs'. However, the survey adds, 'some small vessels ascend upriver even to the bridge'.

At Black Pool there was a ballast quay, and whilst hired hands and the crew took on ballast, vessels were also provisioned. I take it from this that the stretch of river between the town and Black Pool was so shallow that the brig could not risk increasing her draught of 8–10 ft by taking on provisions up at Carmarthen but had to bring these down in the ship's long and jolly boats. Moreover, the fact that a ballast quay existed there suggests that many journeys started or ended at Green Castle rather than up at the town quay.

Farming

Welsh agriculture remained primitive well into the nineteenth century; holdings were generally small and farming techniques static, bequeathed from one generation to the next.

Most of the land was in the occupation of small tenant farmers who paid an annual rent. The damp climate and hilly terrain meant that pasture predominated over tillage. The rearing of sheep and cattle also sustained a range of subsidiary industries vital to the Welsh economy, such as the wollen industry.

The eighteenth century had seen far-reaching and rapid changes in English agricultural techniques, encouraged by the need to satisfy an increasingly urbanised, industralised and growing population. The new ideas were slow to make any impact on Wales, where roads were narrow and poorly maintained, the great landowners often absent and the farmers lacking in capital and initiative.

Enclosure was the radical change to the countryside which replaced the open field system of farming. Instead of open land there were fields with fences or hedges around them. This led to villages losing their land and grazing rights and left many unemployed. Enclosures are associated with the late-eighteenth century, but the changeover had been going on since the Middle Ages, from which time open fields, commons and waste lands had gradually been enclosed.

Further enclosure was necessary for the agricultural revolution. Farming was being revolutionised as the population grew. The techniques for growing the food necessary to feed the increasing population were improving but they meant that open fields had to go to enable foodstuffs to be produced in greatly increased quantities. Farmers needed large, consolidated plots of land so that new machinery and crop rotation schemes could work. For centuries land had been divided up into small strips. and farmers tended to own lots of scattered strips, which was highly inefficient. Between 1760 and 1830 Parliament passed the Enclosure Acts, which divided up common land, redistributed plots and required farmers to build a fence around their lands. The

Killing a pig at Penyclun. Left to right: *Ernie Jones, Hannah Jones (his sister-in-law), William Jones, Pentrewyman.*

The original thatched cottage at Danlanfach. Gentleman unknown.

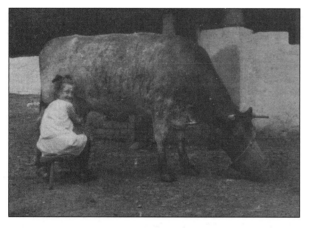

On their way to milk by hand at Gilfach, 1930. Left to right: Sarah the maid, Mollie Evans.

Mollie Evans milking Violet besides the mounting steps at Gilfach in 1924. The barn is the present Cysgod y Bedol.

Tom Howells, Danlanfach, cutting hay, 1950s.

Harvest time at Cwrt Hir, September 1954. Left to right: Harri Howells, Tom Bowen (servant), David (Australia).

Supper after haymaking at Werncorgam, 1938. Left to right: *Jim Baker, Jack y Gof, Gad Williams, Percy John, Mr Davies Werncorgam, Ieuan ?, Ann Jones, Mrs Davies.*

Thrashing day at Penyclun in the 1930s.

poor, although in theory compensated for the loss of their rights to common land, did suffer. They were often unable to make a livelihood from the small plots they were given. Sometimes there was no compensation.

The sale catalogue of 1812 described Green Castle Estate as:

> ... *a capital Freehold and the Tithe-Free estate in Llangain Parish, on the excellent new road to Llansteffan, to be sold at the Ivy Bush, Carmarthen, on Friday 24 July 1812 at 12 o'clock.*

The estate was to be sold in 17 lots, namely 'The Picturesque Ruins of Green Castle House', the farm house, numerous outbuildings, and 52 fields, comprising 334a.3r.27p, Tir Eglwys, Llety Pen hên or Clyn hir, Cornel Cae, a small house lately repaired, with a new barn and other outbuildings, Llety Noyadd a small thatched house, homestead, and outhouses, both Danylan farms, Clomendy, Tyddyn Coch y Barlis and Tir Antoon, Hendy and Penarthur, Dolau Main, Penrhyd Clydan, Waun Meini

Llwydion, Llwyndu, Llwyn (a bush or a grove), Llech (a flat stone) Leah, mill and land, a small cottage with eight fields attached. Acreages are also included, almost identical with those in the terrier of 1779.

A name was allocated to each piece of land. Fields which are near the former wharf continue to bear the names 'Waun Llongau' (meadow of ships), 'Waun Llongau bach', 'Waun Johnny Merchant', 'Waun West Indies'; a cottage and meadows were called West Indies, while between Green Castle and Plas Cwrt Hir (long court) stood two cottages, one called 'The Packet' and the other 'Sailors Rest' (a former tavern) – names which remain the sole memorial to the nautical connection.

West Indies field, Waun West Indies, West Indies cottage and garden and West Indies small fields (map Nos 17, 18, 19, 20 respectively) are all situated together. In fact, 'Waun West Indies' is the Welsh translation of 'West Indies Field', but nevertheless they are two separate fields. The four fields known as West Indies small fields are described as being arable and pasture land. Llether Pwll (No. 14) is both arable and woodland, and the name is appropriate because below this slope is a whirlpool and it is known locally as 'pwll du'. Adjoining this land are two fields (Nos. 15,16) called Waun Llonge bach. These are, again, very appropriately named because there was, it seems, considerable trouble over the silting up of the river from very early times, for Leland (1536–39) describes, about four miles from Llansteffan, 'a place or cliff called Greencastle where ships used to lie at anchor'.

Three main woodlands belonged to Green Castle, namely Allt (hillside or wood), Morva Hywell (No. 3), Allt-y-Ci (No. 23) and Allt Ffordd Wen (No. 28). There is a very interesting piece of local history attached to Allt Morva Hywell. John Wesley (the great Methodist of the eighteenth century) first

Cutting corn with a binder on Parc y Morfa field at Penyclun, with Ernie Jones as the driver.

visited Carmarthenshire well over 210 years ago, and the entry in his diary for Friday, 26 August 1763, reads as follows:

We designed to take horse at four, but the rain poured down so that one could scarce look out. Having then little hopes of crossing the sands, we determined to go round by Carmarthen, but the hostler told us that we might save several miles by going to Llansteffan Ferry. We came thither about noon where a good woman informed us that the boat was aground and would not pass till the evening; so we judged it best to go by Carmarthen still. But, when we had rode three or four miles, I recollect that I had heard speak of a ford which would save us some miles riding. We inquired of an old man, who soon mounted his horse, showed us the way, and rode through the river before us ...

John Wesley in Carmarthenshire 1763–1790,
The Carmarthenshire Antiquary, 1973

Colin Lewis and Lletyrneuadd bull.

The ford ran from a spot south-west of Green Castle to the track running down to the river from Croes-y-Ceiliog. This being so, John Wesley would have ridden through this wood. This fits in well with the distances mentioned by him. The alternative is the ford at Rhyd-y-Gors (ford of the marsh), but this is so close to Carmarthen that it would scarcely 'save some miles riding'.

A great number of fields have their names preceded by the word 'parc', which means simply 'field'. The following are examples of the best known, all of which are described as arable land in the Estate Map Book of 1779.

Parc y Berllan   (No. 4) (orchard field)
Parc y Lloi (No. 12) (field of the calves)

Parc Gwyn Bach (No. 22) (small white field)
Parc Llwyn Gwenin (No. 25) (bee grove park)
Parc Cerrig Mawr (No. 26) (field of the big stones)
Parc y Drysi (No. 33) (thorn meadow)
Parc y Pant (No. 34) (field in the hollow)
Parc y Ffynnon (No. 36) (well or spring meadow)
Parc Ddau Goed Bach (No. 40) (meadow of the two small woods)
Parc Cware (No. 46) (quarry field)

From the manor house at Green Castle, the estate extends over most of the parish and is made up of no fewer than 15 farms. Clomendy Farm gains the reputation from the sale catalogue as being from situation one of the most desirable in the county. It was a very respectable farmhouse with every appropriate

17

Respite from planting potatoes, April 1960. Left to right: Jonathan Davies (Nathan y Bardd, the local poet), Tom Bowen y gwas (farm servant), Harry Howells, May Howells, Cwrthir.

Respite from haymaking. Left to right: Alf Howells, Gwilym Raymond, May Howells, Harry Howells.

Gwyn and Tom Thomas playing quoits on Waun field at Gilfach.

Armando Sarracini, the Italian worker placing a milking machine on a cow at Gilfach. Mid 1950s.

Mr and Mrs Wyke, Green Castle, and baby Gwen, c.1942

The Gilfach Jersey herd tied by yokes. The pipeline above them took the milk to the cooler house.

Mr Douglas Wyke ploughing at Green Castle.

A hedging competition at Green Castle fields – held on the same day as the ploughing match (left).

building, homestead and yards, together with a small cottage called Dan-y-Lan, situated on the distant lands near the Tywi.

The farm was let on lease from Michaelmas 1784 during three lives, all of whom were living in 1819, namely Morris Morris, son of the lessee at the time, aged about 37, Anne Morris, daughter of the lessee, aged about 57 and Eleanor Morris, also daughter of the lessee, aged about 41. The reserved rent was

Mr Douglas Wyke, Green Castle, cutting a hedge just outside the farmyard with the farmhouse in the background near the notorious corner on the B4312 Carmarthen to Llansteffan road, early 1950s.

£57.10s., and the land tax was £1.14s., making a net rental of £59.4s., in half yearly payments, for a total acreage of 140 acres.

An area of 61 acres of Dan-y-Llan Farm was let out to David Morgan, tenant of Tŷ-yr-Eglwys Farm. The rent in 1815 was agreed at £70 per annum, but on account of the bad times during the post-Napoleonic War (1793–1815) years it was lowered to £50. David Morgan was, of course, in charge of Tŷ-yr-Eglwys Farm, which amounted to 108 acres. Again, due to the bad times, the rent was lowered from £130 to £100, clear of all deductions.

There is a reference in the sale catalogue to a farm called Llety Penhen, or Clyn-hir. By today there are, in fact, two farms called Penhen and Clun Mawr adjoining each other on this very same site – however, the farm referred to in the catalogue was at the time described as one of the most compact and neatly formed small farms, perhaps, in this or any of the adjoining counties in the principality. The farm consisted of fields ranging in size from two acres (Parc Scybor) to 12 acres (Parc Ffynnon Gedi).

Llety-y-Noyadd Farm comprised a small thatched house and outhouses. It was let on lease from Michaelmas 1784, for three lives. Esau Jenkins was the present tenant in 1819. According to the census returns of 1851, the premises were occupied by one John Lewis, his wife Elizabeth and their daughter, also of the same name. Mrs Annie Lewis, whose memories appear at the end of this chapter, was a descendant through marriage.

Both Tyddyn Coch y Barlis and Hendy Farms adjoin the River Tywi. The latter is nearly three times the size of the former. Hendy farm, 130 acres in total,

The hounds in front of the cowsheds at Green Castle in the 1950s.

Alf Howells, Danlanfach, the mobile ironmonger. Maggie Howells, his sister, still lives in Llangain and is 95 years of age at the time of writing.

White liming walls at Danlanfach. Left to right: Bert Jones, Tom Howells, Maggie Howells.

Harry and May Howells whitewashing in Cwrthir.

Beryl Davies, Cwrthir on a Massey Ferguson 35.

Tom Thomas, Gilfach preparing a two-year-old horse at Penyclun for Llanybydder Sale, c.1940.

Left: Llangain Show, 1932. David Evans with Gilfach Pearl. At the time it was the opinion of many that Gilfach Pearl was the best shire horse in Wales.

Gilfach Maid of Honour (daughter of Pearl), 1936.

was let on lease from Michaelmas 1784 for three lives, two of whom were living in 1819, namely Abel Williams, aged about 67, and Sarah Williams, aged 38. Among names allocated to the individual fields are Parc Tir Hir, Parc y Defaid, Parc Gwartheg, Parc Cwarre Bach and Tir Garw (rough land). Both farms had a field named 'Erw Goi', one being seven acres one rood in area and the other eight acres, two roods and 17 perches.

Inland, one would come across the four neighbouring farms of 'Pen Rhyd Lydan', 'Dolau-Main', 'Waun Meini Llwydion' and 'Llwyn Llech Leah'. The first of these totalled 56 acres and, like the others, was let on lease from Michaelmas 1784 for three lives. The word 'rhyd' means 'ford', and below the farmyard runs Fernhill Brook, which served, and still does, as the border between the parishes of Llangain and Llangynog. 'Llwyn Llech Leah' was a farm totalling 44 acres, while Waun Meini Llwydion totalled 51 acres. 'Meini Llwydion' is certainly

Tom Thomas, Gilfach, and the thoroughbred Skip being prepared for a sale at Leicester, late 1940s.

Cups won by the shire horse Gilfach Pearl in the 1930s.

Preparing at Gilfach for Llangain Show, September 1939.

The United Parishes Show in the 1930s. Left to right: Jim John, Penywern, Percy John (his nephew), Rees Evans, Gilfach, William Evans, David Evans, Vincent Evans (servant).

Ernie Jones with a shire horse gelding at Penyclun.

Harry Howells bailing on Parcglas field at Cwrthir, 1960.

amongst the most appropriately named farms in the parish, because a direct transaction would be 'Greystones', and still standing on the land is a fine example of a cromlech, or dolmen, from the Old Stone Age. In fact, the field in which they are situated is called Llain Cerrig Llwydion and covers an area of five acres and 32 perches.

Dolau–Main farm, however, was the largest of the four, totalling 111 acres. The property comprised a farmhouse with good cow-houses, granary and other proper buildings.

There is an example of a farm which disappeared in 1953 with the selling of the estate, namely that of Cornel Cae, adjoining the farms of Llety Pen Hen and Tŷr Eglwys. According to the sale catalogue of 1819,

the property comprised a small farmhouse with every requisite outbuilding, homestead and yards. The 23-acre farm was let to David Davies, tenant from year to year at the rent of £16. It was valued at £1 per acre, but on account of the tenant being a careful man and attending to the woods in hand, the quarries and fences, he was continued the tenant at the low rent of £16. A very romantic name given to one of the fields was Park y Delyn (harp meadow). In 1953, the farmland fell into the hands of the neighbouring tenants.

At the beginning of the nineteenth century, the parish had its own mill. An overshot corn water-mill, with a small dwelling-house and some out-buildings,

A cow-back ride – Gillian Davies on Rosebud, September 1964.

Horse and cart, August 1962, with Tom Howells with Gillian Davies, his granddaughter, at Cwrthir, and Dick the horse.

together with six acres of land, comprised the property. Richard Morris, the tenant of Clomendy, was also at this time tenant of the mill.

Details regarding the property at Llwyndu appear to be missing from the sale catalogue of 1819, and although it is indexed as Lot X in the catalogue of 1812, no descriptive particulars are given. However, from the 'Map book of the estate of Fred Bludworth in the County of Carmarthen – 1779' one can read the given acreage for individual fields. This source also contains a reference to one farm which neither the sale catalogue of 1812 nor that of 1819 mentions, namely the 24-acre farm called Bailey Farm, which serves as a neighbour to Pen Rhyd Lydan and Waun Meini Llwydion farms.

The form of an old name may have altered considerably with the passage of time and, even it if has changed little, it may well not mean what it seems to suggest. In *The Annals and Antiquities of the Counties and County Families of Wales*, first published in 1872, Dr Thomas Nicholson permitted himself the following observation concerning a residence in Llangynog:

The mansion of Cwm has a name expressive of its situation and means a vale or dingle. In obedience to a bad taste, it has been disguised into the unmeaning form of Coomb or Coombe – a word belonging to no language and devoid of the advantage even of prettiness. Local names in Wales have generally a significance and should be respected.

On this Major Francis Jones remarked:

With this stricture on a by no means uncommon practice, no self-respecting Welshman can withhold agreement. Even if uneducated, our distant forbears were not illogical, and their choice of place-names was governed by a determination to describe a topographical or other condition in more or less precise terms.

It is worth remarking that the name of a town, village or hamlet is often the earliest surviving written evidence of that settlement. Moreover, the fact that so many early names were given during periods for which written records are rare or non-existent makes them an especially valuable source of information. 'Llan' means church and the 'cain' in Llangain refers to the dedicated saint of the Parish Church. As already indicated, the name Castell Moel is not a direct translation of Green Castle. In fact, where 'green' tends to suggest 'richness' or 'plenty', 'moel' suggests the exact opposite, meaning 'bareness'.

By today, Dan-y-Lan Farm has become Tanlan Fach; Clyn-hir is Clunmawr; Llety-y-Noyadd is Llety'r Neuadd and Bailey is known locally as Beilisyfi, which is a beautiful Welsh rendering of 'strawberry orchard'. Farm names such as Waun Meini Llwydion and Llwyn Llech Leah have been curtailed to Meini and Llwyn.

Place names not only yield information about their origins or about early local inhabitants, they also often reveal considerable detail of their personalities, lives, work, customs and beliefs and of the countryside in which they dwelt.

Field names are valuable in themselves, but many are in danger of being lost. In many areas, the present field pattern is the result of parliamentary

Respite from haymaking on Parcyddwylan field at Cwrthir, July 1963. Left to right: Ann Richards, Harry Howells, Robin Howells, Bryn Raymond, Keith ? , Christine Richards, ? , Philip Davies, Stuart Richards, Gillian Davies.

Cwrthir Farm Sale, 3 October 1964. Note the young smoking farmer to the right of photo holding the half-moon utensil. Jack Davies (the owner) is to the left. Haydn Williams (the author as a boy) is next left and Evan John Williams (the author's father), wearing cap and glasses with both hands resting on a long stick, is further left (centre of photo).

Haymaking at Danlanfach, Summer 1962. Left to right: *Alf Howells, Tom Howells, Glenys Jones, Maggie Howells and Fan the dog.*

Danlanfach Farm sale, September 1962.

Cwrthir Farm sale, 3 October 1964. An Ayrshire cow awaits her fate!

Forlan cottage in the 1950s.

The outbuildings at Hendy, early 1970s.

Acts of enclosure passed in the eighteenth or nineteenth centuries. Many names, therefore, are modern, and even where medieval names survive, they are not usually attached to the precise piece of land which they originally described.

A large number of these field names within Green Castle Estate incorporate a word meaning 'a patch' or 'strip'. For example, a field was named Llain Caradoc (Caradoc's strip) (three acres 11 perches) on Tŷr Eglwys Farm. This might very well take us back to the days between 1760 and 1840, when farming arrangements of many parts of the county were changed. The 'open field' system of the Middle Ages, whereby one farmer had many strips of land scattered in various parts of the parish, was ended. There were also areas of land known as common or waste, where several farmers, sometimes all the villagers, had the right to take their cattle to feed. By the eighteenth century, there was every reason to put an end to this by letting farmers gather their strips

The pond at Hendy, early 1970s.

together into workable units and dividing commons for more sensible management.

Many describe position, size or shape – West Indies Field, Tri Chwarter in Morfa'r Ystrad at Green Castle (fields Nos. 17, 53), Waun Fain – Meini Llwydion Farm (field No. 9); function – Waun

Clunmawr, 1967.

The church and Church House, 1967.

Clunmawr, 2003.

Penhen, 1967.

The Brook, 2005.

Property uncertain, possibly Penycoed.

Lloyd and John Phillips, Hendy, 2005.

Dewi Davies with a small churn – times have changed!

Gilfach, with Glanygolau and Penywern in the background, 2005.

Haversting hay at Clomendy in the 1960s. Left to right: Bert Jones, Gwennie Jones, Evan Jones, John ?.

Clomendy in the 1990s.

Hafodwen, 2005.

The Tywi Estuary as viewed from Clomendy.

Llongau bach and Waun Llongau, Green Castle (fields Nos.15, 16) or character – Waun yr Eithin – Llwyn Llech Leah Farm (field No. 48). Nicknames were common. Some of these were complimentary in their reference to productive land – Parc Glas – Danylan Farm (fields Nos.18, 35) but many more were derogatory – Tir Garw – Hendy Farm (field No. 15), Waun Arw – Pen Rhydlydan Farm (field No. 25), Llain Ddrainog (thorn patch) – Llwyndu Farm (field No. 32). A few fields were also named after persons – Wern David Phillip – Green Castle Farm (field No. 9), Waun Rhys Jones – Hendy Farm (field No. 18).

Useful references are often found to local features now disappeared or forgotten, such as wells and woods – Parc-y-Ffynnon, Ddau Goed Mawr, Ddau Goed Bach – Green Castle Farm (field Nos 36, 39, 40). Again, one comes across such intriguing names as Parc Chweched Ffordd, so called because of the six roads adjoining it, now known as The Beeches.

During the nineteenth century, Green Castle Estate totalled 1,327 acres and, according to the sale catalogue of 1819, had a net rent income of £567. The maps of the individual farms, therefore, offer an almost complete picture of the parish at the time. Thomas Hughes, author of *Tom Brown's Schooldays*, once wrote, as he upbraided the young pupils of his time, 'You don't know your own lanes, woods and fields.' In this respect, the study of the fields and their individual names proved worthwhile as, indeed, any local history study of this kind does.

The Memories of Mrs Annie Lewis, Lletyrneuadd, at 80 Years Old
January 1976

Haydn: I'm researching into the history of Llangain and especially the history of the Green Castle Estate. What would you say has changed the most?

Mrs Lewis: The estate was sold in 1953 and many more people lived on the farms before then. The families themselves lived on the farm and kept two or three boys or one or two maids to work with them on the farm. Things have changed a lot now. The amount of people living on the farms has halved. The farms only have half the amount of creatures, too.

Haydn: Do you remember the servants and maids that worked on Green Castle farm?

Mrs Lewis: There were lots of children and their uncle. Their uncle was with them there for several years. They called him Uncle William. They also received lots of help from the Irish.

Haydn: Now, I remember noticing many Irish people on the 1851 census. What were they doing at Green Castle?

Mrs Lewis: Farm work, potato growing and so on. Many of them worked at Green Castle, so they weren't there that often, you see, but they worked in order to offer their help –– during periods of haymaking, laying potatoes and labouring.

Haydn: Who was Margaret Hartt, then?

Mrs Lewis: I'm not sure. She was an Irish woman. That was during Tom Morris' time.

Haydn: Were you a young girl when she was an old lady?

Mrs Lewis: Probably, yes.

Haydn: *Her name was on the 1851 census; Margaret Hartt, Green Castle.*

Mrs Lewis: Yes. You listen to me. As I told you earlier, the Davies' came to Green Castle in 1904. I was born in 1895 and was only a year old when they arrived at Green Castle. I was very young and have no memory of this.

Haydn: *What about the quarries? There was a quarry around the corner near Green Castle and there is one down by the river. How did they get down to the quarry by the river?*

Mrs Lewis: Where's the map? I'm sure they made their way down near Waun Llongau, you know. That's near the river, isn't it?
Haydn: *I went on a boat up the river in the summer.*

Mrs Lewis: Did you? That's very close to the river. They probably brought small stones and cut them there.

Haydn: *It is known that John Wesley, the keen English Methodist, preached in the area centuries ago. He came to St Clears one afternoon with the intention of crossing from Llansteffan to Ferryside by boat, but a lady told him that the boat wasn't crossing on that day and instead of waiting until the following day he followed the road from Llansteffan to Llangain. Apparently he then asked a man at Green Castle where he could find the ford to cross the river and historians believe that he went down to Allt Heol Morfa and over the ford, which is shown on this map. We saw this map earlier. Surely it's important to think that John Wesley crossed the river further down from Green Castle?*

Mrs Lewis: Yes, at some period it is likely that somebody had a boat to cross over to Croesyceiliog. But how would they go to get lime? There wasn't much of a river there if they were crossing with lime!

Haydn: *That's true. There wasn't much of a river to be found at that time.*

Mrs Lewis: I think that the whirlpool is located exactly where the corner is.

Haydn: *Pwll Du is on the corner?*

Mrs Lewis: Yes, to the side of Waun Llongau.

Haydn: *Was Pwll Du dangerous?*

Mrs Lewis: Look here, now. As you said earlier, you come from town, from, say, Johnstown. The river flows just to that direction, I'd say, like so, and turns like that. Well, I think to that side.

Haydn: *Is it called Pwll Du?*

Mrs Lewis: Yes, it's known as Pwll Du. The water that turns like so forms the black whirlpool.

Haydn: *Do you remember anything else?*

Mrs Lewis: I remember when we were young children; Bess was the youngest girl in Bolahaul, you know.

Haydn: *Bolahaul is on Lletyrneuadd's land?*

Mrs Lewis: Yes, it's down there underneath Chweched, you see. Now I remember, she was the youngest at Bolahaul, and she was here day in, day out. She was about the same age as my elder sister. Both used to go to town together and raced on their bikes to Smyrna Square; they would get there in less than ten minutes in those days; there was no traffic on the roads. Now Bess wanted to take us for a ride down to Llansteffan; her parents had a cart and a donkey.

Haydn: *Of course there were no cars at that time, were there?*

Mrs Lewis: Good gosh no, not a single one! Bolahaul boasted a lovely garden and her mother used to go down to Llansteffan to sell the produce to the visitors. Now, there was this old man, Tomos Tacery, who was a very keen gardener. He'd take a cart full of things to sell. Then he'd eat a meal in the Cothi Tavern. Do you know where the Union Hall is? There's one house stood by itself on the left-hand side. And we went over to Ferryside in the boat (and that was a big story with us) there was mud on the other side and the man with the boat carried the women over the mud! What a funny sight it was!

Haydn: *Did you ever pick cockles there?*

Mrs Lewis: Yes, yes, but this side.

Haydn: *Going back to Bolahaul, it was of course, a small cottage on Lletyrneuadd's land? A lot of these cottages have disappeared now, have they?*

Mrs Lewis: Yes, many of them.

Haydn: *Bolahaul being one of them; do you remember any of the others?*

Mrs Lewis: Yes. Now, before I go on (you don't need to record this) but Bill, Mari, Ann, Marged, John and Tom and Bess; there were that many children and Bess was their youngest. John and Tom went to

Australia. And then, another one lived in town. Now, another lived in Ponthenri and Mari lived in Pontyberem. Mari got married to Cwrt Hir's son. Mari's husband was from Johnied. Well, you know, some people from Ponthenri had come down to act in dramas in the church hall, years ago. Well, you know Ifor Thomas the producer; his wife was Ann Bolahaul's daughter. We used to go and listen to them.

Haydn: We'll take the Beeches. It used to be named Chweched, didn't it? Why did they name the cottage Chweched?

Mrs Lewis: There are six roads there!

Haydn: Are you sure? (teasingly).

Mrs Lewis: Yes.
Haydn: Yes, there's one leading towards the church, one towards the Gilfach, one towards Llwyn that goes down to the new shop – the old Post Office at the bottom.

Mrs Lewis: One that leads down to Llwyndu.

Haydn: The back drive, is it?

Mrs Lewis: Yes, and one towards Beili Bach road and one towards the vicarage.

Haydn: There's the six. Quite an appropriate name. What about Beili Bach? Banc y Beili you said, was it?

Mrs Lewis: Beili Bach. It was a very old place.

Haydn: What was there?

Mrs Lewis: A small house.

Haydn: Wasn't the first school down there?

Mrs Lewis: Yes, I think the school was on the left-hand side.

Haydn: The present school was built in 1875; she's celebrating her centenary this year.

Mrs Lewis: Yes, the vicarage and the school were built around the same time.

Haydn: Yes, they were built the same year exactly.

Mrs Lewis: What are they doing with the old school now then?

Haydn: I have no idea. Llangain School was built in 1875. Do you have any special memories of attending the school?

Mrs Lewis: Yes, the first schoolmaster that left

Llangain for Cardigan.

Haydn: This was at the turn of the century, was it?

Mrs Lewis: I'm not sure. I must have been quite young because one day a few of the older children came around and asked us what we wanted – hammer or sweets. I couldn't understand what they meant, you see, because when you were younger you sat with your sister or someone else. Gosh, I thought to myself, I don't want a hammer, and instead I said 'sweets'. I know what they are! And what they were doing, you see, was giving small packets of sweets to the children as a presentation because Ifans was leaving. And apparently the 'hammer' was a long thing like that with sweets and chocolate on its small end. I don't know what year that was; I couldn't tell you. You know, there were two teachers and the schoolmaster there at that time. There must have been between 80 and 90 children. There were many large families on the farms and in the small houses. There was a small house in Penbanc, opposite the school gate.

Haydn: Is the Green Castle farmhouse part of the old ruins?

Mrs Lewis: I don't think so. But, you know, it's better than what you build now perhaps but the buildings out there; they're unique! There were so many nice rooms upstairs, the boys wanted to sleep outdoors you see. They were better than the house. The house was very old.

Haydn: Would you see the boys going to church on a Sunday?

Mrs Lewis: Yes.

Haydn: Was the church full in those days?

Mrs Lewis: Yes. The Dolaumeinion family and the boys attended regularly.

Haydn: Who else? There were large families on the farms.

Mrs Lewis: There were so many; it made a huge difference. My sister's husband was brought up in Dolaumeinion. There were around 10 children, you see.

Haydn: Who was the priest at that time?

Mrs Lewis: Evan Jones, Mrs Jones Bryderi's father.

Haydn: Evan Jones? He built Bryderi didn't he?

Mrs Lewis: Yes.

Haydn: Didn't they walk to church in those days?

Mrs Lewis: There weren't any cars, you see.

Haydn: How often did you go into town?

Mrs Lewis: Saturday was the day to go.

Haydn: Because of the market?

Mrs Lewis: Yes. Well this one time in the *Journal*, you know – there are old articles and so on in the *Journal*. I always read those. There was a piece in it a while back about how the mart commenced in Carmarthen, and it's ridiculous that they now wish to move the mart from the town. Carmarthen will be finished!

Haydn: Do you remember going to the market?
Mrs Lewis: To the mart. I never went to a monthly market. I went to the mart – to look after young calves until they were sold.

Haydn: Did many people take their animals to the mart?

Mrs Lewis: Yes, indeed, sheep and calves. Well, say you enter the mart where the clock is. You go back towards Water Street. That was full of young calves, about ten in every cage.

Haydn: All from different farms...

Mrs Lewis: Yes, yes! From across the area. You won't get a mart that's more central than Carmarthen. It can't be moved from the town. It is probably of more use to the town than Tesco is. What do you think?

Haydn: I agree.

Mrs Lewis: Do you? Or are you just saying so?! Because, I'll tell you, it has probably been here for over 50 years!

The Memories of my Mamgu Pantydderwen at 83 Years Old
January 1976

Haydn: Can you remember anything significant about Green Castle, Mamgu?

Mamgu: I can't tell you more than what Mrs Lewis told you about the area. Of course, I had a great time at Green Castle; lots of fun. I remember one day there were foxhounds about and there was bread placed in buckets ready to be put on the fireside to make toast. One of the best beagles came along, put her nose in one of the loaves and left with a piece of toast!

Haydn: Where were you?

Mamgu: In the kitchen, and I went after her, of course. Then some of the boys came along with the Buckleys. There was a lot of fun.

Haydn: Did you ever walk down towards the river?

Mamgu: Yes. I loved walking down after supper at night. There would be a few lads from Carmarthen there with their coracles. Gosh, they used to give me bucketloads of fish. I used to enjoy feeding the piglets and the calves and to see the lambs.

Haydn: Above Green Castle?

Mamgu: Yes, in the field near the top of the farmyard there was a mound, you know. The lambs used to run circles around the mound and some ran up. They used to run into each other. Such vivid pictures! I used to love the little lambs.

Haydn: What about some of the fields?

Mamgu: It was a lot of work but I enjoyed it.

Haydn: Did you call the fields the same names as they were known years before?

Mamgu: No, I don't think we did; fields and homesteads as you saw them on the map had been brought down since many years.

Haydn: Waunllongau?

Mamgu: Oh yes, I enjoyed visiting Waunllongau to see the cows.

Haydn: Was there ever a pub down there?

Mamgu: I don't know. Some say there was. I had to run down there if a flood came or they would all be under water.
Haydn: What did you mention earlier, about the horse?

Mamgu: They had come; around 1929 or 1930.

Haydn: Floods?

Mamgu: From here to town was completely under water. I can't recall a greater flood since that time. The sheep and horses and so on were carried down the water.

Haydn: Do you remember anything about the quarry?

Mamgu: No, I don't remember the wall being built.

Haydn: The wall close to the road?

Mamgu: Yes. I remember boys working up on the

fields near Ysgubor Fach and up so far as the church road. I had to carry food and tea for them. Jac the Carriers and his bus stood next to the farmyard's gate and gave me a lift. Boy, those were the days!

Haydn: Ships used to sail up the river and stop beneath Green Castle before making their last 'stretch' towards the town.

Mamgu: Yes, I think they did but I don't think they landed there often, but it seems as if there were two or three pubs here because they waited and the boys came out. Well, when there was a quay, you see, flour, wheat and milk – everything was brought over by boat. That's why they named that place Waunllongau. There used to be a landing space there, but that's gone with the water.

Haydn: Would you agree that the church was the focal point of society in those days?

Mamgu: There were harvest services in the church and we had to prepare early for these; do the milking early or there would not be any room. Two priests would preach, apart from Mr Evan Jones, the local priest.

Haydn: What else was held at the church?

Mamgu: We used to hold nativity plays and whist drives years ago, but when the war broke out in 1939 everything stopped and it hasn't revived since.

Haydn: And what about Smyrna?

Mamgu: Smyrna, like the church, was in its realm at that time and was full to the brim. It was a surprise to find how many went to both places, considering they were so close within a small parish. It is thought that Llangain was the smallest parish in the area.

Haydn: Where do you remember the smithy to be?

Mamgu: In Pant-yr-Ynn. That's where it was. I'm not sure what's there now. A garage, I think.

Haydn: Did many go there?

Mamgu: All the farmers did. Jac Ifans did a bit of everything there; he'd shoe every horse there. Your mother went down there once to collect a mare. Took her down in the morning to be shoed, and your mother went down to collect her in the afternoon. The factory was down there, and then she did some work for us. I remember doing some work there. Then on to St Clears with the flannel, socks and woollen shirts and so on. We'd stand next to the monument on the roadside selling flannel, wool and so on.

CHAPTER 2

Church and Chapel

St Cain's Church

Worship has been offered to Almighty God through long centuries on this hallowed spot. The scene has, of course, changed much since:

... the faith of the good old men, who, as far back as the sixth century, found out, on the hill by the Tywi side, a place for the Temple of the Lord, where they might worship Him. (The Welshman, 1871)

But the ages have given unbroken witness on this site to a great worshipping tradition.

The word 'llan' is derived from the Celtic period and originally meant a monastic enclosure. It referred to the whole enclosure, incorporating the communal buildings, the individual 'beehive' corbelled huts of the monks and the burial ground. Now it means the church. Hence, Llansteffan means the church of St Stephan, Llan-gynog the church of St Cynog and Llan-llwch the church of the swamp, or lake, being the cymric form of the Gaelic 'loch'.

Some of the Carmarthenshire churches are dedicated to the sons and daughters of Prince Brychan of Brycheiniog (Breconshire, now part of Powys). St Brynach is reputed to have died on 7 April, about AD570. He was a contemporary and friend of St David, who died on 1 March AD603. Brychan's children became devout monks and nuns. Thus his sons, Cynog, Clydwen and Dingad, are honoured in the church names of Llangynog, Llanglydwen and Llandingad and his daughters, Tybie, Cain, Cynheiddon and Tyddystl, in the names of Llandybie, Llangain, Llangynheiddon and Capel Tydyst (which formerly existed near Manorafon).

The most interesting of the saints associated with Brychan, Brycheiniog, are St Brynach and St Keyne (Cain). St Brynach is one of the major saints of West Wales, with five dedications in Pembrokeshire and

St Cain's Parish Church, Llangain, 1989.

two in Glamorgan. St Keyne is the best known of Brychan's reputed daughters, and her 'life' is one of those included in a collection compiled from older sources in the fourteenth century by John of Tynemouth. St Keyne appears in dedications under a variety of different disguises. In Wales, she appears as Cain, Ceinwen and Cainwyry. There is no doubt that Llangain and Capel Cain in former Carmarthenshire are to be associated with the cult of St Keyne.

The Early History

In the sixth century, South West Wales was as rugged and dramatic as it is today. It had the good fortune to be a region relatively free from the impact of the Romans' coming and going, yet was a region where two major sea-routes crossed; that from the North to the South West of Britain; and that from Ireland to the Bristol Channel. Thus Christianity was able to survive and develop in such an area, where accessibility to Ireland – and places further away – meant contact, bringing enrichment as well as challenge.

As Wales gradually fell before the Normans in the eleventh century, the Church in Wales was brought into the English system of dioceses and parishes. The Norman kings and their successors, the Plantagenets, pursued the purpose of establishing a strong central government in which church and state worked together, each fortifying the other. It was, however, an aim that proved difficult to achieve, since the Welsh had a strong vein of obstinacy supplemented by a deep-rooted nationalism. This proved so powerful a combination that Wales has the honour of knowing that it was never completely subjugated by anyone.

Llangain Church in the Middle Ages

The parochial origins of Llangain Church are obscure, and this is especially so since most of the medieval sources refer to a chapel and not a church. The earliest reference to it is as the church of St Kein. This is an undated document of c.1150–76, when a man called Arthur Drue – who was probably Lord of Llangain (or Maenor Gain) – made a grant to Carmarthen Priory. The grant gave the church arable land in the forest of Trefcarn, immediately east of the church. He also gave a tenth of the pannage (i.e. rights for pigs to graze within the forest) in the same forest, and, moreover, the tithe of the pasturage in the event that the pasture was covered with cattle.

This informative document shows that at this time Llangain Church lay within or to one side of a large forest – Trefcarn – which presumably extended down to the river, over towards Old Castle and Green Castle. We may surmise that the pasturage lay to the north and west of the church. The dating of the Drue grant is difficult: it was certainly confirmed by

Henry II (1154–74), but the original grant could well predate Henry's reign. One of the witnesses to the charter – Roger Norreys – was constable of Carmarthen Castle. We cannot tell exactly when he was constable, but Sir John Lloyd, in his *History of Carmarthenshire*, suggests a date of c.1150.

Whatever the date of Drue's original charter, we can be confident that it was confirmed by Henry II, and the date of confirmation is probably between 1154 and 1176. Henry's charter confirms the granting of various lands, churches and chapels, which included the following:

I have also given and granted to them (the canons) one ploughland in Eglwysgain with the chapel situated within the bounds of the same lands which Alfred Drue gave to the same canons...

It is clear that Llangain remained a holding of Carmarthen Priory until that house fell in the Dissolution (1537–38). The lands were recorded in Pope Nicholas' *Taxatio Ecclesiastica* of c.1291. In 1395, Richard II confirmed that the Priory had in its benefices:

... which we learn are, by the licence of our said ancestors, appropriated to their Priory, to wit, in Llanllwni Church, in Llanfihangel rhos y Corn Chapel, in St Peter's Church, Carmarthen, in St Mary's Chapel in the said town, in the chapel of the castle of the same town, in Llanllwch Chapel, in Abernant Church, in Conwyl Chapel, in Maenor Gain Chapel, in Llandeilo (Abercycwyn) Chapel, in Canon Hill Chapel (Capel Iwan, Carm), in Newchurch; in St David's Church, Abergwili, with all its chapels (Llanllawddog, Cefncoed, Llanfihangel Pen-rhos, and Llanfihangel Llechmaelor), in Llanfihangel-ar-arth Church, in Pencader Chapel, and in Llanbyddair Church...

These same holdings remain in the Priory's ownership and are listed in the valuation – known as the *Valour Ecclesiasticus* – undertaken at the time of the Dissolution.

The Later Centuries

The outbreak of the Civil War in 1642 saw Wales, with the exception of Pembroke, strongly in support of the king, the gentry being predominantly Royalist. Only a handful were prepared to support Parliament in the struggle.

As a result of a new Act for Wales (1649–50), 71 commissioners were appointed and 25 Puritan ministers, or 'approvers', were selected. These approvers were responsible for the filling of those churches ordered vacant by the commissioners. Carmarthenshire did not have a single representative. The clergy were ejected from parishes such as Llansteffan, St Clears, Myddfai and Llangain. Many

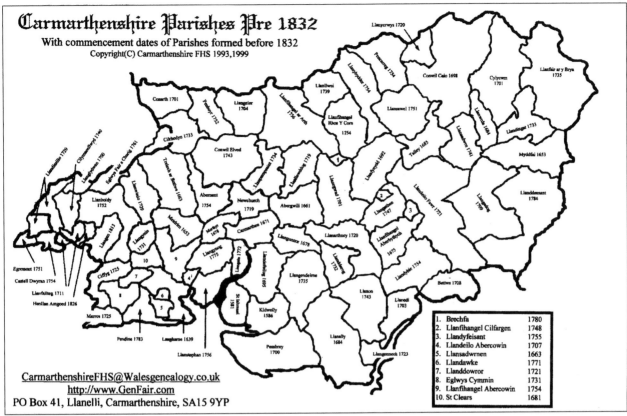

Carmarthenshire parishes pre-1832 (with the commencement dates of parishes formed before 1832).

were ejected for 'delinquency', 'malignancy' and 'insufficiency'. The words do not necessarily imply anything more than that these clergy were Royalist and anti-Puritan. When a stricter terminology was required, the accusers made use of the charge of 'drunkenness', especially, in the case of clergymen who hospitably entertained their Royalist friends. When Cromwell died in 1658 the hope of perpetuating the Puritan system of religion died with him.

Although Bishop George Bull was over 70 years of age and in frail health when appointed in 1705, he took a very serious view of his duties. The presentments of churchwardens at his primary visitation in 1705, at St Peter's Church, Carmarthen, are of great importance. They supply evidence as to the state of the churches in the various parishes at the beginning of the eighteenth century. At Llangain the 'minister' (the officiating clergyman, whether a vicar or curate) is described as 'a studious, painstaking man, of sober life, and unblemished character'. He preached every Lord's Day and administered the Holy Sacrament monthly. There being no glebe house, he resided on his own farm outside the parish.

Vicars

–1683	David Rees
–1721	M. Jones
1730–50	John Jones, curate in charge
1751–96	David Thomas
1797–1805	William Evans, assistant curate
1806–16	William G. Davies, perpetual curate
1817–64	John Thomas, perpetual curate
1865–69	David Jenkins, BD
1869–80	Joseph Williams
1880–99	David Evans
1900–34	Evan Jones, BD
1935–48	D.T. Price, BA, MTh.
1948–61	Melvyn Thomas, BA
1961–64	D.S. Lewis, BA
1964–77	A.J. Jones, BA
1977–85	V.H. Jones, BA
1986–95	Leslie Evans, BA, LTh.
1995–	Illtyd Protheroe, Dip.Theol.

Llangain Church amalgamated with Llangynog in 1964, but in 1977 the local churches were regrouped and Llangynog Parish joined Llanfihangel Abercywyn with Revd Canon Conrad Evans, while Llangain amalgamated with Llanllwch. On his retirement in 1983, however, Llangynog rejoined our church with Llanllwch. The Revd Sian Jones, BA, BTh., having experienced her student diocesan placement in the parish in 1987, returned as deacon to the parishes in 1988 and is at the time of writing is vicar of Llansteffan with Llanybri and Rural Dean.

It is interesting to note that the Revd A.J. Jones and Canon V.H. Jones, who were brothers, succeeded each other as incumbents at Llangain.

Quotations

The people have built perhaps the prettiest church of its size in the three counties. (THE WELSHMAN, 28 JULY 1871)

Mae yr eglwys newydd hon yn un o'r tlysaf yn y Deheudir, y ffenestri o wydr tebyg i Eglwysi Cadeiriol.

(YR HAUL, 1871)

Commemorative Stone

Llangain Church is a well-proportioned church, built in 1871 within 40 feet of the site of the former dilapidated church. The length of the church from east to west within the walls is 75 feet, while its breadth from north to south within the walls is 20 feet. A grant was made by the Incorporated Church Building Society, London, to the sum of £50 in 1869, on condition that 70 additional sittings were made available in the new church, with 52 sittings reserved for the poor. A commemorative stone beneath the east window bears the following Welsh inscription: 'ER GOGONIANT I DDUW CYSERGRWYD EGLWYS SANT CAIN GORFFENNAF 27 O.C. 1871' (St Cain's Church was consecrated to the glory of God on July 27 1871).

The reopening of Llangain Church from *The Welshman*, 28 July 1871:

There are a few parishes yet remaining in this county where new churches are very much needed; and though they be poor and thinly populated it is possible for them to do the right thing in the all-important matter of providing decently and reverently for the service of God, in their parish churches, providing one or two conditions exist. The first is, one good working man to take the matter up, and the second is, a good feeling towards the church amongst the people generally. We cannot believe that any parish is destitute of these essentials to success, and therefore hope that in the course of a year or two at the very outside, the work of church restoration in the county of Carmarthen, at all events will be complete. When we think of the efforts made by our pious ancestors in the very infancy of the Christian faith, when we remember their lavish provision of church accommodation in proportion to the wants of the then existing population, how much more ought we, who live in days when the church exhibits such strong vitality and the calls of the people for her ministrations are so much increased, to grapple earnestly and hopefully with the work which is set before us. The people of Llangain have not been insensible to these influences.

They got a report and plans from Mr Withers of London, but then the great money difficulty cropped up and almost dismayed them. The plans seemed beyond their means and Mr Withers was asked to modify them somewhat. This, however, he flatly refused to do, and urged the people to go on. So they took his advice and went on, determined to trust in Providence as to the result. Mr Gwyn and a few other capital business men soon floated the affair; and though they did not receive the support they reasonably expected from various quarters, still they progressed, surely if somewhat slowly.

About £1,200 was the sum which they wanted, and we believe they were as successful in collecting the money as people usually are under such circumstances. They now have cause to congratulate themselves on their self-sacrifices and exertions for the church which they have jointly produced will always be a pleasure to them both to think of and to look at.

The stone comes from a quarry by the river side; but some of the old stones were also used. There is an abundance of freestone dressings, which give the structure a most attractive appearance. The most prominent object is the tower, square in the base, girt with strings of ornamental stone, and surmounted with a nicely designed piece of white but hard stone, beautifully tooled, and gradually tapering. At the top is a small piece of ornamental iron work, on which is poised a gilded weather cock. Two bands of worked stone run round the church, in character with the tower; and along the roof runs a ridge of ornamental tiles. In short the exterior is as complete as it can be, even to the nicely worked vestry chimney, and we cannot enumerate everything. The roof is effectively drained by pipes which conduct the water to gutters in the floor. The upper lights of the windows, too, are elaborately worked in white stone. The entrance is not under the tower but through a neat porch. On getting full into the building one has a clear unobstructed view right up to the chancel, and the effect is satisfactory and pleasant to the eye... Mr Gwyn has determined to lay out the churchyard in character with the church. The surface will be turfed and designed in the style of a cemetery; inside the boundary walls, ornamental shrubs will be planted and at one part a row of elms set. Opposite the porch a piece of ground which cannot be used for purposes of internment will be converted into a shrubbery. Thus, in a few years, the whole of the churchyard will be enclosed by a belt of foliage.

The day of the opening was deliciously fine, and visitors flocked to the place from all parts. Some we recognised as coming from very long distances. The doors were not opened till the last moment, and then the clergy, about twenty in number and clad in surplices and hoods, led the way; the crowd followed soon filling the church to overflowing. There were not less than 300 persons inside, for the aisle was crowded from end to end. The clergy sat in the chancel stalls and the service was shared between them. Unfortunately, there was no harmonium and the only singing heard was in the ordinary hymns. Here, however, full amends were made for want of harmony in other portions of the service. Mr Gwyn led off the tunes with perfect success, and as they were such as one usually hears in country churches – fine, old-fashioned, sweeping melodies – the congregation knew them thoroughly, took them up at once, and sang them with great heartiness and fervour. It was a great pleasure to hear the flood of vocal harmony, for the example of the good country folk was catching, singing was fashionable for the day, and everyone joined in. The ceremony of consecration has been described so often that we need say nothing about it again. After the Holy Communion had been celebrated, the new piece of churchyard was consecrated, and the company then adjourned to a neighbouring barn, where a most tempting luncheon had been prepared on a lavish scale by the parishioners. This was dispensed to everyone who needed it, and the people returned invigorated to the afternoon services, at which the eloquent Rector of Neath preached. There was some talk of open-air preaching, and it would have been advisable in the morning for there were many people who could not enter the church, and were obliged to sit in the churchyard. The sermon in the morning was preached by the bishop; but it contained nothing particularly striking. The erection of this handsome building which won high praise from all who saw it, does infinite credit to everybody concerned; and it is to be hoped that from its completion will date a new and a better era for the old church of the people, in the parish of Llangain.

Llangain Church Decoration, *Carmarthen Journal*, 29 December 1871:

This church, which has been very recently restored, is at all times well worth a visit from anyone who cares for correct ecclesiastical art. The restoration has been effected in a manner which reflects the greatest credit on the architect, and the furniture is quite in keeping with the arrangements of the church. This is chiefly noticeable in the sanctuary, to the eye wearied with the shameful desecration it is so often compelled to see in this holy place.

There is something refreshing in the beautiful reredos and handsomely vested altar at Llangain. The former contains, in the centre, a plain cross; the four spaces being filled up with the emblems of the Evangelists; whilst on each side are the Agnus Dei and the Pelican. A beautifully worked frontal and super frontal adorn the altar, and on the left side of the sanctuary is placed a credence table. The choir stalls, lectern and pulpit, though perfectly plain, are marked by neatness and good taste, and the low open seats and large font complete a very pleasing picture. That so pretty a church should be well decorated seems natural, and the visitor will find nothing to complain of in this respect. In the east window and directly above the altar is suspended a large cross of white wool with a border of holly; a scroll on the cross contains the appropriate text in Welsh, 'I am the Bread of Life'. From the pillars of the reredos hang two banners, one bearing the sacred monogram, the other the Constantino Cross, and these are connected by a wreath of evergreens running over the top of the reredos. A shield and banner with appropriate devices adorn the lectern and pulpit respectively. The font is wreathed with evergreens and the margin decorated with moss and flowers. Various texts in Welsh and English are placed in the super-altar and the walls of the Church. In the west window stands a cross of moss and flowers wreathed with hollyberries.

Altogether the decorations at this church are very effective, and we trust that the good work begun may be carried out each year (or better still at each church festival) with such improvement as the gradual restoration of Christian art may teach the decorators.

Architecture

An old church is a wonderful link with the past. It was built centuries ago and it has seen all the history since. It has been used week after week, year after year, and century after century, without a break. Its shape and its stones were as familiar to people who lived long ago as they are to us today. You can discover the history of a church if you know the rules of architecture, which means the science of building. In different centuries men built in different ways, and the story of architecture is divided into periods according to the style.

Church Architecture

450–1066	Saxon (Romanesque)
1066–1200	Norman (Romanesque)
1200–1300	Early English (Gothic)
1300–1400	Decorated (Gothic)
1400–1500	Perpendicular (Gothic)
1500–1800	English Renaissance
1800–1900	Gothic Revival (Victorian)
1900	Twentieth Century

The style of the present building is Gothic; we cannot say of what period, but there is great warmth and variety in the treatment of the details. Gothic architecture came from one very important discovery – the pointed arch. Saxon and Norman builders always used round arches, which were solid and strong, but the pointed arch was even stronger, with the importance advantage of being lighter. The new shape completely changed church buildings. With the pointed arch even higher, roofs could be built soaring above the nave.

As a result, the lancet window was introduced. Sometimes many lancet windows were put together to form one large one.

The Bell

The spire is a pointed structure which rises above the tower in the form of a tall cone or pyramid. Many people think of it as a finger pointing upwards to the heavens. Inside this spire is the belfry, containing a bell dated 1913. The founder's name, or mark, does not appear on it. In view of this, one wonders whether the bell was cast by a local non-ferrous founder, the number 01 on it possibly denoting the first bell that he made – but this is pure supposition.

The chief purpose of the bell is to call people to worship. According to the church balance sheet of 1939–40, the sexton, whose duties included bell-ringing, was Stephen Davies, who was paid an annual sum of £3.10s. The 'cloch paratoad' (preparatory bell) would be rung half an hour before each service. Before clocks became common, the bell was used to peal the hours. In the Middle Ages, the curfew bell was rung to warn people that it was time to extinguish all fires – the word 'curfew' means 'cover the fire'. The new belfry rope was a gift from Mrs S.J. Davies, formerly of Pantydderwen, on the reopening of the church in 1979.

The Nave

There are three main parts into which the church is divided – the nave, the chancel and the sanctuary. The largest part of the church is, however, the nave. The word nave comes from the Latin word *Navis*, which means a ship. A navy is a fleet of ships, so this name reminds Christians that the church is a ship, and Jesus Christ the captain. The beautiful wooden roof and the thrust of the roof vaulting is a copy of the original and reminds us of the keel of a ship.

The roof is timbered according to the old plan which the architect found in existence; he was so pleased with it, that he determined to perpetuate it. It looks somewhat heavier than the work in most new churches but is very handsome, and of course has a peculiar interest to the parishioners from being a copy of the original.

(*The Welshman*, 28 July 1871)

The ship is one of the oldest images of the church.

Both the ark and the ship, as symbols of the church, are found engraved and painted by Christians of the first ages in the catacombs at Rome.

The nave contains the font, lectern, pulpit, litany desk, pews and, in this particular church, the organ and an oak table as well. The table was given in memory of Hannah Davies, Eithincefn (Ardwyn), by her husband, Stephen Davies, the church sexton during the incumbency of Revd Evan Jones (1900-34).

The Font

In 1705 David Thomas, in his churchwarden's presentments to the Lord Bishop, wrote that 'there is in our church a font of stone set in the usual place for the administration of baptism with a proper cover to it.' When members of the Carmarthen Antiquary Society visited the church on 7 August 1912 they commented that the font was no longer set in the usual place but 'in the unusual place for the growth of flowers outside the church'. During the restoration work of 1978–79, the font was moved from what was once called the shrubbery area to the foot of the tower. The font is Norman and is eight-sided, the sides representing the circumcision of Jesus when he was eight days old. The baptism of Christian children took the place of the circumcision of Jewish children. Another reason why fonts were built with eight sides was because eight was the number of regeneration. The number seven symbolised creation, while the next number, eight, represented the new creation or regeneration. This font, which is

St Cain's Parish Church, Llangain, 1989.

round in shape, reminds us that everlasting life is begun at the font and that the circle is the sign of eternity. Whatever the shape of the font, however, it is always placed near the door, baptism being the door by which we enter the Christian Church.

Memorials

In the nave there are several interesting memorial tablets, bearing witness to faithful parishioners.

On the south wall is a plaque to Charles Bankes Davies of Llwyndu. This monumental slab was an object of mournful interest to many visitors on the reopening of Llangain Church in 1871. The Latin words 'Vivit Post Funera Virtus' mean 'virtue still lives after death'. The tombstone can be seen in the churchyard.

The following words can be seen on a plaque in memory of William Stubbs, Green Castle:

To the Glory of God and in memory of William Stubbs, JP, Mayor of Hastings 1887, 1888, 1889, who entered into rest 3 May 1911, aged 57.
They, Thine forever! Oh! how blest!
They who find in Thee their rest.

On the north side of the nave is a memorial to Lce-Cpl Willie D. Davies (Welsh Regiment) of Green Castle, who died in action in France on 23 March 1918, aged 20.

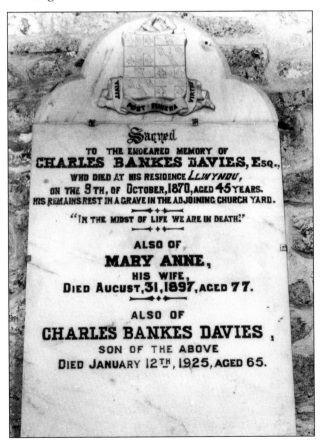

The Charles Bankes Davies Memorial.

Willie Davies
The Welshman 10 May 1918

Soldiers' Death. The sad news has been received that Lance-Corpl Willie Davies, Welsh Regt, the youngest son of Mrs Davies, Green Castle, has died in hospital in France on 25 April. Deceased was twenty years of age. He joined the colours in August, 1916, and went on active service in December, 1916. He was wounded on March 23 1918. A fortnight ago his mother visited him in hospital in France for a few days. There was a very large congregation at the memorial service at Llangain Church on Sunday evening, deceased having been a faithful member of the Church. Out of respect to the memory of the deceased there was no service at Symrna Chapel that evening and members of that chapel attended in large numbers at Llangain Church. The service, which was a most impressive one, was conducted by the Vicar (Revd Evan Jones, BD) who preached an appropriate sermon from the Gospel for the day, St John xvi, 33. Suitable hymns were feelingly sung and the Dead March (Saul) was played by the

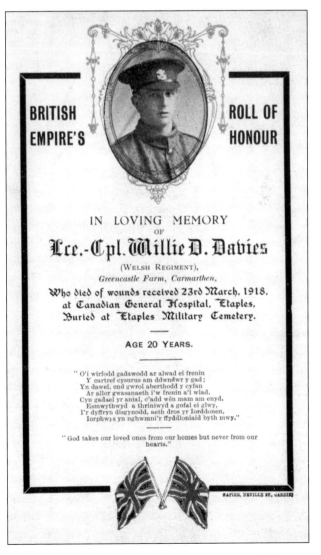

Memorial Card commemorating Lce-Cpl Willie D. Davies, Green Castle (Welsh Regiment).

organist, Miss Morris, Llwyn. Among those present were Mrs Davies, Greencastle (mother), Miss Maggie Davies (sister), Messrs E.J. and H. Davies (brothers), Mr T. Davies, Vorlan, Mrs Davies Vorlan, Mr, Mrs and Miss Jones, Blaencorse, St Clears (uncle, aunt and cousin), Pte E.J. Jeremy, Narberth (cousin), Mr T. Thomas, Penhill (cousin), Mr Morgan Pritchard, Carmarthen. and a large number of friends.

The Lectern and Litany Desk

The lectern is the desk on which rests the bible. In 1955 a Bible was given by Miss Elizabeth Dyer, Delfryn, Llangain, in memory of George Dyer. In 1979 lectern copies of the New English Bible and the Welsh New Testament were given by the author. In 1989 he presented a leather-bound copy of the Beibl Cymraig Newydd. The litany desk is the prayer desk which you may see in the centre aisle of some churches. At this the priest or clergyman says the litany – an 'asking' prayer – in which the people take part. Its place in the nave of the church, where the people sit, reminds us that the priest and people join together in prayers such as the litany for the needs of the world. This desk was given in memory of David Evans, ALCM, LLCM, organist here for 17 years, who died on 1 October 1936. It was presented by his cousins, H.M. and F.M. Jones.

The Pulpit

Prior to 1979 the pulpit, like the church, was built of local stone with dressings of red and grey grinsal stone. In 1979, however, a new oak pulpit made by Mr Ryan Davies, Brynderwen, a local carpenter, was given by Mrs Dilys Davies (formerly of Penhen) in memory of her husband, John Hinds Davies, and Eileen, her daughter. The three sides and the three steps remind us of the Holy Trinity. The pulpit light was given by John and Aneurin Thomas, Ty Canol.

Wardens' Wands

The rods near the front pews, the wardens' wands, are symbols of the churchwardens' office, and are carried by them in the procession before the bishop or clergy in the church. The churchwardens are responsible for the church building, among other things, and assist the parish priest in the performance of his duties.

The Organ

Organs have been in existence since about the tenth century, and were to be found in very large churches by about the thirteenth century. In the eighteenth and nineteenth centuries, however, village orchestras sometimes led the music in smaller churches. In 1979 the harmonium was replaced by a Viscount (Domus

8) electric organ. It is a gift of Mr and Mrs Vincent Davies and family, Llwyn, in dear memory of their son, Gareth, who was tragically killed in a farm accident on 18 August 1978, aged 20. Above the organ is a hymn board given in memory of Henry Evans Brook by his widow on Easter Sunday 1939. There have been numerous organists over the years, but in more recent times they have included Mrs Gwladys Thomas, formerly of Waunfordd, Meryl Jones, Clomendy, who started playing at the age of 15, and Einir Jones, of Cenir in Heol Smyrna (formerly of Penycoed), who has played for over 35 years to date and is the sole organist in the church in 2007.

The Pews

Pews are fixed benches on which people sit. Once there were no seats in churches and the congregation knelt or stood. Later, in some churches, a few seats were attached to the wall for the old and sick, and from this comes the saying 'the weakest go to the wall'. Fixed seats for all the people were introduced in about the fifteenth century. Later, the squire and wealthy patrons of the church had their private pews, often near the chancel. The pews in this church are made of Christiana deal, stained and varnished, and on each pew a small piece of carved woodwork gives a pleasing finish, appealing to the eye, and there is a kneeling board to each sitting.

The Chancel

The part of the church, between the nave and the altar rails, is called the chancel. Another name for the chancel is the choir, because here the choir sings. The fixed seats are the 'stalls', where the choir and clergy usually sit. Until the Reformation (the great religious revolution of the sixteenth century), most churches had some stalls which were separated from each other by projecting 'elbows'.

The chancel arch, of carved Bath stone, is unusually wide for a country church of this size. The two figureheads, depicting a bishop and a monarch, represent the diocesan and state heads of church respectively. The arch and the choir stalls offer the ideal setting for a robed choir.

In fact, the Easter Day service of 1970 was unique because the congregation witnessed the procession of a robed choir, led by a cross-bearer, for the first time in the history of the church. The processional cross was a gift from Mr Tom Williams, Fernhill, who had been the vicar's warden for several years.

The Gwyn Memorial

On the south side of the chancel is a memorial to William Bevan Gwyn Esq, of Pilroath, and his wife, Margaret. The Gwyn family owned seven other farms in Llangain, and it was a member of this family

The Gwyn family memorial.

The reredos above the altar table.

who built Plas Cwrthir towards the middle of the nineteenth century. William Edward Bevan Gwyn was the first resident of the mansion. In 1873 his estate comprised 496 acres. According to *The Welshman*, it was this Mr Gwyn (a churchwarden at the time) who:

... not in consideration of his broad acres but of his broadness of heart and general popularity, is justly regarded as the squire of the parish, was the first to take this matter in hand.

The 'matter in hand' was the building of a new church, and Gwyn was obviously the driving force in seeing the entire project through to its completion in 1871.

A beautiful tiled mural on either side of the east window depicts four angels, with the last words of the Apostles' Creed artistically painted across them:

The Communion of Saints
The Forgiveness of Sins
The Resurrection of the Body
The Life Everlasting Amen.

The entire work is dedicated to the glory of God and to the loving memory of various members of the Gwyn family.

The Sanctuary

The part of the church to the east of the chancel, the sanctuary, is divided from the rest of the church by altar rails, at which all communicants kneel. The word 'sanctuary' means 'holy place' or 'sacred place'. The name is used because this part of the church contains the altar, the most sacred part of the church, and it is here that Christians come during the Holy

Communion service. The richly decorated floor tiles are Victorian copies of a medieval pattern.

The Reredos

The space between the top of the altar and the window-sill above is the reredos. The word means 'back of the altar'. This reredos is of stone and is beautifully painted with symbols of the four evangelists. A man, a lion, an ox and an eagle represent Matthew, Mark, Luke and John respectively. The sacrificed Lamb of God can be seen, along with the pelican feeding its young with its own blood. Both represent the Sacraments, which are themselves outward signs of God's grace. The Alpha and Omega are also shown. The first and last letters of the Greek alphabet, signifying the beginning and the end, they remind Christians that Jesus is the beginning and the end of all things, and suggest His everlasting nature.

A reredos of white stone filled with choice work emblematic of the four Evangelists, runs along the chancel wall. Toward this, we understand the architect has generously contributed. The style of the reredos is very striking and at a distance has a fine effect; the lower portion of it forms a kind of super-altar.

(The Welshman, 1871)

The Sedilia

The sedilia are canopied seats on the south side of the chancel for the use of the priest and his attendant at the Eucharist. Originally they were behind the altar, along the east wall, which was curved in a semi-circle. Some modern churches are returning to this arrangement.

Some sedilia have two seats, others three, and a few have four. Sometimes the seats are of different heights; the highest, nearest the altar, is for the priest, the next for the deacon, who reads the gospel, and

The Sedilia.

Communion vessels in memory of Sarah Jane Davies, Pantydderwen, and wafer box in memory of Andrew MacWilliam.

The altar desk is a small desk of brass needed to hold the Service Book used by the priest at the altar. The old custom, still followed in many churches, was to have a cushion for this purpose. This stand was given in memory of a churchwarden named Edward Williams, Pantydderwen, who died on 4 May 1941, and his wife, Alice Williams.

Communion Vessels

The chalice is Elizabethan and both lid and cup are silver and bear the inscribed date 1576 (the same year as the former Queen Elizabeth Grammar School, Carmarthen, was founded). Of the Amroth type, they bear the maker's mark and the Latin inscription: 'POCVLVM ECLESIE * DE * LAN * GAYNG (The Chalice of Llangain Church).

The cup is no longer in use and a new chalice, given by Mrs Myra Jones (née Lloyd-Davies), Llwyndu, is presently used at the Lord's table.

The two cruets are needed to hold the wine and water for the Holy Communion. Glass cruets are mostly used now and the ones at St Cain were given in memory of Sarah Jane Davies, Pantydderwen, by her grandchildren – Mairwen, Einir, Gareth, Hilda and Haydn. The wafer box was given in memory of Andrew MacWilliam (1957–89) by his parents, the Very Revd A.G. and Mrs MacWilliam.

The Bishop's Chair

The special chairs which stand near the altar are known as bishop's chairs. One is placed at the entrance to the chancel for the bishop to use when he takes a Confirmation service. The other may be used by his chaplain.

the third for the sub-deacon, or server, who reads the epistle. When there was a fourth seat this was used by the clerk.

The Ornaments of the Altar

The altar cross is known as the Calvary Cross because it stands on three steps, thought to represent faith (top step), hope and charity. It is also an empty cross, with no figure of Christ upon it, which seems most fitting for the altar. This speaks of the Risen Jesus, who has left the cross, and who gives those at the altar the power of His risen life.

The altar lights placed on either side of the cross, teach us that Christ, by that cross, has joined in one both Jew and Gentile. Also, He who died on the cross has two natures – He is both God and Man; and that He gives to us His twofold nature in the Blessed Sacrament of the altar. The candlesticks and offertory plate were given by Mai Philipps in memory of her brother, Thomas Morris, of Coomb, Carmarthenshire, a lieutenant with the Sixth Dragoon, killed in action on 26 January 1902.

The altar vases were given in memory of the same Thomas Morris by his mother. To place flowers in vases upon the altar is not an ancient but a modern custom.

The Piscina

In some churches, you may find the sedilia designed jointly with the piscina. The word 'piscina' means 'cistern'. A niche on the south side of the altar, formed like a shallow stone basin with a drain in the bottom, it is used for washing the sacred vessels – the chalice (cup) and paten (plate) – after the Holy Communion service. The drain leads to the consecrated ground of the churchyard outside. The piscina here is probably a replica, since it is in the north wall and has no drain. It serves, therefore, more as a credence shelf for the vessels before consecration.

The Vestry Door

The vestry door was given by his mother in memory of Mark Vowles, 1957–94.

Historical Extracts

The church roof is out of repair, no mansion house, no glebe lands, no tenements belonging to ye parish. Our minister hath not any competent salary for serving ye cure. No school, either public or private, taught in our parish.

Extract from Churchwardens' Presentments, 1684

Wanted a cloth for the pulpit.
No chest for alms.
Some disputes concerning the ancient marks and boundaries of our parish.

Minister resides at St Ishmael about 4 miles distant.
No perambulation within our memory.
Our churchwarden chosen by the minister every Easter.
No school.

Extract from Churchwardens' Presentments,1790

Easter Vestry – *Carmarthen Journal,* **3 May 1889**
The Easter Vestry was held on Friday, the 26th ult., when a fairly representative number of the working bees of the said church were present. The matters transacted were of a purely ecclesiastical character. The Vicar, on taking the chair, said that it afforded him very great pleasure to meet the out-going church wardens at the termination of another year, on their part, of efficient and faithful service to the church. He was glad to be able to say that he had always found the two wardens most energetic in the discharge of their various duties. One of them had for many years now rendered most valuable service in connection with the Sunday school. The churchwardens presented their account, which was examined and found correct in every item. One very encouraging feature in the account of the present vestry was that the deficit of last year had been converted into a balance of £4.6s. in the hands of the churchwardens. It is pleasant to reflect that this favourable balance had not been obtained at the expense of neglecting the fabric of the church or churchyard; neither have the sick and needy of the church been forgotten. Mr W. Davies, of Clynmawr, consented to be re-elected as the vicar's warden, and Mr James Jones, jun., Penyclyn, as parish warden for the ensuing year. Mr W. Jones, of Werncorgam, was elected lay elector. Mr Jones, Penyclyn, said that he could assure the Vicar and all

Llangain Church

Statement of Accounts

1st January—31st December, 1956

Vicar :
Rev. MELVYN THOMAS, B.A.

Churchwardens :
Mr. T. E. THOMAS, Rhydlydan
Mr. D. J. DAVIES, Ardwyn

Secretary of P.C.C. :
Mr. E. T. DAVIES, Clynmawr

Statement of Accounts, 1st Jan., 1956—31st Dec., 1956

RECEIPTS.	£	s	d	EXPENSES.	£	s	d
Defence Bonds	100	0	0	Quota	79	10	0
Interest on Bonds	3	10	0	Insurances	6	12	6
Covenanted Subscription	2	0	0	Help the Clergy Scheme	10	0	0
Refund from Covenanted				Lampeter College	5	0	0
Subscriptions (2 years)	17	2	8	Coal and Gas	18	4	5
Sunday Collections	60	3	0	Reports	2	0	0
Sunday School Collections	2	16	6	Church Tower Repairs	5	15	0
Sunday School Outing Fares	6	8	0	Deanery Fee	0	5	0
Cheque from Church Hall				Stove Repairs	0	10	0
Account	1	2	9	Caretaker	13	0	0
Harvest Thanksgiving				Sunday School Outing	8	15	0
Collections	12	9	1	Children's Gifts	0	16	0
Missions	8	9	5	Memorial Vase	5	5	0
Quota, March	40	17	6	Easter Offering	14	18	3
Quota, September	46	8	0	Bread, Wine	2	12	1
Easter Offering	14	18	3	Missions	8	9	5
Balance in Bank,				Harvest Thanksgiving			
31st Dec., 1955	33	12	10	Expenses	1	0	0
				Easter Cards, Envelopes	0	6	3
				Women's Offering	1	1	0
				Home of the Good Shepherd	1	1	0
				Hostel of St. Luke	0	10	0
				Delapidations	15	19	8
				Cheque Book	0	4	2
				Postages	1	3	2
				Balance 31st December, 1956	47	0	1
					249	18	0
				Defence Bonds	100	0	0
	£349	18	0		£349	18	0

Audited and found correct—T. I. Nicholas

Llangain Church statement of accounts, 1956.

Collections towards Quota

	£	s	d			£	s	d
Llwyndu ...	6	0	0	Pwntanbach ...	...	2	0	0
Plas Cwrt Hyr ...	6	0	0	Dolau ...	...	2	0	0
The Vicarage ...	5	0	0	Glogddu ...	...	2	0	0
Waunfort ...	5	0	0	School House ...	...	2	0	0
Rhydlydan ...	4	10	0	Anonymous ...	...	2	0	0
Ardwyn ...	4	0	0	Cwrt Hyr Farm ...	...	1	10	0
Clomendy ...	4	0	0	Glenydd ...	...	1	10	0
Llwyn ...	4	0	0	Kenneth Thomas ...	...	1	5	0
Hafodwen ...	4	0	0	Mrs. M. Hesford ...	...	1	0	0
Blaentir ...	4	0	0	Bryhedydd ...	...	1	0	0
Derw ...	3	10	0	Blaencwm ...	...	1	0	0
Fernhill ...	3	0	0	Plasuchaf ...	...	0	10	0
Ffynnonfair ...	2	15	0	Clynmawr Lodge ...	...	0	10	0
Tycanol ...	2	4	0	Delfryn ...	...	0	10	0
Clynmawr ...	2	0	0	Upper Llwyndu Lodge	...	0	10	0
Dolaumeinion ...	2	0	0	George Evans, Penhen	...	0	10	0
Penhen ...	2	0	0					
Bethesda ...	2	0	0	Loose Cash ...	...	1	11	6

	£	s	d
Churchyard Fund	11	3	6
Organ Fund	4	9	9

COVENANTED SUBSCRIBERS

	£	s	d
The Vicar	5	0	0
Mr. Lloyd Thomas, Hafodwen ...	4	0	0
Mrs. Key, Cwrt Hyr Plas ...	2	0	0

Lent Missionary Boxes

The Vicarage, 15/-; Rhydlydan, 10/3; Derw, 10/-; Ffynnonfair, 10/-; Pwntanbach, 9/4; Plas Cwrt Hyr, 9/3; Ardwyn, 8/6; Waunfort, 7/6; Brynderi, 7/-; Cwrt Hyr Farm, 6/-; Greencastle, 5/1; Dolaumeinion, 5/-; Clomendy, 5/-; Llwyndu, 5/-; Cochybarlys, 5/-; Llwyn, 4/10; Hafodwen, 4/6; Dolau, 4/3; Clynmawr, 4/-; Bethesda, 4/-; Penhen, 3/6; Clynmawr Lodge, 3/1; Glogddu, 3/-; Cartref, 3/-; Tycanol, 2/-; Delfryn, 2/-; Haulfryn, 2/-; Glenydd, 2/-; Plasuchaf, 1/10. Total, £8/9/5.

Altar Flowers, 1957-58

1957		
April	21	Miss Davies, Derw
	28	Mrs. T. Evans, Penhen
May	5	Miss G. Wyke, Greencastle
	12	Miss Dyer, Delfryn
	19	Mrs. Davies, Plasuchaf
	26	Miss Stewart Haulfryn
June	2	Mrs. Thomas, Tycanol
	9	Mrs. Lloyd Davies, Llwyndu
	16	Mrs. James, Glogddu
	23	Mrs. Davies, Mount Pleasant
	30	Mrs. Platt, Clynmawr Lodge
July	7	Miss I. Evans, Dolau
	14	Miss C. Owen, Cartref
	21	Miss G. Thomas, Waunfort
	28	Mrs. Owen, Cartref
Aug.	4	Miss Davies, Pwntanbach
	11	Miss H. Jones, Clomendy
	18	Mrs. Evans, Dolau
	25	Mrs. Davies, Upper Llwyndu Lodge
Sept.	1	Mrs. Davies, Cwrt Hyr Farm
	8	Miss M. Davies, Penhen
	15	Mrs. Davies, Dolaumeinion
	22	Mrs. Rees, School House
	29	Mrs. Davies, Penhen
Oct.	8	Miss Thomas, Clifton
	13	Mrs. Thomas, The Vicarage
	20	Mrs. Yorath, Cochybarlys
	27	Mrs. Davies, Clynmawr
Nov.	3	Mrs. Davies, Ffynnonfair
	10	Mrs. T. Hesford, Llanstephan
	17	Miss Lloyd-Davies, Llwyndu
	24	Mrs. Wyke, Greencastle
Dec.	1	Mrs. Thomas, Hafodwen
	8	Miss S. Jones, Clomendy
	15	Mrs. Davies, Ardwyn
	22	Mrs. Thomas, The Vicarage
	29	Miss A. Davies, Glenydd
1958		
Jan.	5	Miss Hodges, Belmont
	12	Mrs. Thomas, Belmont
	19	Mrs Thomas, Rhydlydan
	26	Mrs. Jones, Brynderi
Feb.	2	Miss Harries, Blaentir
	9	Miss Evans, Llwyn
	16	Miss Evans, Llwyn

Llangain Church statement of accounts, 1956 (internal).

present that it had given him and his brother-warden very great pleasure to be able to render the best service they could to the church at Llangain, however imperfect it might be. He trusted that in the course of the next twelve months, by the kind assistance of the congregation, they might be able to effect few further improvements in the churchyard. He begged to remind them that the success of the church depended to a very high degree upon the loyal and faithful co-operation of all its members. He had much pleasure in thanking all the congregation for the cheerful and liberal support which they had given them in the past. The Vicar thanked the churchwardens most sincerely for their past valuable service to the church, and the kind, willing assistance they had invariably given him. He felt certain that 'Progress in all good works' was their motto for the coming ecclesiastical year.

Harvest Festival, *Carmarthen Journal*, 10 October, 1890

Thanksgiving services were held at the above Church on Wednesday, 1st inst. At 10.30 morning prayers were read by the vicar and the Revd Griffith Jones vicar of Mostyn. The latter delivered an instructive sermon, which could not fail to deepen in his intelligent and devotional audience their sense of thankfulness to the 'Giver of all good gifts'.

Then the Holy Communion was celebrated. It was a pleasing sight to observe such a large number of young and old, rich and poor, kneeling at the Lord's table, and uniting to bless the Father of all mercies for all the blessings of this World, and, above all, for His inestimable love in the redemption of the world. At 2.30 the Revd S. Jones, RD, Llangunnor, read the service, and the Revd G. Jones preached in English and the Revd J. Marsden, of Llanllwch, in Welsh. The Revd J. Marsden dwelt with great force and eloquence on our duty to thank our Heavenly Father for the manifold, apparently too often forgotten, blessings we daily receive from our merciful Creator. Evensong was said by Revd J. Marsden, and the lessons were read by the Revd D.S. Davies, vicar of Llanybri. The vicar of Mostyn delivered one of the most eloquent and soul-stirring discourses heard in the district for many years. There was not a dry eye in the crowded audience. Miss Easter Gwyn, with much efficiency, presided at the organ during the day. The choir rendered most able and faithful service at each service in leading the praises of the congregations. The Church decorations for this year's festival surpassed our most sanguine expectations. The decorations, whether viewed separately or as a whole, could not fail to elicit our warmest admiration. Undoubtedly great care, trouble, and taste were bestowed by the decorations in the selection and

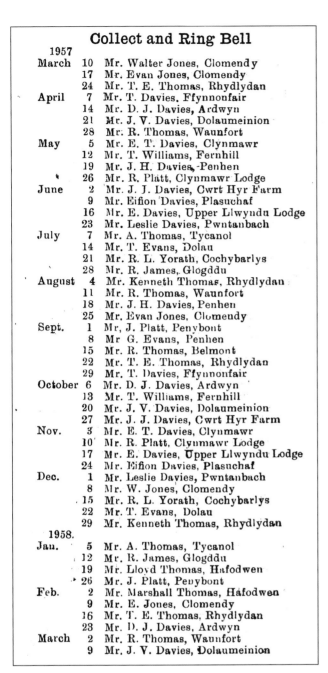

Collect and Ring Bell

1957

March	10	Mr. Walter Jones, Clomendy
	17	Mr. Evan Jones, Clomendy
	24	Mr. T. E. Thomas, Rhydlydan
April	7	Mr. T. Davies, Ffynnonfair
	14	Mr. D. J. Davies, Ardwyn
	21	Mr. J. V. Davies, Dolaumeinion
	28	Mr. R. Thomas, Waunfort
May	5	Mr. E. T. Davies, Clynmawr
	12	Mr. T. Williams, Fernhill
	19	Mr. J. H. Davies, Penhen
	26	Mr. R. Platt, Clynmawr Lodge
June	2	Mr. J. J. Davies, Cwrt Hyr Farm
	9	Mr. Eifion Davies, Plasuchaf
	16	Mr. E. Davies, Upper Llwyndu Lodge
	23	Mr. Leslie Davies, Pwntanbach
July	7	Mr. A. Thomas, Tycanol
	14	Mr. T. Evans, Dolau
	21	Mr. R. L. Yorath, Cochybarlys
	28	Mr. R. James, Glogddu
August	4	Mr. Kenneth Thomas, Rhydlydan
	11	Mr. R. Thomas, Waunfort
	18	Mr. J. H. Davies, Penhen
	25	Mr. Evan Jones, Clomendy
Sept.	1	Mr. J. Platt, Penybont
	8	Mr G. Evans, Penhen
	15	Mr. R. Thomas, Belmont
	22	Mr. T. E. Thomas, Rhydlydan
	29	Mr. T. Davies, Ffynnonfair
October	6	Mr. D. J. Davies, Ardwyn
	13	Mr. T. Williams, Fernhill
	20	Mr. J. V. Davies, Dolaumeinion
	27	Mr. J. J. Davies, Cwrt Hyr Farm
Nov.	3	Mr. E. T. Davies, Clynmawr
	10	Mr. R. Platt, Clynmawr Lodge
	17	Mr. E. Davies, Upper Llwyndu Lodge
	24	Mr. Eifion Davies, Plasuchaf
Dec.	1	Mr. Leslie Davies, Pwntanbach
	8	Mr. W. Jones, Clomendy
	15	Mr. R. L. Yorath, Cochybarlys
	22	Mr. T. Evans, Dolau
	29	Mr. Kenneth Thomas, Rhydlydan
1958		
Jan.	5	Mr. A. Thomas, Tycanol
	12	Mr. R. James, Glogddu
	19	Mr. Lloyd Thomas, Hafodwen
	26	Mr. J. Platt, Penybont
Feb.	2	Mr. Marshall Thomas, Hafodwen
	9	Mr. E. Jones, Clomendy
	16	Mr. T. E. Thomas, Rhydlydan
	23	Mr. D. J. Davies, Ardwyn
March	2	Mr. R. Thomas, Waunfort
	9	Mr. J. V. Davies, Dolaumeinion

List of sidesmen to collect and ring bell for 1957.

arrangement of the articles, fruit, corn, and flowers, by which the sanctuary was adorned. The font and western window were decorated by the Misses Morris, of Llwyn, windows in the nave, Miss Morgans, Glogddu, Miss Morris, Penhen, Miss Williams, Clomnendy, Miss Jones, Danlan, and Miss Lewis, Waunmably, pulpit, Miss Easter Gwyn, lectern, Miss Ethel Gwyn, choir stalls and altar rails, Miss Lloyd, Clynmawr, chancel window, Miss M Lloyd, Clynmawr; super altar, Mrs Evans, the Vicarage. Clergy and their friends were entertained at the Vicarage.

Reopening Services, *Carmarthen Journal*, 5 November 1915

Harvest thanksgiving, combined with re-opening services, after restoration of the Church, were held at Llangain on Thursday 28th November 1915. The service in the afternoon was read by the Revd Evan Jones, vicar, and the lessons were read by the Revd B. Parry Griffiths, vicar of St Peter's Carmarthen and the Revd Canon J. Lloyd RD, vicar of Llanpumpsaint. An able sermon was preached in English and Welsh by the Ven. Archdeacon R. Williams, vicar of Llandeilo. The service in the evening was read by the Revd W.Ll. Rees, vicar of Llangunnick, and powerful sermons delivered in Welsh by the Revds B. Parry Griffiths and Canon Lloyd. The church was crowded both in the afternoon and evening and Miss Morris of Llwyn ably presided at the organ, and the singing was under the leadership of Mr T.M. Jones, churchwarden, Dolaumeinion. It had been found necessary that certain repairs should be done to the church, and all the Church people in the parish unanimously joined to contribute, both by money and labour, towards the work, and substantial contributions were received from Mrs Morris, Coomb, Sir O. Philipps; and Mrs Stubbs, Hastings; and others outside the parish. A building committee was formed with Mr J. Lloyd Thomas, JP, Gilfach, as chairman; Revd Evan Jones as secretary; and Mr T.M. Jones, churchwarden, treasurer, and the work, which has been completed, is a great improvement, both inside and outside the church. It is generally recognised that Llangain has one of the most beautiful country churches in the diocese. The inside work was entrusted to Messrs Bartlett Bros, Carmarthen.

Carmarthen Rural Dean
Fatal End to Seizure
Carmarthen Journal
Revd Evan Jones, Vicar of Llangain

We regret to announce the death, which occurred early on Tuesday morning, of the Revd Evan Jones BD, of Llangain, and Rural Dean of Carmarthen, which occurred at this residence, Brynderi, Llangain, at the age of 69 years.

Mr Jones had a seizure whilst preaching at the morning service at Llangain Parish Church, on Sunday, 4th inst., from the effects of which he never rallied. He was one of the best known clerics in the Diocese of St David's and had been vicar of Llangain for the past 39 years, and his many sterling qualities had gained for him the esteem of all sections of the community over a wide area.

He graduated at St David's College, Lampeter, and was ordained deacon in 1890, and priested the following year. During his 44 years in Holy Orders he held one curacy and one vicariate. He commenced his career in the parish of Llanedy, and was in charge of the populous district of Hendy, where he laboured with energy and such success for nine years. In those days one of the largest Church schools in the diocese were at Hendy, and the young curate worked strenuously to keep them going and cleared the heavy debts with which they had for years been burdened.

39 Years at Llangain

The Revd gentleman was appointed to the benefice of Llangain in 1899, and accomplished excellent work during his long tenure of the incumbency. He collected a goodly sum towards augmentation of the living, the income of which has more than doubled ever since Disestablishment. Many improvements were carried out to the church and churchyard. In 1920 Mr Jones was appointed as Diocesan Inspector of Schools for a great part of the Archdeaconry of Carmarthen, which office he fulfilled to the satisfaction of all concerned until 1926. In 1921, the late Bishop deputised the Vicar of Llangain to act as organiser of the 'Llan' in the diocese, and after some months of energetic endeavour, the circulation of the Welsh Church newspaper was substantially increased. Mr Jones was a member of the Governing Body of the Church in Wales.

The revd gentleman was appointed Rural Dean of Carmarthen in March, 1931, in succession to Canon Benjamin Davies, MA, now of Wrexham. He discharged the duties of Rural Dean with the thoroughness that characterised all his efforts, and was revered by his fellow clergy in the Deanery, who found in him a counsellor and friend. To his Parishioners he was a faithful and diligent priest and his passing will be keenly felt for a long time.

Public Services

In addition to his parochial duties, Mr Jones took a keen and abiding interest in the social welfare of the district, and was for some years a member of the old Carmarthen Board of Guardians, and the Carmarthen Rural District Council. He was a member of Group II, School Managers, and since 1923 had been a Commissioner of Income Tax for the Derllys Division. He was a staunch supporter of the National Farmers' Union, and had done much to improve the housing conditions on properties he was interested in the district. Mr Jones had for a long period been a frequent contributor to the columns of The Welshman.

Well-known Point-toPoint Rider
Carmarthen Journal, c. 1948
Mr Austin Bevans Wed at Llangain

At Llangain Parish Church on Tuesday, Mr Austin Bevans, son of the late Mr Andrew Bevans and of Mrs Bevans, Cwrt Malle, Llangain, was married to Miss Lila Davies, daughter of the late Mr Benjamin Davies and Mrs Davies, Dolaumeinion, Llangain. The bridegroom is well known as a point-to-point rider and as a prize-winner in jumping competitions at West Wales shows.

Officiating were the Revds D.T. Price, Vicar of Llangain; Gwyn Williams, Vicar of Llangynog, and L.P. Rees, Vicar of Llanddarog. The bride was charmingly attired in a cream brocaded dress with lace hat to match, and carried a bouquet of cream and pink carnations. She was given away by her brother, Mr James D.V.

Davies, and was attended by her sister, Miss Irene Davies, and the bridegroom's sister, Miss Mair Bevans, who wore a helio dress and old rose dress respectively. The duties of best man were carried out by Mr Emlyn Bevans (brother of the bridegroom) and the groomsman was Mr Eric H. Davies, Barclays Bank, Llandelio (bride's brother). A reception was given at the bride's home, after which Mr and Mrs Bevans left for their honeymoon, which is to be spent touring.

The Restoration of 1955

After extensive renovations the Bishop of St David's reopened the church and dedicated a number of beautiful gifts. These gifts were: sanctuary and chancel carpets given by Mr Davies, Pentre, St Clears; pulpit carpet given by Mrs Morris, Bronwydd Road; altar prayer book given by Mrs Morris, Francis Terrace; altar linen cloth given by Mrs Davies, St Non's Avenue; altar rail carpet given by Miss Gwyneth Davies, formerly of Penycoed Farm. At Evensong, the sermon was preached by a former vicar, the Revd D.T. Price, Trinity College. Large congregations attended throughout the day.

The Restoration of 1978–79

Sunday worship continued in the church hall for eighteen months while major restoration work was embarked upon in 1978. This included hand picking

---

Eglwys Sant Cain – Llangain

Thanksgiving Service
for the
RESTORATION of the CHURCH
and
DEDICATION
of
New Organ, Pulpit, Carpet and other Gifts
THURSDAY, OCTOBER 11th, 1979
at 7 p.m.
by
The Right Reverend
ERIC M. ROBERTS, M.A.,
Bishop of St. Davids.

The Order of Service for the Restoration Thanksgiving, 11 October 1979.

Llangain Church Choir (with some members from Llanllwch) on reopening in 1979. Left to right: Neryff Davies, Eiry Davies, Meryl Jones, Revd Victor Jones (vicar), Davies, Eleri Jones, Kathryn Thomas, Rhiannon Thomas, Helen Thomas, Julia Perkins, Arthur Thomas (vicar's warden), Helen Williams, Rt Revd Eric Roberts, Lord Bishop of St David's (centre), Sian Griffiths, Donna Jones, Nicola James, I.J. Williams (people's warden), Richard Jones, Ieuan Davies, Roger Thomas, Robert Thomas, Berin Jones, Robert Davies, Leyton Davies, Robert Mathews, David Mathews, Haydn Williams (choirmaster), Carl Atkins.

Llangain Church restoration work party 1978–79. Left to right: Les Davies, Ken Jones, John Davies, Elwyn Davies, Hugh Thomas, ? Johnston, Revd V.H. Jones (vicar), Vincent Davies, Revd Alun Howells, Vicar of Meidrim (organist), Arthur Thomas (vicar's warden), Jim Thomas and Danny Morris (official carpenters), Rt Revd. Eric Roberts, Lord Bishop of St David's (centre), I.J. Williams (people's warden), Evan John Williams (Smyrna Chapel deacon), Robert Davies, Haydn Williams (choirmaster), Wyndham Thomas, Evan Jones, D.J. Marks (headmaster), John Jones.

and pointing every single stone throughout. Not only has this added to the picturesque appearance of the interior but has also solved the problem of dampness which existed previously.

All the pews were removed, entirely restored and replaced, with a newly cemented aisle dividing both rows of pews on either side of the nave. The font was moved from its original setting in the tower to the south wall, replacing the choir vestry. This gave the nave an equal number of pews on either side. A new pine ceiling was built in the belfry and terrazzo tiles placed on the floor. Wood panelling was introduced throughout the nave. The carpet was a generous gift by Mr Evan Jones and family, Clomendy, in memory of his parents and sister.

The interior was decorated and intricate details on the reredos were painted in red, black and gold. Embroidered cushions were made for the Sedilia and the Bishop's Chairs, under the supervision of the late Mrs Non Servington-Lewis, Swn-yr-Ehedydd. The entire building was re-wired, new heaters installed and repairs carried out to the roof and masonry.

An old path leading from the main entrance to the vestry door was reopened and tarmacadam laid down. The tarmacadam was the gift of Mr and Mrs Hugh Thomas and family, Clunmawr. The new gates were kindly given by Eira and Mair (formerly of Penhen) in loving memory of their father and sister Eileen.

The completion of the restoration work was marked by a reopening ceremony on Thursday, 11 October 1979 at which the sermon was preached by the then Bishop of St David's, the Rt Revd Eric M. Roberts, MA. It was also a service of dedication of the new organ, pulpit, carpet and other handsome gifts which the church had been embellished with by parishioners and friends.

Lastly, a tribute must be paid to the men who gave freely of their time and talents to the restoration work throughout the long winter and summer months. Danny Morris and Jim Thomas were the carpenters whose craftsmanship can be seen in abundance today.

This labour of love, along with the other kinds of contributions, was done in the hope and with the intention of preserving this fine edifice for the worship of Almighty God by those who come after them.

> We love the place, O God,
> Wherein Thine honour dwells;
> The joy of Thine abode
> All earthly joy excels.

A Church Built on Community Spirit
Carmarthenshire Life, **July 1996**

One hundred and twenty-five years ago, on a glorious July day, over 300 people packed into a Carmarthenshire church to celebrate the indomitable ability of small communities to triumph in the face of obstacles.

The particular obstacle overcome by the people of Llangain was the sheer cost of rebuilding their old and dilapidated church. In 1871, £1200 was a huge sum for a rural parish of no more than a few hundred souls to find, but find it they did and the result is St Cain's Parish Church, as well-preserved an example of Victorian Gothic as you could hope to find anywhere in Wales.

Later this month the people of Llangain will once again be hoping for clear skies and the blessing of sunshine as they gather together to celebrate the church's 125 anniversary. Local historian Haydn Williams, who is the author of the definitive guide to the church, has designed a commemorative plate which has been manufactured by A&M Griffiths of Felingwm Pottery to mark the occasion.

The place that Llangain Church has in the hearts of local people is obvious from the number of gifts made to the church over the past 125 years. There is scarcely a stick of furniture, church ornament, book or cushion cover which has not been either donated or made by a local benefactor.

In 1871 a reporter from The Welshman *wrote of the reopening ceremony:*

'The erection of this handsome building which won high praise from all who saw it does infinite credit to everyone concerned and it is to be hoped that from its completion will date a new and better era for the old church of the people, in the parish of Llangain.'

The Church Alphabet

A stands for altar, **B** stands for bell,
C for the church and the chancel as well.
D is the door – won't you please come inside?
E is the eagle with its wings stretched out wide.
F stands for font – by the door it is seen,
G stands for God – He's the same as has been!
H stands for hymns; the Incarnate we praise,
JESUS His name, unto Him hearts we raise.
K is the Kyrie we sing and we pray,
L is the lectern – its lessons obey!
M is Magnificat – Mary's song we adore,
N's Nunc Dimittis – Simeon's anthem for sure.
O is for organ and **P** stands for pew,
Q is our Quota from all it is due.
R's the responses we're all taught to say,
SUNDAY we love for it's God's Holy Day.
T is our teacher, so faithful (s)he comes,
Unction's the oil, to all sick, comfort brings.
V is our vicar – he's 'Father' to all,
W's the wardens – they're always 'on call'.
X stands for Xian while **Y** stands for yew,
Z starts the zeal – let's all it renew.

The Church Hall

Church members met after morning service on Sunday 21 November 1948, the purpose being to exchange views towards building a church hall.

The official opening of the Church Hall, 24 July 1951. L–r, back row: T. Davies, A.V. Key, W.J. Jones, J.J. Davies, D. Lloyd-Davies, Vicar of Conwyl Elfed, Vicar of St David's, Carmarthen; front: T.E. Thomas, Revd Melvyn Thomas (Vicar of Llangain), Rt Revd W.T. Havard (Bishop of St David's), Mrs Lloyd-Davies, Mrs T. Davies, Mrs T.E. Thomas.

After much discussion it was proposed by Mr D. Lloyd-Davies, seconded by Mr W.J. Jones, Pentrewyman, that a hall be built, and the motion was unanimously carried. A church hall building-fund committee was formed, fund-raising events including dramas, concerts, poetry, whist drives and sales of work.

The only site available was on the curtilage of the vicarage by using the outbuildings – stable, cowshed, etc., which might have meant a saving of approximately £300. By early 1950 Mr W.S.P. Cottrell, architect, had advised that the hall be built on land kindly given by Mr and Mrs D. Lloyd-Davies. The new hall, built at a cost of a few thousand pounds, was opened by Mrs D. Lloyd-Davies on 24 July 1951. Tea was provided followed by evening concert.

Throughout the 1950s, '60s and '70s the hall was a hive of activity, with regular social and fund-raising events connected with both the church and village life generally.

With the increasing use of the new Memorial Hall, with its modern and varied facilities, there was less demand for the Church Hall. Its period of usage as originally intended, therefore, turned out to be just 50 years, and the Parochial Church Council decided to sell the building in the early years of this millennium.

Llangain Church 125-year celebration plate (1871–1996).

The following poem is a celebration of Llangain Church Hall, which was the area's adornment when opened in 1951.

Llangain Church Sunday-school Christmas party, 1964. Left to right: Gerald Davies (Sunday-school teacher), Vernon Bignell, Neville Hesford, Keith Platt, Haydn Williams, Elgan Evans, Huw Davies, Roger Platt, Mary Davies, Eirlys James, Menna James, Sylvia Jones, Phyllis Thomas, Clive Bignell (?), Gillian Davies, Wendy Bignell, Wyndham Thomas, Margaret James, Marina Bignell.

Llangain Church Sunday-school Christmas party, 1964. Left to right: Elwyn Davies, Ronald James, David Davies, Ralph Platt, Jack Davies, Emrys Thomas, Mollie Hesford, Lilian Jones, Sally Davies, Mrs Olwen Davies, Mary Davies, Muriel Platt, ?, ?, Mrs Morris, Mrs T.E. Thomas, Revd T.E. Thomas.

Llangain Church Sunday-school Christmas party, c.1967. Left to right, back row: Mark Vowles, Gillian Davies, Wendy Bignell, Margaret James, Wendy Bowen, Elwyn Thomas, Michael Bowen, Gillian Smith, Andrea Bowen; third row: Roger Thomas, Anthony Harries, Haydn Williams, Wendy Vowles, Yvonne, Menna James, Wendy Thomas, Keith Platt, Roger Platt, Mair Davies, Robert Davies; second row: Elwyn Davies, David Davies, Gerald Davies, Revd. A.J. Jones (Vicar), Emrys Thomas, Jack Davies, I.J. Williams; front row: Mitchell Vowles, Gareth Davies, Raymond Smith, Clive Bignell, Robert Beddow, Neryff Davies, Kathryn Thomas, Helen Thomas, Richard Thomas.

Aerial view of Llangain Vicarage, 1967. Prior to 1875, the vicarage was at the Bryn (above Fernhill). Note the schoolhouse vegetable garden in the background and the side of No. 6 Maesyrawel.

Neuadd Eglwys Llangain

*Ar lechwedd y Lleiniau mae Neuadd
A'i muriau uwch Ceunfan y fron,
A dywed trigolion Cymdeithas
Mai addurn y fro ydyw hon,
Does angen i mi ddweud ei chyfrinach
Hi ydyw brenhines y Llain,
Mae pawb heddiw'n llon ac yn sibrwd
Am Neuadd hoff Eglwys Llangain.*

*Pwy tybed na _yr am fath ymdrech
Bu glynu a'i llanw'n ddi-drai,
A chlywyd pêr odlau'n yr awel
A'r dyddiau yn araf nesáu,
Os urddwyd y fro â phroblemau
A'r werin yn dristfawr ei gwen,
Fe lwyddodd yr Eglwys serch hynny
Cawd Neuadd ar leiniau 'Penhen'.*

Nathan Davies

Smyrna Chapel

Nonconformity flourished early in this area. Between 1661 and 1668 about 40 members were brought in front of the court at Carmarthen and punished for refusing to conform. Evangelist Stephen Hughes had a great welcome here in 1672 and preached in a licensed house owned by Evan Morris. Until 1700 this was a church without a meeting-house, even though half of the parishioners were Independents. That year it succeeded in getting a chapel.

Anwes Chapel, built in the middle of Llanybri village, belonged to Llansteffan Rectory and was consecrated to the Virgin Mary. The year it was built is not known, but references to it are made as far back as 1388. Its name at that time was Morbrichurche. By 1552, it was Marbell Church. When the sum of £2 a year became too much to pay the rector of Llansteffan for reading the prayers there, he refused to read them. As a result his congregation decreased and the building went to ruin. By some means or another, William Evans, Pencader, succeeded in transferring the church into the ownership of the Independents and, when it was refurbished through a contribution from the Presbyterians, the congregation walked in to take ownership of it. The last service held in the Old Chapel was in 1960.

In 1813 the majority of the members of the Old Chapel proceeded to form their own church. David Davies, the minister at the time, was a teacher at Carmarthen College with David Peter. A Ty Cwrdd (meeting-house) called 'Capel Newydd' was built at the furthest end of the village and John Rowland, a student, became its first minister. He remained for

The original Smyrna Chapel, built in 1835.

The present Smyrna Chapel, built in 1915.

six years, ministering in the same village as had his old teacher, before moving to Cwmllynfell.

William James, a native of Trewyddel in Pembrokeshire, became minister in 1826. He used to preach in Capel Newydd on a Sunday morning and in the parish of Llangain in the afternoon. By 1834 the minister had persuaded the locals to build a chapel in the parish of Llangain. It was opened in February 1835 and called 'Smyrna'.

The community spirit, however, is epitomised in the story of the wife of Wauncorgam who invited the minister to choose any animal in the farmyard and sell it at the highest price possible – her contribution to the new chapel. This encouraged many to do the same and pursue the dream of building a chapel on the hilltop. It was at this time that the whitewashed stable and the schoolroom above it were built. There

is, therefore, an obvious link with that distant past. According to the Revd James Charles, Waunmably (a relative of the famous Thomas Charles of Bala), John Richards of Ethincefn (now called Ardwyn) would bring home some stones at the end of each working day and eventually there was almost enough to start building a chapel. His wife, a tall, dignified lady who was the caretaker, attended chapel in her traditional Welsh costume but would change her clogs for sandals at the doorway. One of the sons won the crown at the National Eisteddfod.

William James died in 1862, after a fruitful ministry in the area for 36 years. In 1864 both Capel Newydd and Smyrna invited Thomas Williams, a student from Brecon College, to be their minister. He worked with all his energy and, following in the footsteps of his predecessor.

With the success and increase in non-conformity congregationalism he immediately went about rebuilding Smyrna at a cost of £200. In modern day jargon a 'bigger and better' chapel was built which was wider in structure. By opening day, on 19 September 1865, the debt had almost been cleared, surely an accurate reflection of the hard graft and enthusiasm that had been injected into the venture by the membership which totalled 172. In addition it is known that there was a regular number of children in attendance and listeners in general amounting to 180, therefore giving a total of 352.

The Revd Thomas Lewis, from Solfach in Pembrokeshire, became the minister in 1872. It was during this period that Capel Newydd, Llanybri, was rebuilt. The present chapel was opened in 1874. Bethel was formed as a church in 1881. Within a year of arriving in the area, Lewis' family contracted

Pte David I. Griffiths (Davey), DCM, Cochybarlys, SWB, who fell in France on 3 October, 1918, aged 20.

The grave of Pte Griffiths, Cochybarlys, at Ypres, Belgium.

Mr and Mrs Davies, Wauncorgam Fach, and Harry, who died in action during the Second World War (Smyrna memorial).

typhoid fever, and his wife, his daughter and his mother-in-law died within three weeks of each other. However, his spirit was not diminished; he threw himself into his work and his ministry was a great success.

Before the end of that year, an invitation was extended to the Revd David Thomas from Tonypandy to be minister. This was the first 'calling' to involve the Bethel officials.

He accepted the invitation and was inducted on 15 and 16 March 1882. Smyrna was refurbished and new seats and a gallery were added at a total cost of £150. Membership had now risen to 200 with seating available for 262. The reopening services took place on 30 and 31 May, 1883. Mr Thomas was a faithful minister in the area until 1905, when he had an accident and lost his health completely.

The Nonconformist Statistics for Carmarthenshire available from a survey conducted in 1905 shows the entire property as having an estimated value of £750. The exercise also elaborated on the thriving Sunday School by giving figures of 60 scholars attending under 15 and 55 above, giving a total number of scholars of 115 with 13 teachers and, therefore, classes.

The Revd James John from Crwys came in 1908 and the induction services were in July of that year. His first task was to preside at the funeral of his predecessor. It was during Mr John's committed period as minister that the present chapel was built in Smyrna. He called the new chapel at Smyrna 'Fy Mreuddwyd Gwyn' (my white dream). The architect was George Morgan & Sons of King Street, Carmarthen; the builder, David Jones of Lammas Street and the decorators, D. Jones and Son of King Street. It was reported in 'Y Tyst' on 22 September 1915, that the newly built chapel was the largest and the most beautiful that the Congregationalists owned throughout rural Carmarthenshire.

A most enjoyable evening was spent at the Council School on Christmas evening when an excellent literary entertainment was held in connection with the Smyrna Congregational Church. The Rev. James John, pastor, presided. The entertainment consisted of solos, duets, quartets, octets, recitations, dialogues and a humourous sketch entitled Y Cawr Anwadol (The Fickle Lover). This created tumultuous cheers while all the items were highly appreciated by the vast crowd which had congregated from the neighbouring districts. For many years past it has been a custom to hold an entertainment in connection with the chapel and we hope that by next year we shall be able to hold it at the new chapel which is now under construction.

The programme was in the hands of the Sunday School Secretary Mr Gwilym Evans, Dyffryn, Llanstephan Road, who carried out his duties in an admirable way, while Miss S.A. Evans of the same address, presided very ably at the piano. The usual vote of thanks and the

singing of 'Hen Wlad Fy Nhadau' (land of My Fathers) terminated a most interesting and enjoyable evening.

(The Welshman, 1871)

The Opening Services took place in August, 1915 and according to the *Welshman*, 'quite a galaxy of preaching talent had been secured for the occasion, some of the best known ministers within the denomination'. They included Elvet Lewis-Elfed (1860-1953), the well known hymn-writer and poet from Blaen-y-Coed in Carmarthenshire. He was minister at Tabernacle, King's Cross in London at the time. Amongst his famous hymns are 'Cofio'n Gwlad, Benllywydd Tirion' and 'Arglwydd Iesu, Dysg i'm gerdded'.

The *Welshman* continues by reporting that the chapel had been 'transformed into one of the most beautiful in Wales... there was installed a heating apparatus, pipe organ, acetylene gas lighting, and a system of moving doors behind the pulpit which gave access to the vestry behind, and could be transformed into one vast room.

At the time the three chapels formed one of the largest ministerial circles within the denomination. Members lived as far as Laugharne in one direction and to Carmarthen and beyond in another, and were drawn from five parishes. Mr John was a lively minister and in 1931 received a call back to his native Ebenezer, St Davids.

Then the Revd Hopkin Evans came from Nantyffyllon near Maesteg in 1933. He was the only minister to live in Môr Awelon, Llansteffan – the manse was presented as a gift to the three churches by Mrs Cliff John in 1932. Mr Evans spent almost all his ministry at Smyrna and associate chapels, serving the area for almost forty years. He was a man of many talents not least as a historian and dramatist. The drama group formed by him and centrally based in Llansteffan flourished for many years and was popular with local people

The chapels were unable to find a minister after the retirement of the Revd Hopkin Evans, and between 1973 and 1976 the services were taken by various preachers. It soon became apparent to all concerned that it would be difficult to find an ordained person to minister over all the chapels. It was inevitable that the circle had to break. It became necessary, therefore, for Smyrna to go it alone and join Lammas Street Chapel, since the minister there was prepared to take responsibility for another chapel.

The Revd. J.Towyn Jones, FRSA became the Minister at Capel Heol Awst in 1974 and his original Christmas productions became significant events in the annual calendar of Carmarthen and the surrounding area. Since the 1990s the Advent Concert at Smyrna has become equally popular and successful with renowned artists such as 'Y Tri Tenor' drawing large audiences in recent years.

Above, left and right: *The interior of Smyrna Chapel.*

The partnership between both chapels since 1976 is indeed a healthy one and the support shown to each other is typical of a close and happy relationship. Since 1998 this has extended to include Elim Chapel in Ffynnonddrain near Carmarthen.

It is interesting to note that at least three ministers were nurtured at Smyrna, namely, Revd James Charles, Denbigh, Revd H. Smyrna Jones, Anglesey and Revd. G. Brynmor Thomas, Carmarthenshire, whose father was secretary for over fifty years at the turn of the last century.

This poem extols Smyrna Chapel, praising its fine appearance, its hallowed name and how it has served Llangain over the years.

Capel Smyrna Llangain

Gapel hoff, wyt hardd dy olwg
Addurn penna'r bryn wyt ti.
Mae dy enw'n gysegredig
Ac yn borth y Nef i
Gwyn fu dydd dy adeiladu
I hen seintiau bore oes.
A fu'n ffyddlon wasanaethu –
R'hwn a'i fywyd drostynt roes.

Eang yw dy fwyn groesawiad
Llydan yw dy borth o hyd.
Ti ddiwellaist lawer enaid
Ar ei daith i arall fyd.
Brafed yw dy sylfaen heddiw
Peraidd yw dy ddwyfol sain.
Aed newyddion dy areithfa
Tros randiroedd bras Llangain.

Boed i'r gwlith Nefolaidd ddisgyn
Megis cynt yn araf ddwys.
Tywys eto'r pererinion
I gyd-dynnu'r ddwyfol gwys.
Melys fyddo deddf dy allor
I addolwyr oesau'r byd.
A'th wirionedd fyddo'n lusern –
I lewyrchu ar bob pryd.

Nathan Davies

Ministers

1835–62	William James
1864–71	Thomas Williams
1872–81	Thomas Lewis
1882–05	David Thomas
1908–31	James John
1933–72	J. Hopkin Evans
1976	J. Towyn Jones

Chapel Secretaries

1835–		
1877–1930	William Thomas	Brynmor
1930–47	William Thomas	Siop Newydd
1947–60	Henry Jones	Minyrafon
1960–65	Tom Nicholas	Derw
1965–90	Ieuan Hobbs	Ty Isaf
1990–97	Dan Evans	Cyncoed
1997–2005	Terence Hesford	Yr Hafan
2005	Gillian Edwards	Tir Brwyn

Smyrna Jubilee

Debt Extinction Celebration
Services at Llangain

There were large congregations at the Jubilee services held at Smyrna Welsh Congregational Chapel, Llangain on Thursday, 18th inst., to celebrate the extinction of debt on the chapel, which was re-established in the year 1915. The esteemed ministers, the Revd J. John conducted the services and among those who took part were: The Revds., Elvet Lewis, MA London, Rees Williams, Maenclochog, Sam Williams, Landore, W.D. Rowlands (Water Street), Carmarthen; Harding Rees, Llanstephan, George B. Thomas, Penygroes. Other ministers present were the Revd. Edwin Jones, Liverpool, and Revd. J.P. Evans, Penygraig. There were substantial collections.

The minister, Revd J. John, who also has charge of the Welsh Independent Church at Llanstephan and Capel Newydd Llanybri, is a native of St David's, Pembrokeshire. He was ordained to the ministry in Shenandoah, Pennsylvania, USA, but five years later returned to the country of his birth and became first pastor of Bethlehem Church, Eyre Street, Cardiff. After three years of successful service there, Mr John removed to Gower to become minister of Three Crosses Congregational Church. Nine years later the churches constituting his present charge gave him an unanimous invitation, and he was installed as their minister in May, 1908.

Opening Service
Carmarthen Journal, 1915

An event of considerable interest in the Church life of Llangain and Llanstephan and district was the opening on Wednesday of the new Welsh Congregational Chapel at Smyrna, in the parish of Llangain. The opening services were largely attended, and several of the most prominent preachers of the denomination took part. The new edifice is erected on the site of the old chapel, which was built in 1834, and is a branch of the new chapel at Llanybri. Fitted with electric light, it has seating accommodation for 450, and the cost of erection was nearly £2,200. The pastor is the Revd James Johns, Llanstephan, who is also in charge of the new chapel at Llanybri and Bethel, Llanstephan. The three churches provide one of the largest fields of labour for the Congregational denomination in the whole of Wales, and the members reside in an area extending from the Laugharne river to the Town of Carmarthen, a distance of ten miles. The area covered includes five parishes. Mr John has taken a keen interest in recruiting in the locality and has addressed many meetings in West Wales. His only son is a lieutenant in the 15th Service Batt. Welsh Regiment. The contractor for the erection of the chapel was Mr David Jones, Lammas Street, Carmarthen, while the decorators were Messrs D. Jones & Son, King Street, Carmarthen. The number of members is about 180.

This poem sings the praises of Smyrna's little old vestry. It was sacred to the forefathers and there are sweet memories of it. The poet wishes that the old customs associated with the vestry would come back.

Hen Festri Fach Smyrna

*'Festri fach' rwyt gysegredig
Eisoes gan y tadau gynt.
Bu dy furiau'n wynfydedig
I'r hoff ddeiliaid ar eu hynt.
Melys ydyw'r mwyn atgofion
Am dy egwyddorion ffri.
Ac yn swyn y pur awelon
Seiniwyd cân am Galfari.*

*Os unigrwydd dreigla'r dyddiau
Am yr hen flynyddoedd gynt.
Pan fu'r mawl ym mri'r telynau
Megis sain Nefolaidd wynt.
Anwyr hoff tan wên fu'n trydar
Oddi mewn i'th gorlan glyd.*

Yr Hen Stabl, the old whitewashed stable opposite Smyra Chapel.

*Llonni wnest yr egin cynnar
Ar eu taith trwy'r anial fyd.*

*O na bawn fwy tebyg iti
I wynebu'r byd o'i loes
Boed bendithion gynt ddadebru
Llwybrau hedd o oes i oes.
Llawer crwydryn llesg a bawlyd
Droediodd heibio'th fangre gu.
Heb gael trem ar dir y bywyd
A heb gael d'adnabod di.*

*Deued eto'r hen arferion
Oedfa'r wythnos yn ei bri
Ti mi wn fu'n eiriol droeon
Dros rinweddau'r hyn a fu.
Er yn hen a llwyd dy furiau
A'th ddelfrydau mêl yn sarn.
Byth ni dderfydd grym dy arfau
'Festri fach' hyd ddydd y farn.*

Nathan Davies

Henry Jones, Minyrafon
Carmarthen Journal, 1963

It is with regret that we record the sudden and unexpected death of Mr Henry Jones, at his home at Minyrafon, Llangain.

Mr Jones was 86 years of age, and throughout his life he had given faithful and devoted service to Smyrna Chapel. He was a deacon from 1926 and chapel secretary from 1947 to 1960. For nearly half a century he had been responsible for the guidance and training of the children at the Sunday School. Deceased was very thorough and methodical in all his duties and his exemplary work towards the cause of religion will serve as a pattern to the younger generation. He has also served as the sub-postmaster of the village for the past 56 years.

The funeral, which was largely attended, took place at Smyrna Chapel on Tuesday 9 July, and the services were in the charge of the minister, the Revd J. Hopkin Evans.

Smyrna Minister and Deacons, 1940. Left to right, back row: *William John (Forlan, 1939), David Davies (Bryn, 1939), Thomas Howells (1939), David Davies (Wauncorgam Fach, 1939), James Thomas (1939), John John, 1939 (Arweinydd y Plant 1923); front row: Henry Jones, 1926 (Hyfforddwr y Plant 1900), William John (Cwrthir) 1926 (Trysorydd 1924), Revd Hopkin Evans (Minister) 1933, William Thomas 1902 (Arweinydd y Gan 1888; Ysgrifennydd 1930), William Evans 1926.*

Sunday-school class at Smyrna Chapel, c.1938. Left to right, back row: *Tom Roberts, Jac Jones, William John (Sunday-school teacher), Ernie Jones, Glyn John;* middle row: *Nellie Williams, Dora Lewis, Rachel Lewis, Maggie Howells, Edith Howells, Mary Davies;* front row: *Lawrence? Walters, David Jones (Dai bach y teilwr), Nathan Davies (y bardd).*

Post-war Sunday-school outing to Porthcawl, 1946. Left to right, back row: Teg ?, Ieuan Davies, Jacky Davies, Jacky Jones, Emrys Davies, ?, Tudor Williams, Vincent Williams, Tom Evans; front row: Meriel Lewis, Beryl Howells, Lena Lewis, Nesta Williams, Katy Davies, Hywel Williams, Olwen Davies, Glenys Howells, Elvira Davies.

Smyrna celebration services for the 50th anniversary of the new chapel (1915–65). Left to right: Llungwyn Jones, Edwin Jones, Brynmor Thomas, ?, Tom Thomas, Tom Nicholas, Jones y Ffordd, Emrys Hesford, Tom Howells, Elwyn Thomas, Revd Hophin Evans and Mrs Evans, Islwyn Jones (headmaster), William Bowen, Revd J.J. Evans, Revd T.V. Lewis, J. Jones y Down, ?, County Cllr T.Ll. Harries, Revd Eurfyn Morgan, Ieuan Hobbs.

Sisterhood meeting at Smyrna in the mid-1960s. Left to right, back row: May Morris, Ida Hobbs, Anne Hesford, Eiry Jones, Linda Davies, Beryl Davies; middle row: Mollie Thomas, Rachie Lewis, Annie Davies, Olwen Evans, Mrs Mason, Heulwen Morris, Maggie Howells, Amy Davies, Betty Thomas, Celia ?, Rhiannon Morris, Dorothy Clement; front row: Dilys Jones, Sally Jones, Ruby Howells, Mrs Hopkin Evans, Gwladys John, Edith Evans, Minnie John, Blodwen Hesford, Meriel Lewis; sitting on floor: Delyth Jones, Iona Morris.

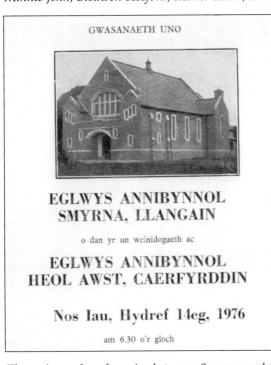

GWASANAETH UNO

EGLWYS ANNIBYNNOL SMYRNA, LLANGAIN

o dan yr un weinidogaeth ac

EGLWYS ANNIBYNNOL HEOL AWST, CAERFYRDDIN

Nos Iau, Hydref 14eg, 1976

am 6.30 o'r gloch

The union order of service between Smyrna and Heol Awst Chapel, Carmarthen, and induction of the Revd. J. Towyn Jones, FRSA, as new minister on 14 October, 1976.

Lena Lewis, Lletyrneuadd, Smyrna Chapel organist for over 50 years.

Easter at Smyrna, 1972. Left to right, back row: *Yvonne Davies, Bronwen Morris, Iona Morris, Gwenllian Walters, Gillian Davies, Delyth Jones, Beryl Hicks, Hywel Williams;* middle row: *Eleri Morris, Hefin Morris, Dorian Bowen, Yvonne Bowen, Paul Thomas;* front row: *Elona Phillips, Edwin Jones, Rhiannon Morris, Mrs Hopkin Evans, Dilys Jones, Elonwy Evans, Beryl Davies, Emrys Hesford.*

Presentation to Mrs Hopkin Evans at a Sisterhood dinner in the Werndale Guest House, Bancyfelin, 1972. Left to right, back row: *Sally Jones, Dorothy Morgan, Mair Morgan, Gillian Davies, Iona Morris, Janet Morris, Sara Morris, Delyth Jones, Valerie Davies, Eiry Jones, Rhiannon Morris, Mair Jones, Elona Phillips;* middle row: *Sally Jones, Sal Rogers, Annie Davies, ?, Amy Davies, Nellie Williams, Heulwen Rees, Beryl Davies, Glenys Jones, Maggie Howells, Rachie Lewis, ?, Mrs Hughes (?), Awena Thomas, Minnie John, Edith Evans;* front row: *?, Mrs Nurton, Molly Thomas, ?, Catherine Williams, Ruby Howells, May Morris, Mrs Hopkin Evans, Dilys Jones, Gwladys John, Mrs Griffiths, ?, Bethan Davies.*

Smyrna minister and deacons, 1980s. Left to right: Ieuan Hobbs, Gwyn Walters, Beryl Davies, Revd J. Towyn Jones, Nellie Williams, Jack Jeremy.

He was assisted at the house by the Vicar of Llanstephan the Revd J.T. Jenkins, and at the chapel by the Revds Towyn Evans, Cana, E. Richards, Bancffosfelen, and Ll. Jones, Trewyddel. The Vicar of Llanagain, The Revd D.S. Lewis, was also present, together with Mr T.L. Thomas, assistant postmaster, representing Mr Johns, the head postmaster of Carmarthen.

Cyfarch Mr Ieuan P. Hobbs

This is a tribute to Ieuan Hobbs, who was secretary of Smyrna Chapel for 25 years. It acknowledges the many demands made on him and thanks him warmly for his contribution, his loyalty and his unfailing readiness to deal with matters.

Ysgrifennydd Smyrna Llangain
1965–90

Aeth chwarter canrif heibio
Bu llawer tro ar fyd,
Ond dal yn Ysgrifennydd
Wnaeth Ieuan Hobbs o hyd.

Mae llawer o alwadau
Ar' Sgrifennydd pawb a wyr,
Amhosib ydyw plesio'r pawb
Aelodau bawb yn llwyr.

Dros Smyrna bu yn ddiwyd
Ffyddlondeb oedd ei ran
Ei gyfran dros yr Eglwys
Ddaw'n amlwg yn y man.

Beth tybed fydd yr hanes

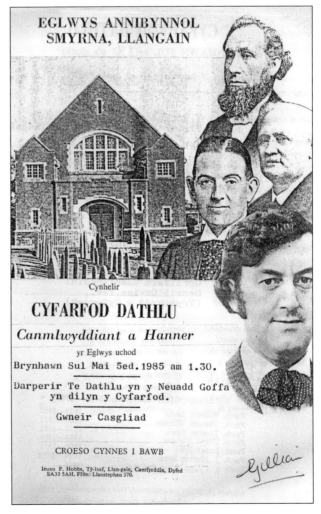

Smyrna Foundation order of service celebrating 150 years on 5 September 1985.

Land donated by Mr and Mrs E.J. Williams, Penycoed, to provide additional burial to Smyra graveyard.

Gorffwysfan Llwch (cremation resting place) donated by Mr Glyn Williams, Broadlands, in memory of his wife, Eira Elonwy Williams.

Yn Smyrna maes o law?
Amlwg fydd gwasanaeth Ieuan
I bawb pwy bynnag ddaw.
Diolchwn bawb o galon
Am eich parodrwydd llwyr,
I drafod ein gofynion
Boed fore neu foed hwyr.

A'n diolch gwir i'r ddynes
Fu'n dawel wrth y llyw,
Hir oes, da iechyd hefyd,
Boed i'ch fendithion Duw.

Dan Evans

Memories of Miss Maggie Howells, Arfryn, Heol Smyrna (Formerly of Danlanfach), aged 95 2005

Miss Howells is Llangain's oldest parishioner.

Haydn: What are your first memories of school?

Maggie: I walked to school every day from Danlanfach – past the church and through Lletyrneuadd and over a stile opposite the school.

Haydn: Did you take a packed lunch?

Maggie: Yes. No school meals in those days. I had a tiny milk churn and I would warm it by the school fire.

Haydn: Who were your teachers?

Maggie: Miss Griffiths and Mr Rees Thomas. Then came another Thomas after him. He was called 'Tomos tal', since he was tall.

Haydn: What kind of subjects were you taught?
Maggie: Well you see, I was in poor health. If I was in school for a week then I would be away for a fortnight or so. I had to leave altogether at ten years old. My brother Harri would carry me piggy back because of my leg deformity. The doctors were saying that I would either get better or live just to see around 21. Well, my health improved and here I am all these years later! Mind you, I often think now being unable to do things for myself and alone that it would have been better if things had turned out differently. But there again, who would have looked after my parents and then my mother in her latter years? The carers do for me now what I used to do for her.

Haydn: What can you tell me about Pantydderwen?

Maggie: I remember Henry Jones offering us the opportunity to move there. My mother wasn't keen. Her argument was that if they did go there, she would be confined to the house since there are steps in front to go down to the road and there were some steps going up to the flower and vegetable garden. In any case a downstairs room such as the parlour would have to be adapted to her needs.

Haydn: My Great Aunt Getta while living there with my grandmother had to eventually have her bedroom downstairs in the parlour. So I understand what you are saying. She was admitted to Argel in the end but only remained there a short while before her death on 1 December 1962.
Maggie: There was another Getta in Pantydderwen after Henry Jones. A Getta Williams and Rose, her daughter.

Haydn: There weren't many houses here in those days. Take me on a journey! What places to you remember?

Maggie: After Pantydderwen there was only the school, vicarage, Chweched and Penywern. That's all there was on that lane. Then down to Gilfach, Hendy and Cochybarlys. Then you would cross a stream to Clomendy and onto my home and Penyclun, Clunmawr, Penhen and Church House.

Haydn: What properties do you remember in the direction of Llansteffan?

Maggie: There was nothing until Delfryn, but I remember Haulfryn and Cartref being built and, of course, Brynderi. Evan Jones, the vicar, built it in the 1930s and Lilian, his daughter, and her husband lived there. Miss Grant, her cousin from Lampeter, came there after she lost him. Then you reach Delfryn, Beilsyfi, Rhydlydan and Meini. Oh dear, no one farms these days! The first people I remember at Rhydlydan were Mr and Mrs Rees. I went down there past the church and onto Chweched and onto the main road by Beilibach (behind Delfryn).

Haydn: What can you tell me about the woollen factory at Bwthyn y Felin?

Maggie: Tom Williams was the owner and he employed about four people there. It closed after the war. Now let's go on to the Brook. There was a shop at Belmont and it was called Siop Newydd in those days. Opposite was Y Dolau and Ty Newydd below it. The Post Office was at Min yr Afon for about 50 years! Alongside you had Brook Forge, where Jac Ifans was the Smithy. We would often take our pony there. The undertaker lives there now. Glanmor and Wendy have changed the name to Welsh – Swn yr Einion. That's pretty.

I tell you an interesting thing! They used to carry the coffins to church and chapel in those days and shoulder high, too. The bearers would change around like a relay race according to the distance of the telegraph posts and therefore be relieved of their duties every so often. I remember the funerals of both William Thomas, Shop Newydd (Belmont) and Tom Williams of the factory.

Anyway, from Swn yr Einion there you would go along the main road to the Glyn and Ty Canol and onto Morfa Bach. The Brook and Morfa Bach was Llangain in those days. There was a shop further along from the Post Office owned by the Lewises below the road opposite the entrance to Panyrathro.

Haydn: Now let's turn around and go back to beyond Penycoed, my old home. What was there in the direction of Carmarthen?

Maggie: There were two cottages by Penycoed bends – Penybanc and Danybanc. There was a little shop with Jane Stewart and Bess, her daughter, was to continue that tradition in Haulfryn.

Now then, Green Castle. I remember Johnny Davies and your grandmother there. Willie, his brother, was killed in action. He was only 20. Then the Wykes came there. Wyke was a good farmer and to see his straight potato rows in the garden above the bend was a treat! After the bend you would go towards Plas Cwrthir. Now my parents lived in a cottage called Packet House before moving to

Miss Maggie Howells on her 95th birthday in 2005 being presented with a bouquet of flowers by Cllr Haydn Williams, Chairman of Llangain Community Council.

Danlanfach. It was in the field opposite the entrance to the mansion.

Haydn: Who was your first minister at Smyrna?

Maggie: Oh, Mr John. You know he walked all the way from Llansteffan to conduct services. The old vestry above the small stable was used to prepare food when Eisteddfodau were held in the chapel.

Haydn: Did you ever attend the church since it was nearer to your home?

Maggie: Oh yes! Although I was a member at Smyrna, we would support the church. My father would go to Smyrna Sunday school in the morning and the service in the afternoon but would attend Evensong at the church instead of walking back up to chapel again. It's a pretty church. Both places were full in those days, unlike nowadays. People don't care about such places today!

Tell you another thing. That vicarage should never have been pulled down by the council! Why didn't they convert it to an old people's home? It would have served the same purpose as the bungalows at Maersyrawel that they did build. No need for a crowd there, but say a dozen or so residents.

Memories of Tom and Mollie Thomas, Gwynfan
(Formerly of Gilfach), aged 89 and 90 respectively, 2005

Mr and Mrs Thomas celebrated their diamond wedding anniversary in 2003 and are the oldest married couple in the parish.

THE BOOK OF LLANGAIN
THE BOOK OF LLANGAIN

Haydn: What are your first memories of your childhood days in Llangain?

Mollie: I remember helping on the farm. Milking by hand then.
Tom: Then came the pipeline system and the milk tankers.

Haydn: Who was the schoolmaster when you went to school?

Mollie: Tom Thomas first.
Tom: Not Tom her husband now ! (laughs).

Mollie: Then there was a relief who was known as Phillips bach. Rees, my brother, was quite a favourite with him. Then came Sam Rees!

Haydn: Did you behave in school?

Mollie: Oh gosh yes! He was a disciplinarian. No nonsense. Pupils had to behave. He was a good master and able to put things in our heads.
Tom: He was a keen gardener, too, and introduced a school garden. The boys did the work and he reaped the harvest – gooseberries and strawberries.

Haydn: Did you take a packed lunch with you?

Mollie: No. I used to walk back to Penywern and had lovely soup most days. Some of my friends would come too. The Johns were very kind.

Haydn: Who was the caretaker at that time?

Mollie: I remember Jane Stewart, Danybanc, doing it. Bess, her daughter, delivered the mail around the parish. Later she sold sweets, cigarettes and Sunday papers at Haulfryn on the main road.
Tom: Woodbines! They were sold as 5s. in paper packets.
Mollie: Ben Davies, Ystradwalter (Watt Davies' brother, Dewi's uncle) was working with us on the farm. On one occasion, when he had ran out of cigarettes – there was a shop at Belmont (Siop Newydd) in those days – my brother, Rees went there to fetch some for him. On his way back over the fields there was a beautiful walled pond at the bottom of the farm. Now when Ben opened the packet there was one cigarette missing. 'Oh, I saw a fox on the road,' said Rees. You know what he had done? He had placed it on the water surface and watched it float its way down the pond and out through a pipe!
Tom: Miriam, the shopkeeper, made homemade wine. She would make you try some. She was dangerous! A large glass like this, Haydn, would bring your knees up high!
(At this point I was offered a glass of Gwynfan's home-made elderflower wine, which I highly recommend since it went down a treat!)

Haydn: Do you remember some of the cottages that have now disappeared?

Mollie: Bolahaul was across the field opposite Penywern. They used to carry water there. Penllwyngolau was where Glanygolau is today. The Vowles home. Danybanc just beneath the double bend by Penycoed. Opposite it was another cottage called Penybanc. I don't know who lived there but the house was there where the rough land is now after the double bend. There was also a cottage where the thatched house is now, after Green Castle bend.

Haydn: Smyrna chapel has played an important part in your life, hasn't it?

Mollie: Yes, it has! I was 'received' as a full member by the Revd William John, the Minister. Edwin and Dilys Jones, Islwyn, and John, Y Bryn, were accepted at the same time. The three have passed away. John was a character. He was Eira's brother and Eric's Jones' brother-in-law. We walked to chapel three times a sunday.
There were 50 in Sunday school. Henry Jones was one of the teachers in the 1930s. But once the war broke out things changed. Hopkins Evans was there for a very long time and then Towyn Jones came in 1976.
Tom: There was a service on a Tuesday night and you had to be there about threequarters of an hour before it started, otherwise you wouldn't have a seat. Completely different from what it is like nowadays.

Haydn: Was the small stable well used?

Mollie: Howells Danlanfach was one that brought a pony and trap. Also the Thomases of Waunmably. They later went to live to Rugby.
Tom: There was room for four horses. The stalls are still there. Above it was the old vestry with its own fireplace. I was the one that pulled down the chimney when it was no longer needed and placed some tiles there. I remember a man called Ben living alone there.
Mollie: When we had three services for our Annual Services (cwrdde mawr) and one held the previous evening, dinner was prepared there. We would carry the bread and butter and sliced meat over to the chapel and fetch the boiling water up from the cellar. How things have changed!

Haydn: You were both very involved with the building of the Memorial Hall. Tell me about that.

Mollie: I remember my father saying that there was

66

Mr and Mrs Tom Thomas Gwynfan (formerly of Gilfach) with Cllr Dilwyn Williams, Chairman, Carmarthenshire County Council, on their diamond wedding anniversary, 2004, displaying a congratulatory card received from Her Majesty, Queen Elizabeth II.

an interest amongst a few to build the hall for the district to offer a fitting memorial to those that had lost their lives. Well then we had another war and things were placed on hold. Then in the 1950s it was resurrected.

Tom: Along with John Platt cleared all the trash in that corner in preparation to level out the ground ready for building. They found a human skeleton!

In those days there was a hedge bordering the road. By jumping over a stile you could make your way down to Lletyrneuadd. Now just at the front corner of the new entrance we discovered a woman. Platt and I went to tell Mrs Rees Schoolhouse. She came back with us and to her horror identified her friend by the glasses, handbag and shoes. She had been missing for months, believed drowned in the Tywi, but she had been there all the time!

Mollie: I remember holding whist drives to raise money.

Tom: Yes. Events were often held in the Drill Hall – the barracks at Carmarthen. Tom Williams, Fernhill,

was the driving force behind such events. There had to be regular fund-raising events.

Mollie: It was a pity they pulled down the vicarage. It was a wonderful building. I remember a few vicars too – Price, who came from Aberaeron, Y Ficer Bach (Melvyn Thomas) and Sid Lewis. His wife died here and then he went to Penybont.

Haydn: How do you feel about being the oldest married couple in the Llangain?

Mollie: Well, we recently celebrated our diamond wedding anniversary. That was nice. The years have gone so quickly. But Maggie is the oldest in the area. It's a pity that she is failing now because she has been so good and so faithful to Smyrna throughout her life. Not missing a Sunday. But as for memory she is wonderful, better than me! I hope I will live to see your book.

Tom: Yes, indeed, but we take one day at the time now!

Llangain schoolboys with Mr James Evans (headmaster), c.1900.

Llangain schoolgirls with Mr James Evans (headmaster), c.1900.

CHAPTER 3

Primary School

Historical Background

The year 1846 marked a turning-point in the history of education in Wales. In that year William Williams, a native of Llanpumsaint who was MP for Coventry, obtained the appointment of a Royal Commission to enquire into the state of education in Wales.

Three young barristers named Lingen, Symons and Johnson were chosen for this task, and they in turn appointed ten assistants. They did their work with great thoroughness and in the following year published an extraordinary report, known as the Lingen Report.

The picture they drew of education in Wales was of the darkest kind. They reported that over 78,000 children were receiving some sort of education in day-schools, but they severely criticised the general standard of this education and commented on the incompetence of the teachers and the inadequacy of the school buildings and equipment.

The report went further and said harsh things about the habits, manners and morals of the Welsh people. One of the commissioners thought that the peasants (he included among them nearly all who spoke Welsh) were 'almost universally' immoral. The commissioners considered that the state of the people was due to the use of the Welsh language, which kept them ignorant and prevented them from improving themselves. So black did they paint the condition of the Welsh people that English periodicals declared that Wales 'was fast settling down into the most savage barbarism', and that the habits of its people were 'those of animals and do not bear description'.

The report aroused great indignation throughout Wales, and leading Welshmen, both in Wales and in England, hastened to defend Wales and its people. It was pointed out that not one of the commissioners knew a word of Welsh, and also knew very little about schools. They were all Anglicans and had no sympathy with Nonconformity. They were accused of having emphasised the faults of the schools and of entirely refusing to recognise their merits. They also took their evidence almost entirely from clergymen of the Church of England, JPs and employers. However bad conditions may have been, there seems little doubt that this report was one-sided. The report came to be known as Brad y Llyfrau Gleision (the Treason of the Blue Books).

The immediate effect of the report was unfortunate. Out of disgust with the Lingen Report, Nonconformists were unwilling to accept state grants for schools and it increased the bitterness between Nonconformists and Anglicans. Gradually, however, this feeling passed, and during the 1850s the British and Foreign Society and the National Society set up a number of schools in North and South Wales. Also, in 1848, Trinity College, Carmarthen, was set up to train teachers for South Wales, and a similar college for North Wales was set up at Bangor in 1862. The final steps in the provision of elementary schools in Wales were the same as for England. The passing of the Elementary Education Act (sometimes called the Forster Act, after W.E. Forster, who steered it through Parliament) was the most important reform in the history of education.

Forster's Education Act, 1870

The Act of 1870 provided that:
a. Elementary schools were to be built in all districts where efficient schools were not already provided by religious bodies.
b. The new schools were to be controlled by locally elected school boards, which were given power to levy rates to pay for them.

The Act was a landmark in educational development because it created a nationwide network of elementary schools. These schools, at first, did not provide free education, nor was elementary education compulsory. In 1880, however, elementary education was made compulsory to the age of ten, and in 1891 it was made free. In 1899 the school-leaving age was raised to 12, to 14 in 1918, to 15 in 1944 and finally, in 1972, to 16.

Treason of the Blue Books

William Morris, one of the ten assistants appointed for the Lingen Report, 1846, later known as the Treason of the Blue Books, made the following entry about Llangain on 16 November, 1846:

The Revd John Thomas, curate of this parish, said, 'that there was no day and only one Sunday school in the parish. The parish clerk had given up the day school because he was not sufficiently remunerated for conducting it and was then a labourer, though a good scholar and quite capable of keeping a school. The schoolroom in which the school was held was used by the parishioners to put up their horses when going to

Llangain School and School House.

Llangain School House.

church, there being no stable for the purpose – a school-room was very much wanted for the parish. There was a great desire for education among the people, but they were too poor and a schoolmaster could not subsist unless he had a stipend from the government or some other source. The rate of wages had lately risen very much.'

James Owen, a labourer who was working on the road, said that:

... day labourers were getting from 9d. to 1s. (5p) a day with victuals (food provisions); farm servants from £10 to £15 a year; and female servants from £3.10s. to £5 a year. There was a great desire among the working people to get education for their children. The people were quiet and steady; but there was an increase of drunkenness with the advanced rate of wages.

The Revd William James, minister of Smyrna Chapel (1835-1862) said that:

... commodious schoolrooms and able teachers were very much wanted in the country, as all classes wished to give their children some amount of education; that wages had advanced greatly and that 1s. a day with victuals now was the common rate. Owing to the increase of wages, he was afraid that drunkenness also was on the increase.

Chairman   W.E.B. Gwyn Esq. Plas Cwrthir
Vice-Chairman   Mr William Lewis Church House
Hon. Sec.   Mr John Thomas Gilfach

Dimensions of the Llangain Board School

	Length	Breadth	Height	Cubical Area
Schoolroom (room mawr)	30	18	15.6	8,370 cu.ft
Classroom (room bach)	14	16	15.6	3,472 cu.ft

This shows the main room as measuring 30ft long by 18ft wide with a headroom of 15.5ft, making a cubic area of 8,370 cu.ft. The classroom next to the school-room is 14ft long by 16ft wide with, again, a head-room of 15.5ft, making a cubic area of 3,472 cu.ft.

The accommodation, taking the formula of 8 sq.ft per child, offers room for 67.5 pupils in the main room and 28 in the small classroom, making a total capacity of 95 pupils.

Head Teachers

1876–82	John John
1882–94	John Davies
1894–1902	James Evans
1902–18	Rees Thomas
1918–24	Thomas Thomas
1924–61	Samuel Rees
1961–70	Islwyn Jones
1971–73	Goronwy Phillips
1974–90	David Marks
1990–2004	Malcolm Griffiths
2004–	Angharad Jones

School Managers

School managers came into being following the 1902 Education Act.

1903–34	Evan Jones	Vicarage
1935–40	D.T. Price	Vicarage
1940–46	Arthur Lewis	Lan y Gors
1946–64	Ernie Jones	Pen y Clun
1964–67	Dilwyn Jones	Ucheldir
1967–74	Ieuan Hoobs	Tŷ Isaf
1974–77	J.J. Williams	Cefnglas

N.B. Area Schools governing bodies and Llangain had its own in 2000.

Log Books

In the book, or books, because there are several of them, the headmaster of the time was required to record certain events. These included records of attendance, which were often followed by some explanation if attendance was poor – bad weather, children helping with the harvest or an epidemic of measles or scarlet fever or other illness. Many of these diseases had to be notified at the time to the

Contract for the erection of a Board School in the parish of Llangain, Carmarthenshire

between

Messrs Peter Bowen, Thomas Davies and their Sureties

and

The Llangain School Board

Dated 28 April, 1875

This Indenture made the Twenty Eighth day of April, one thousand eight hundred and seventy five. Between Peter Bowen of Llanybri in the county of Carmarthen, mason and builder. Thomas Davies of Blaencwm in the parish of Llanstephan in the said county of Carmarthen, carpenter and builder. Thomas Davies of Penlanfach in the parish of Llangunnock in the same county, farmer and David Lewis of Meinillwydion in the parish of Llangain in the same county, farmer of the one part and the School Board for the district of Llangain in the said county of Carmarthen of the other part. Whereas the said Board, having with the consent and approval of the Education Department resolved to erect a schoolhouse and premises in the district of Llangain aforesaid, obtained senders for the execution of the works, have agreed with the said Peter Bowen and Thomas Davies for executing and completing the said works comprised in the specification marked 'A' and referred to in certain drawings numbered from 1 to 6 and which specification and drawings have been sealed with the seal of the said Board and signed by the said Peter Bowen and Thomas Davies for the sum of Six Hundred and Forty two Pounds and have named the said Thomas Davies (Farmer) and David Lewis as their sureties for the due performance thereof.

1. *That the said Peter Bowen and Thomas Davies shall and will to the satisfaction of the said Board on their sureties in a workmanlike, substantial and lasting manner and with the best materials on or before the last day of November next erect, execute and complete the schoolhouse and premises and all other works specified and referred to in the said plans and specification including all contingent and incidental works and in case the same shall not be completed on or before the last day of November next then the said Peter Bowen and Thomas Davies shall forfeit and pay the said Board the sum of One Pound for every day after that date during which the said work shall remain incomplete and unfinished.*

2. *That the said P.B. and T.D. shall in carrying out the said work fulfil the directions and instructions of the said Board or their said surveyor.*

3. *That the said Board for the consideration aforesaid shall and will pay to the said P.B. and T.D. the sum of Six Hundred and Forty two Pounds in such instalments and at such times on the certificate of their said surveyor that the works comprised in this contract or intended so to be completed and finished.*

4. *Lastly for the due performance of this contract the said P B and T D, T D (farmer) and D L their sureties do jointly and severally for themselves their heirs executors and administrators are held and firmly bound by these presents in the sum of Five Hundred Pounds to the said Board to be recovered by the said Board or their successors as and for liquidated damages in case the said P B and T D shall make default in the premises.*

Provided always that should any dispute or difference arise or happen between the said P.B. and T.D. and the said Board touching or concerning the said works hereby contracted to be erected, altered, repaired, executed and completed as aforesaid or touching or concerning any other matter

In witness whereof the said parties to these presents have hereunto sat their hands and seals the day and year hereinbefore written it.

Signed, sealed and delivered by the within named P.B., T.D. and T.D. in the presence of

Mr W.D. Evans, Solicitor, Carmarthen.
10/5/75

Mr Rees Thomas (Headmaster 1902–18) and Mrs Thomas, Schoolhouse.

County Medical Officer. Teacher absences were also recorded. Visits from HMIs (school inspectors) were noted, and often their written report on the school was included in the log-book, hand-written by the inspector or transcribed by the headmaster. Often other, more interesting, items were included as well, with mention being made of both local and national events of the time.

I have taken several extracts from the books to give a glimpse at the curriculum offered and at some of the events in the lives of those involved in the school during the last quarter of the nineteenth and twentieth centuries.

Log Entries

28 February 1876
The Llangain Board School opened this day as a Public and Elementary one. There were 32 present. Mr Lewis, one of the board, attended this morning.

12 March
The weather is very cold. Few of the children are absent. I gave a reading lesson to the first class this morning from a piece called 'Greek Pilgrimage to the Jordan'. The home-lesson (homework) was lesson 3 and 4 from Gill's *Popular Geography*. The most of them said their home-lesson in the morning.

26 April
There are two funerals in the neighbourhood and few of the schoolchildren are kept at home because their parents intend going to them.

27 April
David Davies is reported to be sick. John Evans absent – setting potatoes. John George absent – harrowing.

1 May
The children in the lower class were tried individually to see whether they know the figures by this time. They have been constantly taught to know them from the blackboard as well as on the slates.

3 May
Several of the schoolboys were punished this morning for being late; not one had an excuse to pardon him. Jonah Davies Greencastle is away harrowing. The second lesson had about a dozen words to get up and then the lesson was read round the class. The first class did their arithmetic this morning each one very attentive to his work. The schoolchildren were very quiet and attentive.

11 July
Haymaking is going on this week in this parish, the children being useful at this crisis are kept at home.

14 July
The Llangain School Board broke up for a fortnight's holiday on the occasion of hay harvest.

14 August
This time of year when the harvest is, children in this parish are kept home by their parents to render such assistance as is required.

14 September
Lady Hamilton, The Plas, Llanstephan, and Miss Wellington visited the school this afternoon.

29 September
Obtained five maps for the school. Map of the World, Europe, England and Wales, Ireland and Scotland. Also pen-holders, pencils, and slates. School pretty full, 43 scholars present.

3 October
Thanksgiving at Smyrna Independent Chapel. A large number of the children absent in the afternoon attending it. Mary David, Dole, absent this week with a sore foot. Thomas Lewis, Church House, left today for Laugharne Grammar School.

4 October
School closed today. Harvest Thanksgiving Services in Church. Dinner being given to all strangers

attending the services. Consequently the School could not be carried on, it being used for this purpose.

27 October
Thomas Stuart, a lad in this school, whilst playing this morning fell into the pool of water adjacent top the playground wall. This pool being deep and without enclosure is very dangerous to the little ones. Cautioned all the scholars to keep away from it.

2 November
All the boys in the Upper Class absent this afternoon after the hounds. Some has asked leave of absence, the other were punished having gone to school at 3.30p.m., afterwards sent home.

14 November
Hiring fair at Carmarthen. Most of the children attending the Fair, others kept at home as the servants were away. Consequently the School was closed.

31 January 1877
The School was closed this day through a Ploughing Match being in the neighbourhood.

Summary of the Inspector's Report, January 1877:
The present master has had charge of this school for about three months as many of the children had never been in school previously the instruction as yet is very elementary. The work has however made a fair start and is likely to improve. The pits near the school should be filled up, at present they are somewhat dangerous.

The surface drainage in the yards is not satisfactory. A cupboard should be provided for the school books, slates etc and a fire guard to place before the open stove.

I am to state that Mr John is not qualified for recognition under article 60 and I am to enquire whether the Board will undertake to secure the services of a certified teacher with as little delay as possible. Mr John's appointment should have been notified to this Department persuant to article 17{c}.

11 June
Large School attendance – 60 scholars present. Edward Jones and Mary Davies Penywern admitted this morning. David Jones, Factory, through playing with stones, accidentally received a severe blow in the mouth.

29 June
Funeral of a child from The Brook. Consequently the attendance was rather small.

6 July
The attendance this week has fallen off considerably in consequence of hay-making having commenced.

William Morris, Penhen, William Lloyd, Glog, and several others were kept at home the greater part of this week assisting their parents with the hay. Now hay-making has commenced there will be a continual decrease in attendance until the harvest is over. Average attendance this week 35. The Misses Davies Llwyndu visited the sewing class in the afternoon.

18 October
Mr John Rees Hendy called in school this afternoon. Punished Abram Jones for throwing stones at a stranger passing at noon.

26 October
Although it has been very wet through the week but few of the Scholars absent. Annie Griffiths absent through the week through illness. Mr William Lewis, Church House, and Clerk to the Board, called at the school this morning and ordered that fire should be kept now and during the winter season.

Attendance plummeted just before Christmas 1881 since there was an epidemic in the parish. The school was closed for six weeks until 31 January 1882. Only five pupils attended that day anyway.

The inspector's report at that time mentions that, on the whole, the school was in a pretty fair condition considering the district had suffered much from this epidemic. However, a year later, having only been there since March 1882, Evan John Davies was praised by the HMI for considerably improving the general efficiency of the school. The handwriting was very good and the arithmetic and reading had made creditable progress. The grammar was good and the needlework very fair. He suggested that a paid monitor should be of great service to the headmaster.

On 2 March 1882 Evan John Davies started as headmaster. He had been a pupil teacher at St Clears Board School and an assistant master at Blaencwmin British School.

By 1884 the school had made further progress and was in a good condition, and by the following year the HMI clearly stated that Llangain Board School was a very good country school. A very creditable examination was passed in the elementary subjects, English and geography. The average attendance was 55. Number presented in standards, 42; Infants, 11; Percentage 92. Grant earned £52.17s.8d.

Log Entries

2 August 1889
On Tuesday and Thursday the Church and Chapel Sunday schools respectively took their annual trip to Llanstephan. As all of the Scholars belong to one or the other of these institutions I thought it advisable to close the school both days.

Summary of Inspector's Report November 1889
This is an exceedingly good country school. The scholars were well behaved, and passed a most satisfactory examination in the Elementary subjects. Good intelligence was also shown in English. The results in Geography were, on the whole, very fair. The Needlework was creditable. The infants had been well instructed in the elements of reading and writing but numbers should improve.

Percentage of passes = 96. Excellent Merit Grant. Grant £54 or at the rate of 20/- per unit. Staff: Evan John Davies, Second Class Certificate.

Log Entries

6 May 1891
Children obtained half a holiday to mark the success of Lettice M. Evans, Standard 5, who won a Scholarship of £15 at the Carmarthen High School. Could ill afford it but thought it possible that good might result to her schoolmates, it may act as an impetus. Besides some mark of 'honour' was due to the girl for her industry.

19 June
I had to inflict corporal punishment on five boys this week for catching hold of a cow's tail in an adjoining field and driving her. Thomas Davies, Standard 3, was kept in on four evenings for want of industry in school and homework.

26 June
This week we had new blinds for the two windows facing the west, they were sorely needed as the sun's rays made the children who sat beneath these windows have headaches besides dazzling the eyes of the teacher.

The sanitary inspector, who called at School House on the night of 31 October 1893, informed Evan John Davies that there were several cases of 'scarlatina' and advised some parents to keep the children from school.

Within weeks there were cases of whooping cough as well, and the entry in the log-book for 17 November mentions that there was no improvement in the attendance or abatement in the two epidemics. The school work suffered greatly in consequence.

There was still much sickness among the schoolchildren in January 1894. Children, while prohibited from attending school, were allowed to mix, and even attended places of worship, rendering the good effects of isolation to nil.

Having been appointed to Pontyates School, Mr John Davies was presented with a handsome marble timepiece and the mistress with an electroplated tea and coffee service on 27 April 1894. A Mr Thomas Owen took temporary charge of the school until James Evans, certificated teacher, began his duties as

head teacher on 17 September 1894. He remained in the post until 1902.

Mr Evans adopted a new system of marking registers – early scholars were marked in red ink and the late ones in black. Those who obtained ten red marks in a week received an attendance card and everyone who had 25 cards during the following eight remaining months were given a book prize. The system, it seemed, worked well in other schools.

Log Entries

15 November 1895
Work is improving slowly, but the staff is inadequate to do the work thoroughly. The Board has kindly acceded to my request for another monitor and J. Jones will become a Pupil Teacher if he succeeds in passing the examination. J.R. Evans had been chosen to sit for examination as Candidate on Probation.

21 May 1896
The attendance today was exceptional; 85 in the morning and 86 in the afternoon. Mr Richards of Llandeilo was here photographing the schoolchildren and that accounts for the splendid attendance.

19 June
The number on the books now is 95, the highest number that has been on the registers since the school was opened.

National and International events are referred to in the log-books. The entry for 2 June 1902 states that 'Peace' had been declared in South Africa. This, of course, refers to the end of the Boer War (1899–1902), when the Boers agreed to accept British Sovereignty.

25 June 1902
King Edward VII has had to undergo an operation, everybody expresses regret at the King's illness. The children from Standards II–VII were taken for a walk to Hendy Bank. Trees, flowers, rocks, farm machinery and hay were examined. This bank is a splendid site on which to teach Geographical definitions.

26 and 27 June
Holidays appointed for the Coronation of King Edward VII who, unfortunately, is so seriously ill that the ceremony is postponed. At Llangain a tea was given to the children attending this school, together with their parents and friends, the people who attend Llangain Church, Smyrna Chapel and any other inhabitants of Llangain. The Revd Evan Jones, Vicar, kindly lent a field for the occasion. As the hay harvest is at hand, the sports could not very well be postponed. The day was passed in a very quiet, though enjoyable, manner.

Llangain School, 1919. Left to right, back row: *?, Tom Jones, Jim Lewis, Alf Howells, Jack Bowen, Dai John, Jack Wilkins;* fourth row: *Mr Tom Thomas (headmaster), Gwladys Jones, Sally Bowen, Bessie Thomas, ? Davies, Harri Davies, Tom Rees, Jack Thomas;* third row: *Maggie Jones, Irene Jones, Rachel Lewis, Gwladys Walters, Mary Mason, Sally John, Gwen Rees, ?, Miss Griffiths;* second row: *?, ?, ?, ? Rees, May Davies, Maggie Howells, Bessie John, Elizabeth Jones;* front row: *?, ?, ? John, Glyn John, Ieuan Hobbs, Bertie Mason, Jack Jeremy.*

Mrs Morris of Coombe gave medals to the children and contributed £2 towards the tea fund, as she does not intend giving the usual treat this year. The reason being that her son Liew (Llew) Morris was killed in South Africa last February. A book entitled *King Edward's Realm* was given to the eldest child in each family in the district.

Mr Rees Thomas became head in October 1902. A year later the new sewing mistress was Mrs Hannah Jones, Pantydderwen. She was married to Henry Jones, the local postmaster. Their daughter was Mrs Rene Harding, late of No. 20A Dôl-y-Dderwen.

A new grate was placed in the big room on 12 January 1904 in lieu of the stove, which was out of order. Ventilation had improved, according to the inspectors' report of 16 February 1906, but the woodwork and walls needed painting, the conveniences needed to be better kept and the pump repaired.

An evening concert was held on 12 February 1909 to raise funds for the formation of a school library. A sum of £6.0s.3d. was realised. The HMI, in his report in May of that year, said that: 'The School Library just established should prove helpful and of much value'.

Similar fund-raising concerts took place in March 1911, when efforts to raise funds for a piano realised £17.10s.0d. Through the musical enterprise of the headmaster, the piano was purchased in the autumn. St David's Day was a holiday at that time!

Also, there was a week's holiday in June in honour of the coronation of King George V. The coronation was celebrated at Llangain with a tea provided to all the inhabitants of the district and with rustic sports. Mrs Morris Coombe and Mrs Reid, of Spilman Street, Carmarthen, contributed £3 towards the funds instead of giving the usual school treat. Mrs Morris also gave a flag and scroll.

Lady Philipps of Coomb presented each child with a medal, and J.Ll. Thomas Esq, JP, Gilfach, gave each child a coronation mug. The schoolchildren were to be photographed at a later date and the eldest child in each family was to receive a photo of the group as a coronation souvenir. When will the present Prince of Wales be crowned King George VII, I hear the younger readers ask!

By 1917, because of the First World War, there were shortages of food, particularly of bread, and from early 1918 meat, butter and margarine were

Llangain School, 1922. Some recognised faces are Sally Bowen (left of Mr Tom Thomas, headmaster), May Mason (to his right), followed by ?, Gwladys Jones, Bessie John; Mollie Evans, Gilfach (next but one to the right of Mrs Gertie Thomas, the headmaster's wife) and Ieuan Hobbs (second from left, standing, towards the front).

rationed. With the authority of the Education Committee, school closed on 21–22 March and again on 4–5 July so as to enable the staff to have time to prepare the food and meat cards (ration books) for the parish.

Mr Rees Thomas, the headmaster, was informed on 13 July that he had been appointed headmaster of Coedmoor County School, Lampeter. This is both particularly interesting and peculiar at the same time, because a successor of his was to have a similar appointment in 1974, namely Mr Goronwy Phillips.

Martha Anne Davies, certificated teacher, took over as temporary head teacher for three months before Mr Thomas Thomas, the new headmaster, from Myddfai, started on 30 December 1918. In his brief period of tenure there is one very significant entry in the log-book for 11 November 1918: 'Peace reported. Vicar (Revd Evan Jones) authorised dismissal of children at 11.45a.m. Sang Welsh and English National Anthems.'

Log Entries

8 November 1920
Coal was brought to school at 12.10 (only 6cwts). Fires were lit at 12.30. After fires had been lit the walls were wet with dampness. The Headmaster thought it unhealthy for the children to be in school. They had physical exercise on the playground from 1p.m. to 1.30p.m. – then they had a nature ramble.

11 November
Armistice Day observed in school. The Headmaster told the children about the burial of the 'unknown hero' and of the unveiling of the Cenotaph by the King.

11 January 1921
Received weighing machines and height measuring standard from Llanstephan C of E School last Friday afternoon. All the children were weighed and measured today.

28 August 1924
The Revd Evan Jones (Manager), on behalf of the Scholars, staff and parishioners, presented the head teacher with a dining-room clock and Mrs Thomas with a silver sugar-basin and cream jug on a silver stand. This was to mark their departure for Pontyates.

[Once again it is bizarre to note that a future headmaster was to arrive at Llangain from Pontyates in 1961, namely Mr Islwyn Jones.]

The Reign of Sam Rees, 1924–61

Mr Samuel Rees, certified teacher, commenced duties at Llangain CP School on 1 October 1924, along with Miss Amy David, supplementary teacher, transferred from Llangynog C of E School.

As usual there were regular visits by the attendance officer, school nurse and medical officer. On 15 July 1926, the school dentist called for the purpose of extracting, under anaesthetic, the decayed teeth of David Thomas Bowen and David John Gwyn Davies!

Log Entries

26 May 1926
Mollie Evans (Gilfach) has been taken to the Carmarthen Infirmary for an operation.

29 October
Mrs B.M. Pickrall of the South Wales Temperance and Band of Hope Union gave a lecture to the Senior Classes on Temperance and Hygiene this afternoon.

29 November
A Boulton Elevator was fixed in the school yard to replace the pump, which was in a very poor state.

14 March 1927
A Farmer's Union Social was held at the School on Friday, 11 March, and afterwards one of the desks was found to be broken. The Secretary has informed me that it will be repaired by the local blacksmith.

14 September
Two girls from Standard Six, Millie Evans and Dilys John, have left this school for the Carmarthen County Girl's School.

22 September
A half holiday was granted owing to the Annual Llangain Show being held.

14 June 1928
The head teacher has received a letter today from the Carmarthenshire Education Committee congratulating him on the excellent attendance at the school during the year ended 31 March 1928.

Miss Kate Evans, whose previous school was Penywaun, started as an uncertificated assistant on 2 July, since Miss Amy David had finished the previous month.
A new entrance gate was fixed, the playgrounds covered with tarred chippings and the drains improved in December 1928.

Log Entries

7 March 1929
Fifteen dual tables and 30 chairs arrived at the school today. These are to replace the long old-fashioned desks.

23 July 1930
The Headmaster took the Upper School children for the last hour of the afternoon to the flannel factory in the parish of Llangain.

1 December
The school cleaner, Miss Jane Stewart, has resigned after a very long period of faithful service. Miss Margaret Williams, Pantydderwen, Llangain, has been appointed as school cleaner temporarily.

1 March 1932
The greater part of the morning was devoted to the celebration of St David's Day. The children sang and performed little dramas dealing with Welsh life. A half holiday was given in the afternoon so that children could attend functions at their respective places of worship.

29 June
A County Library Centre has been established at this school, of which the Headmaster is the Honorary Local Librarian. The first supply of books arrived today.

A greater awareness of body and oral hygiene coincided with an increased standard of living that was to continue throughout the 1930s.

Log Entries

15 July 1932
The Headmaster received a communication today stating that he had been successful in obtaining the Diploma of the Institute of Hygiene.

14 September
Miss Dilys Mair John commenced work here today for the purpose of gaining experience in teaching without salary.

26 September
A circular has been received from the LEA to the effect that the Cambridgeshire Syllabus of Religious Instruction is to be adopted for use in the school.

16 December
D. King, HMI, visited the school this morning in connection with the proposed new school garden.

23 June 1933
The school has closed for the day owing to the Welsh Gymnastic Display at Swansea under the auspices of the Urdd Gobaith Cymru.

13 November 1934
The Local School Manager, the Revd Evan Jones BD, Rural Dean, passed away this morning.

29 November
The Education Committee has granted a holiday

owing to the marriage of the Duke of Kent and Princess Marina of Greece.

19 February 1935
School closed due to Induction Services at Llangain Church. *[These would have been for the new vicar, the Revd D.T. Price BA, MTh.]*

6 May
A holiday was granted today owing to the Silver Jubilee Celebrations. The schoolchildren were presented with a Silver Jubilee mug by Mr and Mrs J. Lewis, Meini, and were given a tea at the school by County Councillor and Mrs T.Ll. Harries, Pilroath. Souvenirs were presented to the children provided from the grant towards celebration by the LEA.

Lady Kylsant and local residents sent donations towards prizes in the sports which were held during the afternoon and evening. Nine secondary schoolchildren attended the local celebrations besides the school managers and the people in the locality.

A most enjoyable day was spent by all in a day that will stand out in the memory of all who were privileged to attend.

3 June
Jubilee testaments were presented to the school-children this afternoon by Mrs Barret-Evans, Y Glyn, and County Councillor T.Ll. Harries, Pilroath. The Revd D.T. Price, Vicar, and the Revd Hopcyn Evans, Smyrna, were present, and addressed the children. The children sang a number of hymns and songs. The ceremony terminated with 'Hen Wlad fy Nhadau' and 'God Save the King'.

6 November
Holiday granted on the occasion of the wedding of the Duke of Gloucester and Lady Alice Scott.

2 December
Miss E.A. John, Forlan, the new school cleaner, commenced duties today.

28 January 1936
The school closed owing to the funeral of King George V.

12 May 1937
School closed on the occasion of the Coronation of King George VI and Queen Elizabeth.

23-24 June 1938
A concert was given by the schoolchildren on the evening of these dates. An extensive programme was gone through which included the following: folk songs, action songs, dances, recitations, besides the performance of the following plays – 'Llew' by the Infants and Standard 1, 'Snow White' and 'Y Te Parti' by the Juniors, 'Y Darlun', 'Nans' and 'Owain Glyndwr' by the Seniors.

17 July1939
The following report has been received from the Board of Education with regard to the school:

The 45 pupils on roll in this school are organised into two groups under the headmaster and an uncertificated mistress. The premises consist of a large main room, an infant's room; they are, on the whole, in a good state of repair. The ventilation of the infant's room, however, is defective. One section only of the single window in the room is hung to open; a row of hopper inlets is necessary to make the ventilation reasonable adequate.

Work of a very satisfactory character is performed at all stages in the main subjects of the curriculum. In addition, a good variety of interests are developed with the upper section. There is a well kept school garden and a good series of lessons on rural science and biology has been planned to supplement the instruction in gardening.

Considerable interest is taken in dramatic work and puppetry. There are also examples of good imaginative colour work in Art, and the boys receive instruction in light woodwork on the premises.

The School has a very pleasing atmosphere, and the children respond to oral questioning with commendable freedom. They are undoubtedly receiving valuable training in a stimulating environment.

Inspected 7th June, 1939.
Board of Education No. 96 Reg. No. WE 353/96/14

With regard to the above, the headmaster, S. Rees, received a letter from the Director of Education, Mr J. Edward, MA, MEd, stating that it was gratifying to the Authority to note the very satisfactory nature of the report and at the same time added his own personal congratulations.

The rebirth and rearming of a Germany hungering to avenge its defeat in the First World War was growing more apparent in the latter years of the decade. Rumblings of unrest in Europe began with the Spanish Civil War (1936–39). War was declared on Germany in September 1939 and life in Wales was to change forever.

Children began to be evacuated from the cities in August 1939, and Anderson shelters were distributed in areas likely to be bombed. Everyone had a gas-mask and was encouraged to carry it at all times; those for children were given a friendlier 'Mickey Mouse' appeal.

Log Entries

3 March 1939
School closed for the day, for the purpose of fitting of gas-masks.

Llangain school 1927. Mr Sam Rees with Miss Griffith, Mollie Thomas, Gilfach (centre row, second from left), *and Irene Jones* (front row, fourth from left).

Llangain Schoolroom girls, 1935. Left to right back row: *Tegwen ?, Irene Evans, Glenys Lewis, Muriel Lewis, Rosamound Williams;* front row: *Margaret Evans, Elunded Harries, Sally Davies, Doreen Evans, Esther Ford, Elvira Davies, Joan Evans.*

4 September
The school re-opened this morning, but in view of the communication regarding closure of schools in an emergency, the children were sent home and instructed not to attend until further notice.

6 October
Terence Hesford sent home owing to measles in the home. His mother had been told to keep the child home on the 31st until further notice.

Log Entries

24 May 1940
A quantity of school requirements – exercise books, drawing books, pencils, chalk, arithmetic books, reading books to suit different ages, has been sent to Smyrna vestry for the use of the evacuee children.

21 October
School closed for Evacuation Survey for reception of mothers and babies.

23 October
The Evacuated School at Smyrna vestry was at this school during the afternoon session. The children here were taken to Smyrna for the afternoon. This arrangement is to continue.

9 and 10 January 1943
The Home Guard (Local Squad) utilised the school for night exercises from 10p.m. Saturday 9 Jan till 2p.m. Sunday 10 Jan. Miss Evans, the assistant teacher, reported to me on Monday morning 11 Jan that the two top drawers of her desk in the classroom had been opened and the contents moved about. The hands of the school clock had also been removed.

30 June 1944
The Education Committee has granted a day's holiday in recognition of the splendid work in connection with the recent 'Salute the Soldier' week.

Nine evacuees were attemding the school by July 1944 – eight from Essex and one from Croydon. A further two arrived within a week and in the autumn a Miss Carey, an evacuated teacher from East Sussex, commenced duties at the school. By the beginning of December 1944 there were 19 evacuees in school, 15 of whom were transferred to Smyrna vestry while the remaining four senior evacuees, at the request of the HMI, remained as pupils of the school.

For children, life during the war could be both frightening and exciting – in either case it was very different from the comparative calm of the 1930s. Evacuees from the cities found the countryside a novelty, while for those youngsters who remained in the cities, bombed buildings became playgrounds and looking for shrapnel an engrossing new hobby.

The road to victory was long and hard, but after nearly six years of global conflict the Allies prevailed. When the war in Europe came to an end, on 8 May 1945, Churchill conceded that, 'We may allow ourselves a brief period of rejoicing'. The struggle in the East still had to be won, but Japan finally surrendered on 14 August. Victory had come at a price; Britain and her Empire had lost more than half a million people in the war. Worldwide, it had cost the lives of 55 million, mainly in the Soviet Union, China, Germany and Poland. A two-day holiday was granted to the schoolchildren to commemorate the end of hostilities in Europe. On the second day, the children, in addition to the people of the parish and district and evacuees, were treated to a grand tea at the school. This was followed by a long programme of sports in Brynderi field. The proceedings were presided over by County Councillor T.Ll. Harries, JP, Pilroath, and the school managers.

Log Entries

21 January 1946
A new stove has been fixed in the classroom.

3 June
School dinners commenced today. They were being bought from the central kitchen at Carmarthen in Thermos containers.

11 September
Milk is being supplied free to the children.

20 December
Miss M.E. Owen, unqualified assistant teacher, terminated her duties here today. All the children partook of a beautiful Christmas dinner. Cards were hung and before going home each child was given a piece of iced cake.

In mid-January 1947, no one expected the winter to go down in the annals as the snowiest since 1814 and amongst the coldest on record. The cold, snowy weather continued throughout February and into March. Any breaks in the cold weather were short-lived.

On 4 and 5 March heavy snow fell, with severe drifting. The roads became impassable and therefore no children were present in school. A huge quantity of snow must have blown in under the roofs during the blizzard since, with the thaw, there was continuous dripping of water for days, both in the main room and in the schoolhouse.

Log Entries

7 November 1947
The pump on the school yard has been examined by the engineer and found to be out of repair. It cannot

be repaired until the water comes back to the well.

5 September 1949
The school pump is dry since the middle of August.

A Miss Anne Davies, Pleasant View, Trimsaran, started teaching at the school on 17 October 1949. It's funny to read how Mr Rees, over the years, enters any late arrivals amongst the staff, too.

There are a few references to Miss Davies having missed the connection between the Trimsaran to Carmarthen and the Llangain buses. There were legitimate reasons but one does sense an air of disapproval!

As far as I can tell Mr Rees was never ill, although a Mr Douglas Roberts deputised for six months between early December 1950 and the end of January 1951.

Log Entries

22 June 1951
The head teacher and 17 children are on a school trip to Windsor today.

24 July
School closed this afternoon for the opening of the new Church Hall.

12 October
Presentation books have today been awarded by the County Education Authority to Gwyneth May Wyke for six years' full attendance and to Catherine M.E. Jones for three years' full attendance.

22 May 1953
Alderman T.Ll. Harries, JP, Pilroath, on behalf of the Education Authority, presented each of the schoolchildren with a Coronation mug and a packet of sweets. In addition, Mr Harries himself presented each child with a Coronation book.

2 June
The schoolchildren took part in the Coronation celebrations of Queen Elizabeth II at Llangain. A tea was provided and children's sports were held. A huge bonfire was lit in Green Castle field as the end of a most enjoyable and memorable day.

12 June
School closed. A party of the older children, accompanied by the head teacher, went on an educational trip to London to see the Coronation decorations and the Zoo.

1 February 1954
The older children, accompanied by the head teacher, are attending at the Capitol Cinema, Carmarthen, for the purpose of seeing the film *The Conquest of Everest*.
18 June
The head teacher is accompanying a party of schoolchildren to the Bristol Zoo today.

Miss John, Forlan, retired as caretaker in October 1957 and was replaced by Mrs Mary Davies. In February 1958 Miss John finished her duties as canteen general assistant and was replaced by Mrs Lizzie Thomas, Ty Canol. I noticed at this point in the log-books, entries were logged as day, month and year as opposed to month, day and year.

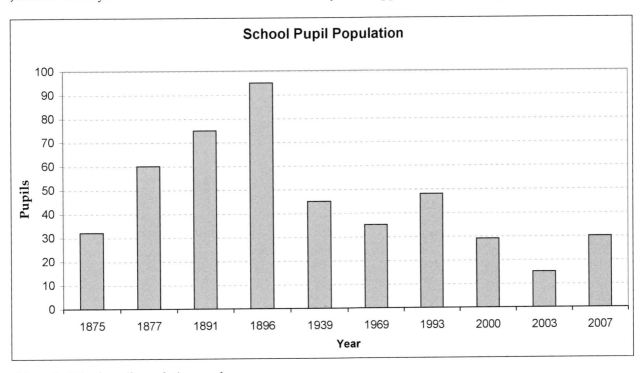

Llangain School pupil population graph.

Log Entries

23 March 1959
Electricity from the mains switched on this morning.

20 April
Peter Davies arrived in school at 10.55a.m. He has been to town with his mother to try a new suit of clothes.

20 May 1960
The head teacher accompanied the older children to Oxford and Blenheim Palace.

3 June
No water in the water mains today. Use of water from the pump in the school yard being made in the canteen.

31 October 1961
'I Samuel Rees resign my appointment of this school after a period of Thirty Seven Years and one month as Headmaster'.

On Friday afternoon, 27 October, a presentation was made to the headmaster on the occasion of his retirement. The presentation was made by Mr T.Ll. Harries, MBE, JP, Pilroath. He spoke in felicitous terms of the untiring work carried out by the headmaster during his long period of service at the school and wished him and Mrs Rees good health and many years of happy retirement.

Others who spoke in similar vein were the Revd Hopkin Evans, Smyrna; the Vicar of Llangain, Revd D.S. Lewis; the two school managers, Mr T. Roberts and Mr E.E. Jones; Mr Williams, Cefnglas, on behalf of the Parish Council; Mr H. Howells, District Councillor; Mrs Rees and Miss E. Davies.

The headmaster, after accepting the present, which took the form of a wallet of notes, thanked all who had contributed to and organised the fund.

The schoolchildren sang a number of songs and the function closed with the singing of 'Hen Wlad fy Nhadau'.

The Sixties

Mr Islwyn Jones, from Gwynfryn CP School, Pontyates, started as headmaster on 6 November 1961. He remained until 1971, when ill health forced his early retirement. During that decade, however, he became very involved with community life as treasurer of Smyrna Chapel, Memorial Hall secretary and Parish Councillor. His first log-book entry was a reference to the school being used as a polling booth in connection with Sunday opening – an issue being discussed more than 45 years ago.

During the summer holidays, 1962, a new Alico stove was installed in the main classroom. This remained in place until the old school closed in 1977. The disused water tank in the girls' yard was removed, the exterior of the kitchen repaired and the old water pump in the front yard removed. He informed the Director of Education about the unsafe nature of the deep well underneath – surely, this was the new head getting things done!

Both teachers started making use of school broadcasts in September 1962. The head teacher's set was used until the school was able to purchase its own. This was done within a fortnight.

The regular visits from the school nurse, school dentist, the local policeman (PC Atkins) and HMIs continued during the '60s as they had done before.

The coldest winter since 1740 came in 1963. The winter began abruptly just before Christmas 1962, and then, on the eve of the new year, a blizzard brought snow drifts 20ft (6m) deep. Villages were cut off, some for several days, and roads and railways were blocked. Telephone wires were brought down and stocks of food ran low and, with farmers unable to reach their livestock, thousands of sheep, ponies and cattle starved to death.

Due to this adverse weather, school reopened three days late after the Christmas holidays. For weeks the snow lay on the ground, since 1963 will not only be remembered for its snowiness but for its hard frosts. Naturally, this affected both pupil and staff attendance and those who did manage to reach school would be sent home in the afternoon since school dinners, which came from Carmarthen, were not delivered.

Miss A.E. Davies terminated her employment with the authority on 26 July 1963, having obtained another post in Cardiganshire. She was presented with a Westminster chimes clock, on behalf of the pupils and adults of the district, as a token of appreciation of her esteemed service over the previous four years. The Vicar of Llangain, Revd D.S. Lewis, also spoke in appreciation.

Mr Allan Wynne Jones, School House, who had graduated from the University College of Wales, Aberystwyth, in 1962, spent a period of observation in the school in September.

The newly built Memorial Hall was immediately put to good use, since the children's Christmas party that year was held for the first time at the nearby venue. Then, when school reopened on 6 January 1964, the school dining scheme moved there. Mrs Thomas, Ty-Canol, the part-time assistant, was then appointed cook. The log-book entry reads: 'The dinner today was of excellent quality. It is a vast improvement to the previous way of eating the dinners – on the school desks'. The cook was now able to excel herself by cooking everything on site in the purpose-built kitchen at the hall. Meals were no longer transported from County Hall!

Mrs Mary Davies, No. 1 Maesyrawel (school cleaner), began her duties as supervisory/clerical

Llangain School on St David's Day with Mrs Margaret Phillips and Mr Goronwy Phillips (headmaster), 1972.

Llangain CP, RFC, 1972–73. Left to right, back row: Colin Davies, Andrew Davies, ?, Alan Davies, Douglas Hicks, Richard Thomas; front row: Kevin Davies, Hefin Morris, Clive Bignell, Mr Goronwy Phillips (headmaster), Robert Davies, Richard Hicks.

assistant on 13 July 1964. Then, in September, a new teacher, Miss Marian Evans, from Llanddarog, joined the staff.

Log Entries

5 November 1964
An evening class in drama was commenced with the Revd J. Hopkin Evans, Minister of Smyrna Chapel, as the tutor.

28 May 1965
On the previous day, Thursday, the Deputy Director of Education visited the school regarding the head-teacher's persistent complaints that the school drains ran out to the main road.

1 September
School reopened after the summer holidays. Miss Marian Evans, the assistant mistress, was married on 7 August to Mr Keith Williams of Cwmtwrch, at Llanddarog.

21 October
School closed this afternoon (Thursday) for a holiday to celebrate the 700th anniversary of Parliament and the following week for the mid-term holidays.

7 November 1966
The Education Committee have agreed to purchase the spare piano at the Memorial Hall for the price of £12.10s.0d. to replace the old one. It was transferred to the school today.

Miss Briallen Davies (ex-Talley CP School) joined the staff on 1 May 1967. Mrs Williams had left the previous Christmas. Miss Davies, however, was soon to become Mrs Jones, as she got married during the October half term that year.

D.J. Evans & Sons, contractors, from Carmarthen, started building the new toilets on the pine end of the school facing Smyrna Chapel.

Mrs Briallen Jones took temporary charge in May 1968, since Mr Islwyn Jones had been admitted to Morriston Hospital for observation. He resumed duties in September after his long illness, but was ill again before Christmas.

Log Entries

6 January 1969
School resumed after the holidays. The head teacher has resumed duties. The new school toilets are in use, and the staff and pupils are very pleased with this essential amenity. The contractor must be congratulated on executing a first class job of work.

Two more pupils were admitted today, making a total of 35. The small classroom is very overcrowded now (19 infants).

21 April
The head teacher has purchased a secondhand television set from 'Modern Radio', Carmarthen, for the sum of £10.16s.0d. (from the school fund). It has been fitted in the small classroom and a geography lesson this morning was very well received by the pupils.

The Seventies

Mr Jac Jones, from Cwmduad CP School, took charge as acting head teacher between the summer of 1970 and 1971. Mr Islwyn Jones had to take premature retirement on grounds of ill health in December 1970 while still a patient at Glangwili Hospital.

The Carmarthen and District school educational excursion to such places as Bristol Zoo, Windsor and London Airport, Bath, Cheddar and Wells continued. A party of 21 children, accompanied by the new head teacher, Mr Goronwy Phillips, and Mrs Margaret Phillips, visited Chester Zoo on 19 June 1972. The train left Carmarthen at 6.50a.m. and returned at 12.05a.m.!. Needless to say, there were many absences the following day due to tiredness and exhaustion! But such trips are invaluable.

The new school year in September saw the arrival of Miss Olive Jones, Peniel, later to become Mrs Dyer. She taught the Juniors alongside the head teacher in the main classroom.

A school rugby team was formed and games were played against other schools, such as Whitland, St Clears (Glasfryn), Llanddarog and Cynwyl Elfed.

The proclamation ceremony for the Bro Myrddin National Eisteddfod, Carmarthen, 1974, was held in the town park on the 16 June 1973. There was a good school representation in the procession and two girls, Caroline Hughes and Sian Hughes, took part in the Flower Dance.

Mr Goronwy Phillips, having been appointed to the headship of Coedmor Primary School, Cwmann, Lampeter, finished at Christmas 1973, noting in the log-book that his period at Llangain had been an excellent experience for him.

Llangain school was soon to reach its centenary and the next head teacher, who arrived with the new local authority of Dyfed in April 1974, fully realised the significance of such a milestone, as his reflections in the log-book show:

Llangain CP School Centenary, 1875–1975
by David Marks
Head Teacher

I had the privileged good fortune of being at the right place at the right time. The Centenary of Llangain CP School was evident and in full view on the horizon, coming closer each day.

My uncertainty and doubt as to completing a 'jigsaw' of the occasion was decisively put to rest when I called

Llangain School centenary celebrations, 1976. Mr Sam Rees, a former headmaster, cuts the celebratory cake with Junior pupils. Left to right, back row: *Eiri Davies, Neil Vizard, Melanie Evans, Philip Bowen, Douglas Hicks, Christopher Heath, Robert Davies, Robert Thomas, Geriant Davies, Paul Thomas, Martin Jones, Meryl Jones, Ieuan Davies, Kevin Evans, Euros Jones, Gareth Davies;* front row: *Eleri Morris, Hayley Evans, Eirwen Clement, Debbie John, Jenny Lander, Karen Lander, Eleri Jones, Suzanne Jones, Gail Thomas, Fiona Marks.*

a meeting of anyone with an interest in a form of celebration. It became, not a question of he who sits and
waits, but one of no sooner said than done.

Fine speeches are a poor substitute for direct action
and the action that evening could not have been more
decisive.

After a free and open discussion, the feeling was that
it would be sad if such a fitting occasion be left unob-
served and forgotten. It was, after all, an opportunity
to show gratitude to those five gentlemen who, on the
eighth of April eighteen seventy five, decided that a new
school room and a house be built in the Parish.

It became a nostalgic and anecdotal exercise. The
history of Llangain CP was well preserved in the memories of former pupils – those locked-in memories, ready
and waiting.

Doing my homework became an enjoyable and stimulating exercise. Many months passed, many verbal
anecdotes recorded, many log-book entries utilised,
until the final piece of the jigsaw was placed neatly at
Llangain Memorial Hall on 7th July 1976.

Great pains were taken to ensure a successful conclusion. That evening was indeed a resounding success.

The attendance was much greater that anyone
expected, beyond one's wildest hopes. The customary
refreshments were shared, not only for the children
present, but also for former pupils, present and past
staff members and the invited guests.

Right: *Centenary (1875-1975) celebration concert leaflet,
7 April, 1976. President: Mr Rees Evans, Cambridge
(a former pupil).*

```
            1875  -  1975
            ――――――――――――――

          C Y N G E R D D

CANMLWYDDIANT  YSGOL  LLANGAIN.

          * * * * * * *

Nos Fercher, Gorffennaf 7fed. 1976.


              LLYWYDD

  Mr. E. T. Rees Evans, Caergrawnt
        (Gynt o'r Gilfach)
          * * * * * * *
            ARWEINYDD

   Y Cynghorwr J. A. J. Harries
        Pilroath,  Llangain
          * * * * * * *
  PRIFATHRO    -    Mr. D. J. Marks
  ATHRAWESAU   -    Mrs. M. Phillips
                    Mrs. O. Dyer
          * * * * * * *
Drysau'n agored am 7.00 o'r gloch
  I Ddechrau am 7.30 o'r gloch
          * * * * * * *
```

Llangain School centenary celebrations, 1976. Mr Sam Rees, a former headmaster, cuts the celebratory cake with Infant pupils. Left to right back row: Julie Evans, Donna Jones, Simon Jones, Jayne Bowen, Richard Jones, Peter Evans, Simon Evans, Richard Thomas, Emyr Jones and Kay John; front row: Rachel Lander, Jayne Griffiths, Joanne Marks, Llions Jones, Louise Davies, Richard Griffiths, Lee John, Stuart Berry, Daniel Heath.

RHAGLEN

AGORIAD SWYDDOGOL

YSGOL GYNRADD

LLANGAIN

DYDD IAU, EBRILL 28, 1977

am 2 o'r gloch

****

PROGRAMME

OFFICIAL OPENING

COUNTY PRIMARY SCHOOL

LLANGAIN

THURSDAY, APRIL 28, 1977

at 2 p.m.

To commemorate the occasion the Director of Education, Mr Henry Thomas, distributed the 'Centenary Mugs' to all those present associated with Llangain C.P. School.

The New School, 1975–

After the Centenary Celebrations in 1975, a new school was built on the former school field, with adjacent land bought to serve as an alternative place of recreation. The new building was completed in 1976 under the continued headship of Mr Marks, and officially opened on the anniversary of the old, namely, 28 April 1977.

Log Entries

17 July 1981
Mrs Margaret Phillips retires after 11 years' teaching at Llangain CP School.

7 September
Mrs Eleri Iorwerth, Infants' Nursery teacher, starts at the school today.

26 September 1983
Mrs Margaret Rowlands takes over Mrs Cramer's duties as midday supervisor.

8 May 1984
Mrs Jean Davies takes over as cook. Mrs Bowen, No. 6 Maesyrawel, commences as kitchen assistant.

Left: The official opening of the new Llangain County Primary School, 28 April, 1977.

Llangain School, Infants, 1981. Left to right, back row: *Mrs Jayne Mattison, Simon Cooke, Ian Rowlands, James Thomas, Ross Jacobs, Nicholas Doughty, Ray Barney, Edward Davies, Mrs Margaret Phillips;* front row: *Elizabeth Perkins, Rhian Davies, Iwan Evans, Sally Morgan, Gemma Jones.*

Llangain School Juniors, 1981. Left to right, back row: *Andrew Rowlands, Alun Jones, Kevin Davies, Geraint Davies, Stephen Jones;* middle row: *Nicholas Berry, Robert Davies, Philip Morgan, Ian Morgan, Roger Thomas, Christopher Jones;* front row: *Sarah Davies, Iwan Dyer, Philippa Jones, Mrs Olive Dyer, Kathy Evans, Dylan Morris, Ayshea Thomas.*

Llangain School, Juniors, 1981. Left to right, back row: *Kevin Morgan, Daniel Heath, Neville Davies, Richard Thomas, Simon Evans;* third row: *Lee John, Peter Evans, Emyr Jones, Richard Griffiths, Richard Jones, Stuart Berry;* second row: *David Davies, Audrey Davies, Geraldine Russell, Jayne Bowen, Gail Thomas, Llinos Jones, Joanne Marks, Julie Evans, Simon Jones;* front row: *Donna Jones, Fiona Morgan, Lynne Davies, Kay John, D.J. Marks (headmaster), Louise Davies, Rachel Lander, Jayne Griffiths, Gwyneth Morgan.*

10 September 1985
Headmaster admitted to Glangwili Hospital. Miss W. Dyer, assistant teacher, takes up temporary duties as headmistress.

Two months later Mr Marks resumed duties and was to continue for another five years until July 1990. Mr Malcolm Griffiths was appointed the next head teacher.

Log Entries

3 September 1990
This is the beginning of my time at Llangain School. I had important help from Mr Marks today. I look forward eagerly to work with Mrs Wendy Roberts, Miss Buddig Jones and Miss Eirwen Clement (NNEB).

21 November 1991
The school had a grant of £200 from the Prince of Wales Committee towards environmental work. It is hoped to plant trees, create a pond and place bird tables and so forth.

4 September 1992
Mrs Jill Davies, Llansteffan, started instead of Mrs Wendy Roberts, who has finished teaching after having a child.

Annual Harvest and Christmas services were held in Church and Chapel alternatively, while Mr Griffiths was head teacher. Harvest in Chapel and the Carol Service in the Church one year and the other way round the following year.

5 December 2001
Miss Rhian Evans, a talented blind woman, came to school. She spoke about her life and played the piano, to the amazement of the children.

Mr Griffiths took early retirement on ill-health grounds in 2004 and Mrs Angharad Jones, from Peniel, who has been acting head teacher since November 2003, was appointed as the first permanent female head teacher of Ysgol Llangain in 2005.

The Sensory Garden was officially opened 3 July 2004 by Cllr John Jones, Chairman of the Community Council. This environmental project was supported

Llangain School, 1988. Left to right, back row: *Mr D.J. Marks (headmaster), Miss Buddug Jones, Richard Keatley, Peter Davies, ?, David Whitbread, Gareth Silverthorne, Paul Barney, Alan Finnimore, Tom Brewer, Colin Whitbread, Philip Williams, Robert Kendrick, Jonathan Jones, Elgan John, Osian Hughes, Tom Burson, David Jones, Miss Meinir Thomas, Mrs Wendy Roberts;* third row: *Nia Pejak, Joanna Brewer, Jenny Allen, Nia Davies, Dawn Evans, Lorraine Evans, Nerys Evans, Anna Henshall, Emma Perkins, Sarah Williams, Helen Davies, Kirsty Finnimore, Gwyneth Hunt, Vanessa Weaver;* second row: *Jessica Davies, Lewis Wicks, Meriel Hunt, Iwan Brain, Lindsey Kendrick, Laura Davies, Rhodri Thomas, Suzy Allen, Robert Davies, Emma James, Rhys Davies, Bethan John;* front row: *Katherine Wicks, Viv Jenkins, David Jenkins, Brynmor John, Sam Jenkins.*

Llangain School, 1992. Left to right, back row: *Miss Buddug Jones, Kai Baxter, Elgan John, Peter Davies, Emma Perkins, Jenny Allen, Kirsty Finnemore, Helen Davies, Nia Davies, Jonathan Jones, Osian Hughes, David Whitbread, Lorraine Evans, Bill Burson, Mr Malcolm Griffiths (headmaster);* third row: *Mrs Wendy Roberts, Mrs Norma Pejsak, Rhodri Thomas, David Jenkins, Richard Keatley, Laura Davies, Joanna Brewer, Dawn Evans, Nia Pejsak, Sarah Williams, Gwyneth Hunt, Vanessa Weaver, David Jones, Brynmor John, Iwan Brain, Mrs Jill Davies, Miss Eirwen Clement;* second row: *Rhys Davies, David Hopkins, Viv Jenkins, Bethan John, Lindsey-May Kendrick, Meriel Hunt, Samantha Davies, Katherine Wicks, Suzanne Allen, Emma James, Cassie Davies, Robert Davies, Lewis Wicks;* front row: *Sarah James, Emily Bowen, Becky Evans, Harry Hopkins, Jason Baxter, Matthew Billingham, Lynwen Thomas, Jessica Davies, Charlotte Davies, Kimberly Morris, Kayleigh Davies, Samantha Davies.*

by parents and villagers. The school has developed an eco-code and, via recycling paper and plastic and conserving rainwater for the school garden, has achieved the Bronze Eco-Schools Award. The painted, pencil-shaped fencing is also a recent development and has been enthusiastically received by both the school and the community.

Regular calls are made by the Revd Illtyd Protheroe, and the Revd Towyn Jones visited on World Book Day 2004 to talk to the children about his current work and his interest in writing ghost stories! The Police Liaison Officer, PC Merion Howells, also

Tree-planting time! Pupils at Llangain School planted a tree for every pupil in the school grounds in 1991. The planting session, part of the school's environmental project, was helped by a £200 grant from the Prince of Wales Commission to buy trees. The youngest pupil, three-year-old Rebecca Evans, is seen planting an oak they grew from an acorn in the school grounds. Ready with the spade is the eldest pupil, 11-year-old Elgan John. Staff on back row: Miss Buddug Jones, Miss Eirwen Clement, Mrs Wendy Roberts, Mr Malcolm Griffiths (headteacher).

Llangain School 'Victorian Age' Christmas play, 2001, in St Cain's Church. Left to right, back row: *Bethan Richards, Gwenllian Williams, Andrew Richards, Heather Fletcher, Lema Imam, Mr Haydn Williams, Jacob Altman, Laura Evans;* middle row: *Elin Williams, Sarah Imam, Jennifer Davies, Megan Williams, Rachel Baxter;* front row: *Aaron Altman, Leah Hartley, Sioned Davies, Megan Davies, Hannah Evans, Morgan Parker, Tomos Van Praet.*

Yr Hen Ysgol – The old school converted into a three-bedroomed house by Ralph and Anne-Louise Morgans with work carried out by Wayne Davies from Bronwydd.

made visits to discuss health and safety issues. The popular policeman retired in May 2005.

The school's computer CD, launched in 2005, gives a variety of information, such as the curriculum taught and school activities, as well as the school's history and a comprehensive range of both old and new photographs.

It is sincerely hoped by everyone concerned that this exciting and thriving school community will go from strength to strength over the next few years by increasing its school population, thereby safeguarding its future.

Memories of Llangain
T. Roy Davies*, Canada (formerly of Old Castle)
Recorded Summer 2004

*Roy is the brother of Peter Davies, Mount Pleasant, Llangain.

The Second World War – Troops at Ystrad
The troops were based at Ystrad down in Johnstown and practised on Old Castle Farm. Now mother used to make batches enough for four. Soldiers came to the back door once and asked 'Can you make them with dried fruit?' She replied, 'I can make them with dried fruit but where can I get dried fruit?' Next morning there was 14lbs on the doorstep! Mother couldn't believe it. You see flour was not rationed during the war but afterwards. She was able to cook. So whenever she needed more dried fruit, she told someone and it was there the next morning. A bag of

rice (10–14lbs) on the doorstep too would get shared around. The pigs did very well by having iron rations as extras.

Another time, close to Christmas, she was away for the day and there was a knock at the front door (not the back door)! My father went to open the door and there were some officers there. One of them, rather shyly, asked, 'Is it your misses that does these batches?' My father thought, 'Oh, my God, what has she done now, she poisoned them or something?' He said to them, 'Yes'. 'Oh good! Do you think we can have some?' came the reply. So from then on, officers at the front door, soldiers at the back door and nobody ever saw each other!

The Home Guard
Dad use to be in the Home Guard. If the soldiers were on night manoeuvres there was an order that he had to inform the duty officer that he was away on homeguard duties. They supplied two regular soldiers fully armed, one at the front and one at the back. My mother hated it because if she went to milk the cows, one of them would be with her all the time but he would never talk to her. Now you know my mother (laughs)!

When Dad came home from duty he would inform the officer and the soldiers would be taken away. His duties, including training, etc., were in the Smyrna area. There was a pillbox there on the chapel side and another one at Penycoed (Carmarthen side). They were both removed soon after the war. As children we were inquisitive and wanted to watch the procedure. They had to use dynamite, so we were kept well back.

Searchlight

There was a searchlight unit between the church and my home. I could go to bed, take the blackout down and read – it was powerful enough. Didn't need any other light. If you look at a map of Llangain, Old Castle is in direct line with Pembrey airfield. Our house was one of the beacons they used to fly over and then the Tywi. We had plenty of hedge hoppers! The bombers couldn't find Carmarthen because of ground mist since it was in a kind of geographical basin. In fact, Pembrey munitions factory was not found by the enemy bombers again because of this ground mist present during the good flying weather. Looking over Llanelli and towards Swansea the night sky would be red. It was the latter burning after the blitz!

To Town

I remember going to town on VE day in May 1944. Now the funny thing was that we were back there again on VJ day some months later. We always went by horse and cart but there was a bus running. Mind you, I walked to and from town many a time since I didn't have the money for the bus. Three miles to Green Castle and a further mile to Smyrna. There was a milestone there and another by Llwyn.

Anyway, on several occasions the food inspector stepped out to stop the bus, but he never seemed to have it right. He only jumped out the last minute and the bus naturally couldn't stop immediately but went on a little further. In the meantime all the eggs and butter had disappeared into the driver's cab. Everything had disappeared and he never found anything!

During the big snow storm in 1947 all roads were blocked. In a few days they got the Carmarthen to Llansteffan road open and, after great effort, we reached the road with our milk. Milk lorries from the factory at Johnstown were running back and forth using certain milk stands, like ours, to collect other farmers' churns, too.

Prisoners of War

The other thing is that people took in POWs. They would work on the farms.

We had an Italian. He came from the POW camp at Llanddarog. Naturally there were restrictions. One was that they were not to travel on public transport. They were allowed to go to town on a Saturday night and when returning they would walk out of Carmarthen past the Cow & Gate and then the bus would stop. They never had to stop it! There would be trouble if they did but it wasn't necessary as long as the initiative didn't come from them. They had it down to a tee!

School

I went to Llangain School when I was five. Miss Stewart taught in the small room. She was fetched from Carmarthen every morning by Ben Reynolds, Beilisyfi. Sam Rees, the headmaster, was in the big room. I walked to school and if the troops were on the march from Ystrad to Llansteffan they would carry me shoulder high and then lower me down by Penycoed. From there to Smyrna crossroads my pockets would be filled with sweets. On reaching the school, the other kids, knowing that I was loaded, would come rushing up to me. I can't believe how much I gave away and thought nothing of it since we shared and shared alike!

Sometimes my dog followed me to school and Sam Rees would tell me to send it home. At the end of the day, she/he? would be waiting for me down the lane by Pantydderwen. I remember a shop there run by a Mrs Williams and I would get 2oz of sweets there once or twice a month. By the way, I remember well that she had a pail of water covered inside the gate to the house during one eclipse of the sun, and when she removed the cover we could see the moon by looking at the water!

The school meals came from town and were dished out in the shed by the front cloakroom. They would cost us 2s.1d. (10p). We would have a meal that was edible and a pudding, not like the junk food of today! 'Afters' would be the heavy steamed pudding, for example. Mind you, that was like lead in your stomach!

Community Spirit

I remember social gatherings at Penhen Farm, where we would have whist drives. We would create our own fun. Children today have no idea! Then we would hold them in the church hall, but they went downhill after the Memorial Hall was built. There were two factions in the area whether one liked it or not.

There were two or three major events on the farming calendar. I used to do some ploughing in single furrows with two horses. Everyone would help each other during threshing and potato picking. There was real community spirit!

CHAPTER 4

Historic Homes

Llangain is blessed with some fine historic homes, whether they are mansions such as Llwyndu and Plas Cwrt-hir, a gentleman's residence such as Brynderi, a manor house like Fernhill or a cottage developed into an attractive public house, namely Pantydderwen. Most are well within the parish boundaries, while others are so close it would be a shame to omit their histories. Indeed, those in question are associated with this book through their postal address even if the Boundary Commission does not allow them to be strictly within the parish of Llangain.

Fernhill

Fernhill, a former manor house dating back to about 1723, is listed as a Grade II building for its architectural and historic connections. The Georgian country house, in its tree-clad dell, famous as the frequent childhood holiday retreat of the world-renowned poet Dylan Thomas (1914–53) in the 1920s, is immortalised in one of his best-known poems, 'Fernhill'. His uncle and aunt, James and Ann Jones, lived there with their son, Idris, and Dylan would spend summer holidays in the rambling country home. It became, therefore, a summertime paradise for the young Dylan and now thousands of schoolchildren and students all over the world analyse his memories of exploring Fernhill:

Now as I was young and easy under the apple boughs
About the lilting house and happy as the grass
was green.

And:

And as I was green and carefree, famous among
the barns
About the happy yard and singing as the farm
was home.

He also remembers the tranquillity of country Sundays, or Sabbaths:

And the Sabbath rang slowly
In the pebbles of the holy stream.

American author David Caputo, while writing on his experiences in the Vietnam war, recalled how he escaped in his mind from the threat of deadly mines, sniper fire and mortar bombings by reading and re-reading the poem at the battle front. The final lines of 'Fernhill' were used as the poet's epitaph on the commemorative plaque installed in Westminster Abbey's Poet's Corner.

Time held me green and dying,
Though I sang in my chains like the sea.

In 1933 he wrote a poem on the death of his Aunt Annie entitled 'After the Funeral', and a short story called 'The Peaches', from one of his prose works, *Portrait of the Artist as a Young Dog*, is also based on his visits to Fernhill. It is, I think, an immensely entertaining story, full of human sympathy and vitality. His belief in ghosts and vampires is evident in the story, as he imagines a demon with 'wings and hooks, who clung like a bat to [his] hair'. Although he loved Fernhill's association with hangman Robert Ricketts Evans, who lived there during the second half of the nineteenth century, Dylan didn't want his readers to realise the connection and painted Gorsehill as his former home. He described it as a dank, dark house and, as he 'climbed the stairs, each one had a different voice. The candle flame jumped in his bedroom, where a lamp was burning very low and the curtains waved…'. Doubtless the young Dylan Thomas found the assistant executioner an inspirational if not horrifying figure, which helped fuel the imagination behind his greatest works.

Dylan's roots were deeply bedded in farming families in the Llangain and surrounding area. His maternal great-great-grandparents were John Williams (1784–1846) and his wife, Anna (1774–1860).

Dylan Thomas and his mother at Fernhill along with Tom Williams, the owner, 1952.

They farmed at Penycoed, on the border with Llangain parish. Their son, Thomas, married Anne Thomas (1815–1902). They were Dylan's great-grandparents. His grandmother, Anna Williams, was born at Pencelly Isaf Farm. Within months of Anna's birth, the family moved to neighbouring Waunfwlchan.

Anna married a George Williams from Alltycnap in 1860 and circumstances made them move to Swansea, where Florence, Dylan's mother, was born in 1882. Family holidays would be at Waunfwlchan and later at Llwyngwyn, which lay on the opposite side of the lane. A great-aunt of Dylan married Daniel Evans, the blacksmith at Brook Forge (today called Swn yr Einion), Llangain, where he would visit while staying at Fernhill.

In 1893 Florence's sister, Annie (1862–1933), had married Jim Jones (1864–1942), the eldest son of Richard and Rachel Jones, Pentrewyman. In turn this brought further family connections with other farms, such as Dolaumeinion and Pwntan Bach (Green Acres). The farms that stayed in the Jones and Williams families to the 1950s were Penycoed, Llwyngwyn, Maesgwyn, Pencelly Uchaf and Pwntan Bach. There were also more distant Williams relations in Pentrewyman and Lletyrneuadd. Dylan Thomas was almost a Llangain boy!

Fernhill is also known, as referred to earlier, for its association with notorious assistant county hangman, Robert Ricketts Evans.

Robert Evans married Maria Davies, the daughter of John Davies, attorney, of Fernhill, who had made Maria the heir to all his property, which extended into ten parishes.

Being the assistant county hangman, Evans, though he had married into wealth, had little income of his own, yet he is recorded as having attended cock fights and gambling matches up and down the country.

His wife, Maria, died soon after the birth of their daughter, Frances, who was made sole heir to the fortune. Before she came of age and into her fortune her father had legal documents prepared so that the girl's property would be transferred to him. Having fallen in love with a Hungarian, a doctor called Blumberg, Frances refused to sign the papers.

Folklore has it that Evans had bars put on the windows, but despite being made a prisoner in her own home Frances showed no signs of changing her mind. Evans therefore built a windowless arch-roofed cell in the courtyard in which to incarcerate the obstinate girl.

The next part of the story is the stuff all fine romances are made of; before the work on the cell was completed Frances' lover appeared, removed one of the window bars and the pair eloped together.

These tales have long been regarded as local tittle-tattle. The truth is that Evans' death certificate shows him as having died at Fernhill, on 26 August 1901, from senile decay and an enlarged prostate, aged 83. His occupation on the certificate is described as being of 'independent means'.

A great-grandson of the deputy hangman, Robert Evans from Llansteffan, insists there is no record of him having taken part in any hangings, nor any record of him imprisoning his daughter in Fernhill. In fact, his daughter arranged his funeral and was left his estate. Robert Ricketts Evans was a colourful character and a well educated and flamboyant gentleman.

According to his obituary, Frances 'did escape one dark night' after learning of her father's determination to force her to sign some deeds, already prepared, whereby he would become possessed of property which she had held in her own right. She did not return home until she received news of her father's illness, and her elopement in 1865 is confirmed in Evans' own diaries!

Death of 'Evans, Fernhill'
End of an extraordinary Career
Carmarthen Journal, 30 August 1901

A notorious personality, one of St Peter's most eccentric boys has just died, viz, Mr R.R. Anderson (otherwise Evans), Fernhill, near Carmarthen. We cannot do better than reproduce the following excellently written biography of this eccentric gentleman published by the Western Mail.

Wales has lost one of the most eccentric of her sons, one around whose memory will ever hang a veil of weird, creepy sensationalism.

Mr R.R. Anderson of Fernhill in the parish of Llangain near Carmarthen, better known as 'Evans the Hangman' has at last 'shot his bolt', as he would himself express it, and left behind him the reminiscences of a career, which for remarkable incidents and wealth of originality in its various phases, stands prominently alone.

Deceased seemed to have an ingrained dislike to pay bills, not because he wished to escape from lawful debts, but because the pestering of creditors and the subtleties which they employed to try and enforce settlement provided his peculiar temperament with a fund of amusement. He had a sufficient number of county court summonses issued against him to paper the whole house with – his favourite mural decorations, by the way, were pictures, some valuable, of prize fights and fighters, bull-baiting, cockpits, hangmen, etc and many of his escapades with bailiffs and creditors' representatives were varied and highly exciting.

To the poor he was a most considerate, compassionate neighbour. Working men hailed with pleasure a job at Fernhill, as the place always afforded so much amusement and plenty of good cheer. Whenever possible the old gentleman would play practical jokes on his visitors. His great aim was to interest them in the narration of

Fernhill, c.1975.

The former coach house at Fernhill c.1975.

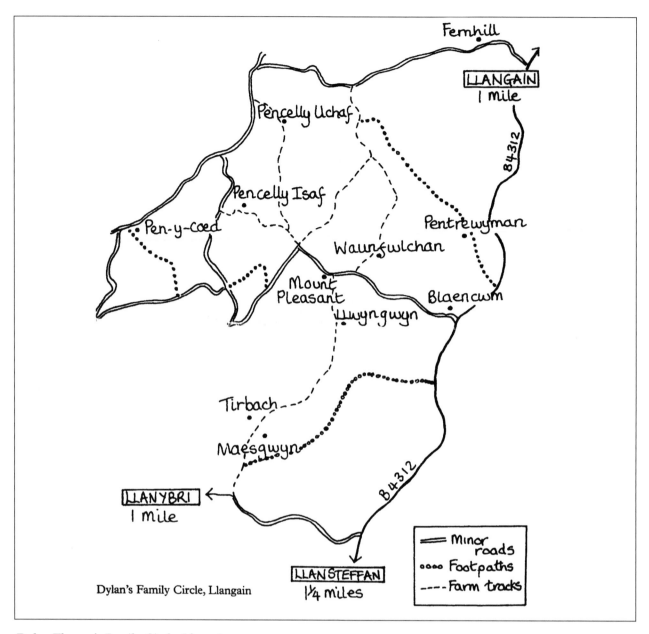

Dylan Thomas's Family Circle, Llangain.

blood-curdling experiences, at the same time raising their spirits with frequent and generous doses of beer, stout and liquors, which he had a knack of continually changing. When he had them fairly 'under the table' he would then excel as the practical jokist. His hangman's outfit – ropes, noose, pulleys, etc, complete were brought into requisition and the affrighted but helplessly besotten victims were put through the whole of the grim process. He has been known, in the plenitude of his eccentric 'playfulness' to even gently kick the chair from under some of his butts, and to laugh immoderately at the screams of the terrorised suspended person. However, he always took care that no serious harm ensued, and the invariable conclusion of the scene was the bestowal of money upon the now sobered victim.

A few hours after the death sentence had been passed, at the Carmarthen Guidhall, on David Rees, the Llanelly murderer, Mr Anderson indicted a letter to the then borough high sheriff, offering his services as executioner, and certain Carmarthen gentlemen can tell a rich, albeit misplaced, joke in connection with the sardonic retort which the high sheriff's letter of refusal elicited from the disappointed applicant. When Berry arrived at Carmarthen to vindicate the law, he was visited at his Majesty's prison by the deceased, and on a later occasion, when he blossomed forth as a public lecturer, he became a much petted guest at Fernhill.

In full consonance with his love of things creepy, he was one of the earliest of latter-day advocates of all round cremation, and in connection with this phase of his character it is well to recall his dealing with the late Dr Price of Llantrisant. These two notorieties were bosom friends, and many are the tales of the eccentricities they held in common. It was Anderson who put the match to the pile on which the body of Dr Price was *publicly cremated on Llantrisant Mountain, an act which created such widespread astonishment at the time and the deceased often used to express the wish to be similarly disposed of outside Fernhill after his own dissolution. He had actually fixed upon a present inhabitant of Carmarthen and old friend of his to apply the torch, but during his last illness he forsook the idea, and the ordinary rites of burial will take place, probably on Friday, in accordance with the wishes of his only daughter.*

The property changed hands in 1929, when a local farmer, Mr Tom Williams of Cwrtmale, bought it. There is a well-known photo of him with Dylan Thomas and his mother when the poet visited Fernhill in 1952. It was to be his last visit there but not the final journey to his family roots, since it is known that he and Florence, his mother, took tea with the Revd Hopkin Evans at Môr Awelon, the manse at Llansteffan. Hopcyn Evans was the minister at Smyrna as well as at Capel Newydd, Llanybri, and Bethel, Llansteffan. A few weeks later, on 9 November 1953, Dylan died in New York.

In 1972 Tom Williams sold Fernhill to former Ghurkha Regiment Major Ken Davies and his wife Maureen of Old Castle, Llangain. They lovingly and sympathetically restored the place over many years and used to show a great number of visitors around, particularly from overseas. These would include students, as well as ordinary poetry lovers.

Since Ken Davies had taught me French at the Queen Elizabeth Boys' Grammar School, Carmarthen, I was fortunate enough to be shown around the entire house in the mid-1970s, and gained permission to make an 8mm cine film of both the interior and exterior of the property to accompany my local history research. For this I am grateful to them both.

Fern Hill

*Now as I was young and easy under the apple boughs
About the lilting house and happy as the grass was green,
The night above the dingle starry,
Time let me hail and climb
Golden in the heydays of his eyes,
And honoured among wagons I was prince of the apple towns
And once below a time I lordly had the trees and leaves
Trail with daisies and barley
Down the rivers of the windfall light.*

*And as I was green and carefree, famous among the barns
About the happy yard and singing as the farm was home,
In the sun that is young once only,
Time let me play and be
Golden in the mercy of his means,*

*And green and golden I was huntsman and herdsman, the calves
Sang to my horn, the foxes on the hills barked clear and cold,
And the sabbath rang slowly
In the pebbles of the holy streams.*

*All the sun long it was running, it was lovely, the hay
Fields high as the house, the tunes from the chimneys, it was air
And playing, lovely and watery
And fire green as grass.
And nightly under the simple stars
As I rode to sleep the owls were bearing the farm away,
All the moon long I heard, blessed among stables, the nightjars
Flying with the ricks, and the horses
Flashing into the dark.*

*And then to awake, and the farm, like a wanderer white
With the dew, come back, the cock on his shoulder: it was all
Shining, it was Adam and maiden,
The sky gathered again
And the sun grew round that very day.
So it must have been after the birth of the simple light
In the first, spinning place, the spellbound horses walking warm
Out of the whinnying green stable
On to the fields of praise.*

*And honoured among foxes and pheasants by the gay house
Under the new made clouds and happy as the heart was long,
In the sun born over and over,
I ran my heedless ways,
My wishes raced through the house high hay
And nothing I cared, at my sky blue trades, that time allows
In all his tuneful turning so few and such morning songs
Before the children green and golden
Follow him out of grace,*

*Nothing I cared, in the lamb white days, that time would take me
Up to the swallow thronged loft by the shadow of my hand,
In the moon that is always rising,
Nor that riding to sleep
I should hear him fly with the high fields
And wake to the farm forever fled from the childless land.
Oh as I was young and easy in the mercy of his means,
Time held me green and dying
Though I sang in my chains like the sea.*

Dylan Thomas, 1945

Pantyrathro

It is marked as 'Pentrathroe' on Thomas Kitchen's map of 1855 and as 'Pant yr Athro' on Colby's Map of 1831. The first known owner was Jenkin Morris, who married Katherine Joliffe of Kidwelly in 1654. It stayed in the family and in 1695 was owned and occupied by John Morris and wife, Florence. She outlived him and was there in 1726. When Thomas Morris made his will in 1772, he left Pantyrathro to his niece and the remainder of the estate to his nephew, the Revd Morris.

On 29 September 1856 a lease for three lives of Pantyrathro was granted to the then owner, Edward Morris Davies, of Uplands, Llandyfaelog, to the Lloyd family (formerly of Penybont, Cardiganshire) and in 1877 was occupied by J. Walter Lloyd, the surviving life, who had married Mary Anne Johnes of Dolau Cothi.

The mansion was later owned by James (Jack) Richards (1832–1909), who carried out restoration works and added the present front and main entrance. He was a local entrepreneur who made his wealth by selling milk and related products to London after the South Wales Railway reached Carmarthen in 1852.

Comprised of 130 acres, it was sold by public auction at the Boar's Head Hotel, Carmarthen, on 18 April 1936. The sale catalogue described five lots –

Pantyrathro mansion, 1930s.

Aerial view of Pantyrathro, showing the B4312 winding its way along the River Tywi, 1967

Mansion and Farm (Lot 1), Clifton (Lot 2), Llety (Lot 3), Ty Gwyn (Lot 4) and Maesteg (Lot 5) between Waunfort and Maesgwynne.

The details of Lot 1 show the house as having an entrance hall, cloakroom, WC and lavatory, bathroom, hall, drawing-room, breakfast room with french windows, library and dining-room with two bay windows. In addition to all this on the ground floor, there was a butler's pantry, passage, larder, kitchen, scullery, dairy, store room, tiled yard with two coalhouses and loft and a wash-house. Reached by an attractive sweep of stairs and a wide landing, on the first floor were the seven front bedrooms and the four bedrooms on the second floor.

The lot description continues as follows:

At the back of the house is a well-arranged Stable Yard with entrance gates leading to the main drive. The stables are a special attraction, being particularly well laid out and comprising: 4 spacious Loose Boxes with exceptional fittings, tiling and flooring. The headroom and lighting are especially good. Overhead is a Hay and Straw Loft with a delivery shoot in the stables. At the entrance stands a flagged and tiled Washery with glass sides and roof suitable for motor car, horse and gear cleaning. The Saddle Room adjoining the stables is fitted with a Cupboard and Hanger. Alongside is a Double Garage and Store Room.

The Farmery approached by a secondary drive comprises the following: Bull house and Calf Shed both with loft and barn. The Corn Mixing Room, Cow house (12 ties), Calves Cot, Stable (4 stalls) and Loose Box all with Granary, Corn and Hay lofts over, Engine Shed, Five-Bay Hay Shed (iron posts with corrugated iron roof).

Alongside are: stone built and Caernarfon-slated Coach-house with granary over, Cow house (7 ties), Calf Pen with loft. Corrugated iron Cow house, Calf shed and Fowl shed, three brick-built and Caernarfon slated Pigs cots and yard; two Open Yards with cattle fattening sheds with Cart Shed alongside.

Pantyrathro Lodge.

The Bailiff's House or Farmhouse at the rear of the farm consisted of 'parlour, kitchen, back kitchen, dairy and four bedrooms together with a garden'.

To complete this Lot there is a reference to the land, soil, grazing and water supply.

The Land is of rich red sandstone loam and lies well together in the form of a square mainly with a south-easterly aspect and standing around the Homestead and across the main road to the river Tywi. The soil is of an exceptionally rich nature and is entirely laid down to grass with the exception of two fields. Included in the grazing are the rich Saltings alongside the river. Water is supplied by gravitation to the Residence and Homestead from a spring on the property, other supplies being received from a stream on the northern boundary and another passing through the land at the south west end.

There were some more change of ownership before Major John Buckley and Mrs Buckley bought Pantyrathro in 1967. They were instrumental in forming the Equestrian Centre, which became well established during the 1970s. The Buckleys built a new house nearby, called Cwrt y Cadno, and lived there briefly before moving to Llandeilo in 1979.

The present owners, John and Merril Parry, converted the mansion into a hotel which is now a hugely popular and successful venue for registered weddings and receptions.

Pilroath

Pilroath is situated at the southern end of the parish above the confluence of Fernhill Brook and the River Tywi. Part of the name preserves the old English word 'Pill', meaning tidal creek or small channel near the coast, an apt description of Pilroath, while 'Roath' (rhoth) is derived from fort/hilltop fort.

The first family to occupy Pilroath, at the beginning of the Tudor period, was an offshoot of the Reeds of Green Castle. They remained there for four generations. In the seventeenth century it was owned by a yeoman family of Llansteffan parish, who sold it to the Morris family of Pantyrathro, on the opposite hill. One George Davies, who was in possession in 1726, became Mayor of Carmarthen in 1729. Around the mid-eighteenth century, it was sold to the Revd Thomas Williams of Wernddu, who was living in Pilroath in 1749 and was there till c.1785.

It then became the home of the Gwynn family, who also owned seven other farms in Llangain. William Bevan Gwynn and Mrs Gwynn were Methodists and members of Moriah Chapel, Llansteffan, and a Sunday school was established at Pilroath. The property later became part of the Cottage estate, Llansteffan, and in 1901 was advertised for sale as 'a fine old Family Residence with extensive outbuildings', comprising 137 acres, and

Alderman T.Ll. Harries, JP, of Plas Pilroath, Llangain, with Mrs Harries and their daughter, Mrs Eluned Rees (wife of Dr Ernest Rees, St. Bartholomew's Hospital), after receiving the MBE from Her Majesty the Queen in 1956. (Dr Ernest Rees is the son of Sam Rees, headmaster of Llangain School 1924–61).

was sold for £5,200 to T.J. Harries, Esq. (J.A.J. Harries' grandfather). He demolished the old house and built the present mansion about 100 yards (30m) away and on slightly higher ground so as to take full advantage of the wider and more splendid views over the estuary and Carmarthen Bay. The only relic of the original dwelling is a large wall which stands just below the commodious outbuildings of former days. Its site is overgrown with trees and bushes, which flank the drive to the present house.

The property was in the Harries family for three generations and was a centre of public service and hospitality for a long time, since both T.Ll. Harries MBE and J.A.J. Harries, CBE, JP, were county councillors and between them served local constituents for 50 years.

Cllr Arthur Harries had Nantllyn built in the mid-1990s as a retirement home. The property is situated at the entrance to the long drive to Pilroath. With failing health, however, both he and his wife, Mair, moved to Dôl-y-Dderwen, Llangain, a few years later.

Llwyndu

The mansion was built in the first half of the nineteenth century, with some later additions. In 1821–23 Captain Henry Harding lived there, and it was afterwards home to Frederick Phillips, JP, who died in 1838, aged 31. It then passed into the hands of Mr Charles Bankes Davies and his wife, Mary Anne. Their six children – Elizabeth (Lilly) and Maria (twin

Pilroath, c.1920s.

Plas Pilroath, 1954.

Plas Pilroath, 1935. **Left to right:** *Mair Harries, Mrs Harries with Henry, Tom Harries, Ben Harries, Eiluned Harries. Arthur Harries is missing from this family photo.*

Southward view at Pilroath showing the Tywi estuary and Llansteffan Castle.

Y Glyn, built in 1924, the home of Mr and Mrs Tom Harries.

Left: Pilroath Lodge, 2005.

Plas Llwyndu with Myra Jones in the front doorway, 2001.

sisters born 21 December 1853), Eugene (born 26 April 1856), Emily (born 21 February 1858), Charles (born 16 December, 1859) and Bankes (born 25 May 1862) – were all christened at Llangain Church, and the four daughters were all married there, too.

Mr Bankes Davies died in 1870 at the age of 45, leaving his wife to bring up the children, then aged 17, 17, 14, 12, 11, and eight. Mrs Davies outlived her husband by almost three decades, and her detailed obituary makes interesting reading. Charles, one of the sons, became the owner-occupier at the turn of the twentieth century.

Obituary Mrs Davies, Llwyndu, Llangain
The Welshman, September 1897

Very many years have passed since a lady so widely and sincerely beloved and esteemed in the parish and district has been called to the Great Beyond. We have no hesitation in saying that no woman ever accomplished the important duties which fell upon her as a widowed mother with great credit to herself and benefit to her children than Mrs Davies did, who brought them up in the way that they should walk. And her labour of love has been crowned in a wonderful degree. She often used to say that she had many reasons to be thankful to her Heavenly Father for the manifest blessings which had rested upon her care and efforts on her behalf and her children, both socially and spiritually.

It was a pleasure for the Vicar of the parish to call Mrs Davies' attention to any case deserving her sympathy and help, as she was invariably a cheerful giver in such cases, in her decease the church at Llangain has lost one of its most faithful members and liberal supporters.

There was no branch of Church work in which she did not love to take part. She was a true friend of the Welsh Church Press. Though her early education, training and the society in which she moved had made her more familiar with English than Welsh, she delighted to converse with her monoglot friends, neighbours and tenants in their native tongue.

Mrs Davies was a warm supporter and constant reader of the 'Llan', and thereby was kept in constant touch and sympathy with people amongst whom she had been called to live, and with the needs and aspirations of the Welsh Church, of which since her infancy, she had been a faithful member. She was utterly devoid of the false pride, which induces some of our nation to ignore Welsh, and to assume that they do not understand their native tongue. Mrs Davies was just, kind-hearted, and Christian-like in all her dealings with her fellow-beings. She lived and departed in the esteem and respect of all her tenants, dependants, friends, and acquaintances and all her children arise up and call her blessed.

Last Friday her mortal remains were laid to rest in the family vault in Llangain Churchyard, in the presence of a large assembly of relations, friends, neighbours and acquaintances, who had gathered from far and near to pay their last tribute of respect to one so dear to many and respected by all. Before starting the mournful procession from Llwyndu, the Vicar gave out the hymn, 'O fryniau Caersalem'. Then the procession started for Llangain headed by the Vicar, The Revd S. Jones, RD Llangunnor; the Revd J. Lloyd, BD, Llanpumpsaint: and the Revd D.S. Davies, Vicar of Llanybri. At the entrance gate of the church the Vicar and the Revd S.

Plas Llwyndu in the 1970s.

The coach house and outbuildings at Llwyndu in the 1970s. Note the Rover 2000, the Ford Escort Estate and the Austin Allegro Van De Plas.

The Beeches, formerly known as Chweched (Six Lanes). This cottage is the upper lodge to Plas Llwyndu.

Llwyndu Lodge, the lower lodge to Plas Llwyndu.

The Beeches won the Pantyrathro Mansion House Floral Trophy Award in the Horticultural Show, mid-1990s.

Jones read the appointed consoling verses. In the church the Vicar read the service, and Mr Puddicombe of Carmarthen played on the organ the 'Dead March' in Saul in his usual able manner. At the grave the Rural Dean officiated most feelingly and impressively.

David William Lloyd-Davies and Margaret Joyce Lloyd-Davies, of Red Court, bought the mansion in 1926 and two of his aunts lived there until 1937. It became the headquarters of a Royal Artillery Ack-Ack and searchlight detachment during the Second World War. Then, after the war, the house was totally refurbished and the Lloyd-Davies family moved there in the early 1950s.

Mrs Lloyd-Davies died in 1957, aged 77, and Mr Lloyd-Davies in 1973, aged 87. Myra, their daughter, who was born in the neighbouring farm, Llwyn, in 1920, then inherited the place. She married Geoffrey Burnett in 1970 but was widowed after a few months. Then, in 1972, she was married to Colin Jones, the marriage lasting 19 years until his death in 1991.

Like her parents before her, who had donated the land for the Church Hall, Mrs Myra Jones was also a staunch supporter of the local church in Llangain and gave the new communion cup when the 1576 chalice became unusable. She passed away in 2005 at the age of 85.

A Spitfire aeroplane crashed into the hills between Llwyn and Llwyndu in the early hours on 6 July 1940. The pilot, George Nelson-Edwards, escaped and was taken to Llwyndu. He retells this adventure in his book *Spit and Sawdust*, written in 1995, from which the following extract is taken.

Since our move to Fairwood, the Squadron had been on continuous night operations, plus, of course, the usual spate of convoy patrols and 'readiness' states during daylight hours. We operated at night along a patrol line code-named 'Crack' between Pembroke Dock and Swansea, where the Luftwaffe had been carrying out intensive mine-laying operations.

As usual we had to rely on visual contact to pull off an interception, and we seldom got any joy. David Haysom had now taken over from Harvey as Commanding Officer and he was determined to get a kill. He managed twice to creep up the backside of an EA, one a JU88, the other unidentified, but he couldn't claim more than a 'damaged' for his pains. We were lucky enough to have Roly Beamont as the new 'B' Flight Commander, who joined us at the end of June from 87 Squadron (Hurricane Night Fighters) based at Charmy Down. Later, of course, Roly made history as the Chief Test Pilot for English Electric, testing the Canberra and the Lightning supersonic fighter.

On the night of 5 July I was detailed to patrol 'Crack', taking off at around 2300 hours. It was a clear night but black as soot. As I turned eastward the Controller's voice came over: 'Several bandits in Swansea/Llanelli area. Vector 100° Angels 15. Buster!' I could see clusters of searchlights beaming up all along my route, when suddenly, in front of me, I spotted an EA caught in a cone. I was at exactly the same height about two thousand yards behind. It was flying inland from my right heading north, and with the aid of the searchlights I tracked it in a left-hand turn, creeping up behind it to within perhaps four hundred yards, closing up fast. Suddenly the searchlights were doused and I was plunging into inky blackness like a derailed runaway trolley-car which had missed the buffers. Recovering from this momentary set-back I made a tight orbit, eyeballs straining from their sockets, trying to pierce the darkness for a sight of the EA, but to no avail. As I turned back parallel with the coast, without warning my Hurricane caught fire, flames spreading from beneath the engine cowling, and it seemed all lit up down below where my feet were supposed to be. In seconds flames were licking round the canopy. I had no choice now, I had to jump before I was barbecued. Screaming invectives at the Controller on the radio to take a fix on my position, I yanked the hood back, half-rolled and dropped clear, not forgetting first, thank God, to unplug everything. Mercifully, the parachute opened. Dangling from the shroud-lines I attempted to survey the scene. All round me there was a vast expanse of dark shadows, which reflected the distant glow of the burning Hurricane as it twisted and spun down towards the coal-black earth. All I could see now were a few stars twinkling above, and the ghostly glimmer of some faraway searchlights.

My eyes grew accustomed to the dark and I could pick out a jagged line of pearl-white breakers along what must be a beach. I'd no idea of my height, but as I sank slowly down I could see that a gentle offshore wind was coaxing me across the coastline. 'Oh God,' I thought. 'For the second time I am heading for a watery grave.'

I feverishly tugged on the shroud-lines to increase my

rate of descent, and nearly collapsed the parachute canopy. Suddenly, the unmistakable smell of crops and the harvesting of freshly mown hay assailed my nostrils. I could now hear the backwash of the surf along the shingle. Quicker than I could sink a pint of beer, I hit the ground with a sickening thud and was dragged along on my back, whilst desperately groping for the quick-release box, without the slightest idea where I was except that a rugged cliff-edge could be only yards away. I found the box and gave the knob a vicious twist, the parachute harness gently slid away into the darkness, leaving me lying in a shallow ditch.

I lay there quietly for a few seconds taking stock. Though bruised and scratched, at least it seemed that I was in one piece. It was pitch black. Staggering to my feet, not knowing which direction to take, I started walking. The ground was stubble and pitted, making it hard going. As I gingerly crept forward I heard muffled movements ahead and thought I saw sinister shadows, even darker than the dark, looming up in front of me.

It's the Welsh Home Guard! I thought to myself in horror. They'll shoot anyone on sight! In a discordant shaky voice I sang out the first few notes of 'God Save the King', then on second thoughts switched to 'Cumre am Bith', in the hope they would take me for a patriotic Welshman, so that perhaps they would spare me the bullet. There followed the instantaneous and sudden rush of pounding feet, as several cows reared up out of the darkness and shied away in the opposite direction, evidently much put out by my song!

I struggled on and eventually spotted a faint light glimmering through the undergrowth. Drawing nearer I saw the outline of some buildings. It was a farmhouse. The farmer took me in, brewed a cup of tea, then ran me in his old jalopy to Llangain Manor (Llwyndu), the HQ of a Royal Artillery Ack Ack and Searchlight Detachment about a mile away, some five miles south of Carmarthen. They gave me bacon and eggs, and I shot my mouth off about searchlights and how they mucked everything up. They hastily pushed me into a truck and drove me back to Fairwood Common, in the eager fervid hope that they would never see me again!

Plas Cwrthir

This Victorian mansion occupies an elevated, sunny position overlooking the lower Tywi valley. It is set in mature wooded gardens and grounds. In 1650 Cwrthir formed part of the estate of Lloyd of Wenallt, Llanfihangel Abercywin, being then a farm, and no records relate to it having been farmed until the nineteenth century, when Colby's Map of 1831 marks the farm as Cwrt Hir.

The present mansion was built near the farmhouse by a member of the Gwyn family of Pilroath. The residence, originally with six bedrooms and built as a double-pile house, was first occupied by Mr William Edward Bevan Gwyn in the late 1840s. He had been born at Pilroath in 1826. In 1873 his estate consisted of almost 500 acres.

The 14 properties comprising the Plas Cwrthir estate were sold on 4 August 1889. The house was described as a 'very charming Country Residence'

Plas Cwrthir in the 1950s.

Plas Cwrthir. The van (right) is parked at the top of the driveway.

Plas Cwrthir showing the new drive through the meadow, 2005

The Davies family on the gravel near front door at Pals Worthier, c.1957. Left to right, standing: Philip Davies, Rhys Davies, Mr David Stanley Davies; seated: Mrs Rachel Davies, Mrs Morfydd Davies.

with attached grounds, and 'a model farmery'. It was again advertised for sale in June 1919, described as a double-pile house with a large hall, drawing-room (23ft by 16ft), dining-room (17ft by 17ft), study (14ft by 10ft), kitchen (16ft by 16ft), larder, pantry, and back kitchen leading to a small courtyard. There stood a large store room with loft, with a larder and pantry on the opposite side of the courtyard and a back house and dairy with loft. The six bedrooms opened onto a central corridor running the length of the house, at the south end a spacious staircase with a large window lighting the hall and upstairs corridor, at the end of which was a linen pantry. It also had grounds, tennis lawn and kitchen garden.

Since then the property has passed through several hands. Mr A.V. Key owned it in the 1940s, before Mr and Mrs D.S. Davies and family moved there in 1958. They found the place in a dilapidated condition, with the roof leaking and no electricity. A tree which had crashed onto the power house in the 1940s had made the occupants revert to oil lamps. It is not known whether the hay found in the attic was used for absorbing the rain or acted as a kind of insulation! Whatever, the family carried out restoration works and Philip Davies, one of the sons, continued to live there until 1994, when Mr and Mrs Dorian Davies, the owners at the time of writing, bought the mansion. Major changes have happened at the Plas in the last decade, with further restoration and extensions, the front drive having been totally rerouted to meander through the front meadow stretching from the house to the main road.

Pantydderwen, 1965. Note the traditional vegetable and flower garden behind the hedge.

Sarah Jane Davies and her sister, Margaretta Jones (the author's grandmother and great-aunt), c.1960.

Pantydderwen with Cartref and Haulfryn in the background. In the doorway are Mrs S.J. Davies and Carl Atkins, her eldest great-grandson, 1970s.

Pantydderwen

Pantydderwen is an old house built around the mid-nineteenth century. The name means 'a hollow or valley of the oak'. It was a typical two rooms down and two rooms up kind of cottage, although there was a dressing-room next to the bedroom on the right as you look at the house, which was used as a small bedroom, the window being above the porch.

It has served the local community in several ways over the years. It was the Post Office for over 20 years, with Mr Henry Jones as sub-postmaster. He was the father of the late Mrs Irene Harding, who lived in Dôl-y-Dderwen in recent years. She was born in Pantydderwen and moved with her family to Minyrafon in the Brook area of Llangain (Isaf), where the Post Office was based for nearly 40 years.

Then the house was used as a little shop when a

certain Edward Williams lived there. He was a churchwarden and the altar desk (the small portable brass lectern for the vicar's communion book) was given in memory of him and his wife. He died on 4 May 1941.

The author's maternal grandmother, Mrs Sarah Jane Davies, lived there with her sister, Margretta Jones, from the late 1950s until 1975, when she moved and became the first resident to live in the new OAPs' bungalows at Maesyrawel.

David and Wendy Jones, the new owners of Pantydderwen, converted the place to a public house in 1979. The landlord was known as 'Dai Shamby'.

They remained there until 1987, when Annie Bath and Susan Foster bought the pub. In 1992 Terry and Dawn Griffiths of Brynderi took over and extended

Tally Ho! A meet at Pantydderwen in the 1980s.

The official opening of Tarfarn Pantydderwen by Roy Bergiers (Llanelli, Wales and British Lions) looked on by David and Wendy Jones, proprietors.

Pantydderwen, 1985.

Community Councillor Ellis Davies, Pantrynn, having a smashing time with the collection for the Adult Day Care Centre, Johnstown, Christmas, 1981. Amongst the onlookers are Wendy Jones (licensee), Nigel Bowen, No. 6 Maesyrawel and E.D. Phillips (Council Clerk).

the property by redefining boundaries, since they owned the neighbouring land. Mr and Mrs Dave Manning became tenants initially and later owners. Substantial improvements and extensions were made by them throughout the 1990s and changes still continue in the first decade of the new millennium.

The house formed a kind of clubhouse for the local 11-hole golf course in the 1990s, and the former reception area/office has been incorporated into a new public bar, the golf course having now closed.

Original Property Layout
Externally, the old cottage extends from the window on the immediate left of the porch to the immediate window on the right of the porch. The north extension is from that point to the patio area. The south extension incorporates the whole area of the new bar (as opposed to the lounge bar). There was once a window in the interlinking doorway now between the bars. This small window overlooked the entire length of the flower and vegetable garden. This is now the pool table area and part of the car park.

Internally, the old cottage would have extended from the fireplace to the arch, although that feature is actually square in shape. The front of the lounge bar would have formed the back of the house. Beyond this point in the old days, however, there was a simple lean-to extension housing a kitchen and downstairs toilet, but it would not have reached the French/patio doors. The staircase started just inside the front door, with, to its left, a doorway into the parlour (the present bar and fireplace area) and a doorway into the living-room (the present area to the right of the front door). The corner of the lounge bar was the 'Cwtsh dan star' (under staircase area).

Some Recollections of My Visits to Pantydderwen
Louie Mellows, Port Talbot, South Wales
2005

I used to visit Llangain regularly as a child because my grandparents, Edward and Alice Williams, lived and kept a shop there. My grandmother was born and grew up in Danlanfach. She would go to market on a donkey to sell produce. Most of her married life was spent in Merthyr, where they farmed. They retired to Pantydderwen. Granny was chapel and grandfather was a staunch churchman, where he was a warden. There is a small brass altar lectern in memory of them both in the church.

Their daughter, Margaretta, lived with them and continued with the shop after their time.

They would knit woollen socks for the local farmers because they had a special machine. Farmers would turn up on horseback outside Pantydderwen, shout out 'Shop!' and my grandmother or great-aunt Getta would go out with whatever they requested.

Mr and Mrs Edward Williams, Pantydderwen, 1930s.

Margaretta Williams and Agnus Jones (née Williams, Louie Mellows' mother).

Do you know, Dylan Thomas, the poet, used to buy Woodbines from them when he was a young gentleman in his twenties and staying at Fernhill?

My grandfather met me off the bus in Lammas Street and then he would take me into the Rose and Crown for his pint and a lemonade for me. My grandmother and I used to go on the bus around

8.30a.m. to market with some chickens she had killed and dressed.

My grandmother used to make beautiful cawl. It was cooked in a cauldron hung by a hook above the fire. I have never tasted cawl like it since. We had lovely times playing games such as Snakes and Ladders and Ludo in the living-room immediately to the right of the front door. By the way, my Aunt Esther was married to a carpenter called Jenkin Evans, who built the porch in the 1930s.

During the Second World War they took in Belgian refugees – a married woman and her sister and one child. We used to fetch water from the village well near Lletyneuadd. Muriel, one of the daughters there, was very ill at one time. She had TB and spent almost a year at Sully Hospital, near Cardiff.

Some of My Recollections of Living in Llangain
Alcwyn Rogers, Canada (formerly of Minyrafon)
2005

I was brought up in Minyrafon Llangain, probably better known at that time as Llangain Post Office. I was born in 1945, attended Llangain CP School and later Queen Elizabeth Grammar School for Boys. I left Llangain when I went to Cardiff University in September 1963 and have not lived there on a permanent basis since that time.

When I grew up, Llangain was a parish and it didn't have a central point. In the Smyrna area there was the Primary School, Smyrna itself, the Church, the Church Hall and a few houses, including the row of council houses opposite the school (Maes yr Awel Nos 1–6). Minyrafon is located in the 'Brook' – an area that has not changed much over the years. It was a hamlet consisting of a number of houses, possibly in the order of ten, and this included Llangain Post Office and Yr Efail (The Forge). The border between Llangain and Llansteffan is the stream (the brook) itself that runs through the hamlet and, ironically, Llangain Post Office was actually located in the parish of Llansteffan. The Smyrna area has changed considerably over the years and is now referred to as the village of Llangain. So, unlike my childhood days, the actual centre of Llangain is no longer in question.

Prior to the 1930s, Llangain Post Office was located at Pantydderwen, near Smyrna. Today, it is the local pub. My grandfather, Henry Jones, was the Post Master and my understanding is that he moved the Post Office from Pantydderwen to Minyrafon. He was the Llangain postmaster for over 50 years and, after his death in 1963, my mother Maggie Rogers succeeded him. The Post Office moved back to the Smyrna area when my parents retired in 1969 and, I believe, it was Gareth Williams that took it over.

Postmaster Henry Jones, Pantydderwen, having finished his mail round (note the flat bag!).

Minyrafon, c.1930. Left to right: *Irene Jones, Margaret Jones, Henry Jones, Samuel Jones* (seated).

An extended family lived in our household. It comprised my grandparents, Henry and Sarah Jones, their daughter, Rene Harding, and Margaret Anne (Maggie) Rogers, who was Henry Jones' daughter from an earlier marriage. His first wife, Hannah, died in 1911 and her grave, as well as those of most of my family, are in Smyrna graveyard. My mother and father were Tom Ivey and Margaret Anne (Maggie) Rogers, and they had two sons, my brother Peter and myself. My brother was born in 1940.

Rene Harding's husband, Arthur Thomas (also called Tom), also lived in the household, but they had no children.

The language spoken in the parish of Llangain and, of course, at home, was Welsh, but, as Tom Harding was originally from Devon, he only spoke English. Tom Harding's work was that of a general foreman and his role was to construct or reconstruct the buildings of his company, the Co-operative. He therefore spent most of his time away from the Carmarthen area, but his occasional presence meant that there was a smattering of English in the household. There is an amusing story of me coming home from primary school and my Uncle Tom who was home at the time, asking me, 'Well, Alcwyn, how did it go today? Were you misbehaving?' It seems that I pondered for a while and replied, 'She's not Miss Behaving, she's Miss Thomas!'

There were about 30 pupils in Llangain School at the time. Part of the time I was there, the more junior teacher, Miss Thomas, looked after the younger children in the smaller room. The headmaster, Sam Rees, looked after the older children in the big room. We were grouped by age, as far as I remember, but there was no real distinction of different classes. I remember Sam Rees as a pretty authoritative figure.

The children from the Brook travelled to and from Smyrna by bus. The afternoon bus left the Smyrna crossroads at about 3:00p.m., whereas school ended 15 minutes later. We from the Brook, therefore, spent 15 minutes less in school each day. This was the case until some of us decided to walk down the old road past Chweched (Six Roads) one day. Anyway, Sam Rees found out about this and thereafter we older children had to walk home each and every day. I remember not being very popular with the others for I had been involved in starting it all!.

As for the children who walked home, there was myself, Glanmor Evans (Brooke Forge, as it was then called), Brian Thomas (Ty Newydd), Aubrey and Ieuan Thomas (Ty Canol) and Dyfrig Hobbs (Ty-Isaf). In addition, we were accompanied by Nancy (Yr Hendy) and Eiri (Y Gilfach) on the walk from the school to Chweched. It was really quite pleasant walking down the old road chatting with my friends. I remember Eiri walking backwards most of the way, for I think she liked to see everything that was going on. Anyway, they were very pleasant days and these are just some of my recollections.

The Post Office

Before the establishment of Post Offices and sub-Post Offices in the later years of the eighteenth century, people had been picking up and delivering their post at receiving houses. These were often inns or post-houses along main coaching routes or, in towns, the coaching inns at the end of the mail-coach routes.

Handling the post was just one of the commercial

Minyrafon and Post Office, 1955.

Llangain Post Office, Minyrafon, with Henry Jones (postmaster 1907–63) and his grandson, Peter Rogers, c.1955.

Minyrafon, c.1946. Left to right: Ira Hobbs, Peter Rogers, Ida Hobbs, Ieuan Hobbs, Maggie Hobbs.

activities undertaken by the receiving house – similar in function a modern sub-Post Office. The postmaster may also have worked as a chemist, builder, bookseller or decorator, or run a general village shop. The Penny Black, the world's first adhesive stamp,

Gareth Wiliams (postmaster 1975–83) in Llangain Mini Market, smiling as he sells his wares!

Llangain village stores and Post Office, mid-1990s.

Cled Davies (postmaster 1987–98) and Suzanne Davies in a festive mood at Christmas time!

was valid for postage from 6 May 1840. Today we take pillar boxes for granted, but in the late 1840s posting a letter could mean a long walk to the nearest receiving house or Post Office. In fact, novelist Anthony Trollope was responsible for introducing pillar boxes to Britain.

An employee of the Post Office for much of his working life, in 1851 Trollope visited the Channel Islands to find ways of improving postal services. One proposal was to install roadside posting boxes. After successful trials in Jersey and Guernsey, boxes were set up on the mainland in 1853. The familiar cylindrical box was introduced in 1879.

A world first for the Post Office in 1968 was the introduction of a two-tier postal delivery service. With the vast quantity of mail then being posted causing delays in its delivery by the following morning, a system was needed whereby mail could be divided so that more urgent items could be delivered the next day and less urgent mail could take longer. The Royal Mail's solution was to use first- and second-class stamps, the more expensive first class indicating next-day delivery. Traditionally, only the portrait of Britain's reigning monarch

or that of someone deceased is shown on a British stamp, but in July 1969 the tradition was broken when, to mark the investiture of the Prince of Wales, his portrait appeared on the 1s. (5p) stamp.

In the year 2000, for the first time, four generations of the royal family were portrayed on the mini-sheet of stamps issued to mark the centenary of Her Majesty, The Queen Mother.

After a period of over 20 years based at Pantydderwen, Henry Jones moved to Minyrafon in the Brook (Llangain Isaf), where the Post Office remained for 40 years. When he died in 1963, his daughter, Maggie Rogers,

Above left: *Llangain postmarks: single-circle date stamp, 20 August, 2003, the last day of opening!*

Left: *Llangain postmarks: rubber date stamp, 29 January 1913.*

Official reopening of the Post Office by Ray Gravell 2 November 2004. Left to right: Cll. John Jones (Chairman of Llangain Community Council), Mrs Jeanette Curtis (sub-postmistress), Mr Gareth Davies (Welsh Affairs Director of the Royal Mail Group), Mr Ray Gravell (Radio Cymru broadcaster and former rugby international), Mr Lyn Davies.

Llangain postmarks: double-circle date stamp, 20 July 2004 – the re-opening of Post Office.

became sub-postmistress, helped by her step-sister, Rene Harding. Sadly, however, Mrs Rogers died suddenly in 1969 and within a year the Post Office had moved across the main road to Penybont before returning to the Smyrna area of Llangain.

The first residents at No. 1 Coedmor Avenue decided to build an extension to house a mini-

market, since this farming community had slowly started developing into a village. Mrs Nancy Davies became the new postmistress.

When Gareth Williams (the author's brother) was sub-postmaster there he converted the garage into a hairdresser's salon which was managed by his wife, Muriel. The salon was later relocated to Brynteg, at the end of Coedmor Avenue, the family having moved there.

With further housing development in the 1980s and '90s, the mini-market was appropriately renamed the Village Stores and Post Office by Cled and Suzanne Davies.

Llangain Postmasters

Year	Name	Location
1907–63	Henry Jones	Pantydderwen/Minyrafon
1963–69	Maggie Rogers	Minyrafon
1969–71	Rita Newnan	Penybont (opposite Minyrafon!)
1971–73	Terry and Nancy Davies	No. 1 Coedmor Avenue
1973–75	Terry and Dawn Griffiths	"
1975–83	Gareth and Muriel Williams	"
1983–85	Morgan and Doreen Griffiths	"
1985–87	Boyd and Anita Ingle	"
1987–98	Cled and Suzanne Davies	"
1998–003	Adrian and Margaret West-Sadler	"

The closure of the Post Office and Stores in August 2003 is, unfortunately, a sign of the times. However, a year later, due to local efforts and the co-operation of the Memorial Hall Committee, it was stationed in the hall on a part-time basis as a satellite office of the Bancyfelin branch, under the direct responsibility of sub-postmistress Jeanette Curtis. It was reopened by Ray Gravelle, former International and British Lions rugby player, on 2 November 2004 during a live two-hour broadcast on BBC Radio Cymru.

Postman's Obituary
Carmarthen Journal, late 1920s

On Monday, the 30th ult., the death took place at Penywern, Llangain, of Mr Daniel John at the age of 71 years. The deceased had acted as postman from Llangain to Coomb for over 30 years, having retired some six years ago. The funeral, which took place at Smyrna Chapel on Friday, was largely attended. The Revd J. John officiated, assisted by the Revd Evan Jones, Vicar of the parish, and the Revd W.Ll. Rees, Vicar of Llangunnock. There were a large number of wreaths sent by relations and friends, including one from Lady Philipps of Coomb. The deceased leaves a widow and a grown-up family to mourn their loss. Mr John had always lived at Llangain and was much respected. When he retired the Postal Authorities bore testimony to his careful attention to duties for the long years he had been in their service.

Dr Dilwyn Jones, Aberystwyth (formerly of the Forlan and Ucheldir, Heol Smyrna), is Daniel John's great-grandson. This obituary, in the form of an old newspaper cutting, was discovered by him, though, unfortunately, the exact date is unknown.

Short Extracts from 'The Peaches'

Dylan Thomas was a Welshman who died in 1953 at the age of 39. He is one of the most popular poets and story-tellers of the century, and his reputation has been highest since his death, though it is probably now declining.

His main characteristic is a bewildering excitability of language, which, with greater sureness of intention and control, might have made him an important poet: as it is, I feel that he is at his best when less pretentious, an entertainer with far more vitality than most. You will see this talent in 'The Peaches', a short story based on his visits to Fernhill, Llangain, in which Thomas' enthusiasm for pushing words around is saved from pointlessness by his keen memory of what it was really like to be a young schoolboy. Few writers have done this so well. There follow short extracts from 'The Peaches':

We drove into the farm-yard of Gorsehill, where the cobbles rang and the black, empty stables took up the ringing and hollowed it so that we drew up in a hollow circle of darkness and the mare was a hollow animal and nothing lived in the hollow house at the end of the yard

but two sticks with faces scooped out of turnips.

'You run and see Annie,' said uncle. 'There'll be hot broth and potatoes.'

He led the hollow, shaggy statue towards the stable; clop, clop to the mice-house. I heard locks rattle as I ran to the farm-house door.

The front of the house was the single side of a black shell, and the arched door was the listening ear. I pushed the door open and walked into the passage out of the wind. I might have been walking into the hollow night and the wind, passing through a tall vertical shell on an island sea-shore. Then a door at the end of the passage opened; I saw the plates on the shelves, the lighted lamp on the long, oil-clothed table, 'Prepare to meet Thy God' knitted over the fire-place, the smiling china dogs, the brown-stained settle, the grandmother clock, and I ran into the kitchen and into Annie's arms.

There was a welcome, then. The clock struck twelve as she kissed me, and I stood among the shining and striking like a prince taking off his disguise. One minute I was small and cold, skulking dead-scared down a black passage in my stiff, best suit, with my hollow belly thumping and my heart like a time bomb, clutching my grammar school cap, unfamiliar to myself, a snub-nosed story-teller lost in his own adventures and longing to be home; the next I was a royal nephew in smart town clothes, embraced and welcomed, standing in the snug centre of my stories and listening to the clock announcing me. She hurried me to the seat in the side of the cavernous fireplace and took off my shoes. The bright lamps and the ceremonial gongs blazed and rang for me.

She made a mustard bath and strong tea, told me to put on a pair of my cousin Gwilym's socks and an old coat of uncle's that smelt of rabbit and tobacco. She fussed and clucked and nodded and told me, as she cut bread and butter, how Gwilym was still studying to be a minister, and how Aunt Rach Morgan, who was ninety years old, had fallen on her belly on a scythe.

Then Uncle Jim came in like the devil with a red face and a wet nose and trembling, hairy hands. His walk was thick. He stumbled against the dresser and shook the coronation plates, and a lean cat shot booted out from the settle corner. Uncle looked nearly twice as tall as Annie. He could have carried her about under his coat and brought her out suddenly, a little, brown-skinned, toothless, hunchbacked woman with a cracked, sing-song voice.

'You shouldn't have kept him out so long,' she said, angry and timid.

He sat down in his special chair, which was the broken throne of a bankrupt bard, and lit his pipe and stretched his legs and puffed clouds at the ceiling.

'He might catch his death of cold,' she said.

She talked at the back of his head while he wrapped himself in clouds. The cat slunk back. I sat at the table with my supper finished, and found a little empty bottle and a white balloon in the pockets of my coat.

'Run off to bed, there's a dear,' Annie whispered.

'Can I go and look at the pigs?'

'In the morning, dear,' she said.

So I said good night to Uncle Jim, who turned and smiled at me and winked through the smoke, and I kissed Annie and lit my candle.

'Good night.'

'Good night.'

'Good night.'

I climbed the stairs; each had a different voice. The house smelt of rotten wood and damp and animals. I thought that I had been walking long, damp passages all my life, and climbing stairs in the dark, alone. I stopped outside Gwilym's door on the draughty landing.

'Good night'.

The candle flame jumped in my bedroom where a lamp was burning very low, and the curtains waved; the water in a glass on a round table by the bed stirred, I thought, as the door closed, and lapped against the sides. There was a stream below the window; I thought it lapped against the house all night until I slept.

Gwilym's chapel was the last old barn before the field that led down to the river; it stood well above the farm-yard, on a mucky hill. There was one whole door with a heavy padlock, but you could get in easily through the holes on either side of it. He took out a ring of keys and shook them gently and tried each one in the lock. 'Very posh,' he said; 'I bought them from the junk-shop in Carmarthen.' We climbed into the chapel through a hole.

A dusty wagon with the name painted out and a white-wash cross on its side stood in the middle. 'My pulpit cart,' he said, and walked solemnly into it up the broken shaft. 'You sit on the hay; mind the mice,' he said. Then he brought out his deepest voice again, and cried to the heavens and the bat-lined rafters and the hanging webs: 'Bless us this holy day, O Lord, bless me and Dylan and this Thy little chapel for ever and ever, Amen. I've done a lot of improvements to this place.'

I sat on the hay and stared at Gwilym preaching, and heard his voice rise and crack and sink to a whisper and break into singing and Welsh and ring triumphantly and be wild and meek. The sun, through a hole, shone on his praying shoulders, and he said; 'O God, Thou art everywhere all the time, in the dew of the morning, in the frost of the evening, in the field and the town, in the preacher and the sinner, in the sparrow and the big buzzard. Thou canst see everything, right down deep in our hearts; Thou canst see us when the sun is gone; Thou canst see us when there aren't any stars, in the gravy blackness, in the deep, deep, deep, deep pit; Though canst see and spy and watch us all the time, in the little black corners, in the big cowboys' prairies, under the blankets when we're snoring fast, in the terrible shadows, pitch black, pitch black; Thou canst see everything we do, in the night and the day, in the day and the night, everything, everything; Thou canst see all the time. O God, mun, you're like a bloody cat.'

He let his clasped hands fall. The chapel in the barn was still, and shafted with sunlight. There was nobody to cry Hallelujah or God-bless; I was too small and enamoured in the silence. The one duck quacked outside.

'Now I take a collection,' Gwilym said.

He stepped down from the cart and groped about in the hay beneath it and held out a battered tin to me.

'I haven't got a proper box,' he said.

I put two pennies in the tin.

'It's time for dinner,' he said, and we went back to the house without a word.

The best room smelt of moth balls and fur and damp and dead plants and stale, sour air. Two glass cases on wooden coffin-boxes lined the window wall. You looked at the weed-grown vegetable garden through a stuffed fox's legs, over a partridge's head, along the red-paint-stained breast of a stiff wild duck. A case of china and pewter, trinkets, teeth, family brooches, stood beyond the bandy table; there was a large oil lamp on the patch-work tablecloth, a Bible with a clasp, a tall case with a draped woman about to bathe on it, and a framed photo-graph of Annie, Uncle Jim, and Gwilym smiling in front of a fern-pot. On the mantelpiece were two clocks, some dogs, brass candlesticks, a shepherdess, a man in a kilt, and a tinted photograph of Annie, with high hair and her breasts coming out. There were chairs around the table and in each corner, straight, curved, stained, padded, all with lace cloths hanging over their backs. A patched white sheet shrouded the harmonium. The fire-place was full of brass tongs, shovels, and pokers. The best room was rarely used. Annie dusted and brushed and polished there once a week, but the carpet still sent up a grey cloud when you trod on it, and dust lay evenly on the seats of the chairs, and balls of cotton and dirt and black stuffing and long black horse hairs were wedged in the cracks of the sofa. I blew on the glass to see the pictures. Gwilym and castles and cattle.

'Change your suit now,' said Gwilym.

I wanted to wear my old suit, to look like a proper farm boy and have manure in my shoes and hear it squelch as I walked, to see a cow have calves, to run down in the dingle and wet my stockings, to go out and shout, 'Come on, you b ----,' and pelt the hens and talk in a proper voice. But I went upstairs to put my striped suit on.

❖ CHAPTER 5 ❖

Community Council

The Local Government Act of 1894 led to all rural parishes where the population was 300 or more, having parish meetings. These meetings had the function of electing Parish Councils.

For centuries prior to this there had been some form of village government. First supervised by the lord of the manor, priority was given to the care of the poor and homeless. Later, this became the concern of the general community, as also did the maintenance of general law and order and responsibility for the village roads, the village pond and common lands. As volunteers took on specific tasks, there came into being, for example, the way-warden and the overseer of the poor. Neither of these offices was other than an honorary post.

During the eighteenth and nineteenth centuries, meetings, attended by the more substantial villages, were held to consider village matters. As these were as much concerned with the church as with the village or community, they were often held in the church vestry. Thus they came to be known as vestries, the true forerunners of Parish Councils.

The Parish Meeting

The parish meeting, the basis of village organisation, now consists of everyone on the electoral register – at least for voting purposes. In 1894 a parish with over 300 inhabitants was entitled to a Parish Council; there could also be a Parish Council if the population was between 100 and 300 and if the parish meeting so resolved. Election to the Parish Council today is by ballot, but the first parish meeting elected its council by a show of hands.

The Parish Council must have an annual general meeting in May, at which the chairman and vice-chairman are elected by the councillors. Members of the public may attend but may not speak unless invited to do so by the chairman.

Parochial Church Councils, which started in 1922, are purely ecclesiastical. There is a parish register for church members and officers. The PCCs absorbed the old vestry meetings.

Historical Origins

Parishes, although ecclesiastical in origin, played an important part in civil administration in medieval times, particularly in relation to highways and poor relief. At the vestry meeting, the parishioners discussed matters of common concern and from among their number elected officers to deal with parish affairs. The main unpaid offices were those of churchwarden, constable, surveyor of highways and overseer of the poor. The Poor Relief Act of 1601 required the overseers to raise money by the levying of a poor rate on the inhabitants and occupiers of land in parishes, thus introducing rating as a means of financing local services.

During the nineteenth century, the influence of parish authorities declined due to the establishment of ad hoc authorities set up for the administration of one particular service. Starting with boards of guardians elected by the ratepayers of unions of parishes under the Poor Law Amendment Act 1834, other authorities were introduced for different purposes. They included public health boards, burial boards, improvement commissioners, school boards and highway boards. The result was that, towards the end of the century, there existed some 27,000 such bodies, with overlapping areas, functions and rate-raising powers.

Rationalisation began with the passing of the Local Government Act 1888, known as the County Councils Act, which divided England and Wales into county and county borough areas with elected councils for local administration. The process continued with the passing of the Local Government Act 1894, which created a new structure in the county areas, consisting of Urban and Rural District Councils except where there was already a Borough Council. Rural districts were subdivided into parishes, each with a parish meeting, and with a Parish Council where the population exceeded 300. The powers, duties and liabilities of the vestry, churchwardens and overseers, except in so far as they related to the affairs of the church or to ecclesiastical charities, were transferred to the Parish Council or, where there was no Parish Council, to the parish meeting. This was the beginning of the modern system of civil parish administration which is now embodied in the Local Government Act 1972.

Parish Councils

Under the 1974 reorganisation all urban parishes were abolished, but rural parishes were retained. Those which were divided by the new county and metropolitan district boundaries continued as separate parishes for each segment. In addition, a few 'rural boroughs', created under a procedure laid down in the Local Government Act 1958, continued as parishes, and some 170 smaller boroughs and urban districts due to go out of existence, under the reorganisation were designated 'successor parishes' by the Local Government (Successor Parishes) Orders 1973 and 1974.

Finance

It is the duty of the County Council (prior to 1994 that of the District Council) to make and levy rates and community charges or (as they are now called) council taxes, and to pay required sums to the Community Council in accordance with the Parish Council's orders, known as 'precepts'. Thus a precept is an order to pay a named sum by a certain date. The amount which the Community Council decides to precept each year is usually decided at the January meeting. The council will consider its likely financial obligations for the forthcoming year, calculating the amount of money required to meet these costs. The Community Council will then ask for that sum, or it will ask for the amount calculated on the rateable value of the properties in the parish.

For a long time, the method of calculating the limits on expenditure was based on a penny rate product. The accounts of the council must be available for inspection (by any member of the public) for 15 days before they go to the auditor. It should be noted that in the early years of Parish Councils, the pound purchased about 40 times as much as it does today. In 1974 came the change to decimal currency, when pounds, shillings and pence were replaced by pounds and new pence (100 new pence = £1).

Minutes

These constitute a record of the deliberations of the members of a meeting, and/or the decisions arrived at. The text of this record is submitted at the next meeting for the approval of those who were present at the meeting recorded. Therefore, the minutes, when approved and passed, are considered to be accurate. For the text of this book, I have used the minutes as recorded.

The Structure of Local Government

The present structure of local government in England and Wales is based on the Local Government Act 1972, which has been amended on numerous occasions since it came into operation on 1 April 1974. Under the 1974 reorganisation, all districts in Wales were divided into communities. Where there was a Parish Council, it became a Community Council. Many districts in England are divided into parishes and in Wales all districts are divided into communities. There are some 10,000 parishes in England. In Wales, there are about 1,000 communities.

Community Councils deal with such matters as footpaths, village greens, parish and community property, provision of street lighting, seats and shelters and some aspects of water supply and the suppression of public health nuisances. They also have the right to be notified of planning applications affecting their area where they have notified the County Council that they wish to receive them, and to submit representations/comments on such applications which must be considered by the local authority dealing with them.

Extracts From Minute Books

The first Llangain parish meeting was held on 4 December 1894 at the school for the purpose of electing a chairman. The Revd David Evans Vicar, was duly elected. The next meeting was on 18 April 1895. In these early years there were two annual meetings, mainly for electing overseers of the poor.

The purpose of the meeting held on 23 December 1898 was to consider the question of establishing a Parish Council. It was decided not to form such a council at that time.

March 1915
It was unanimously passed that a Rural Parish Council petition be presented to the Rural District Council that two footbridges with hand-rails and turn-gate are most urgently required on the footpath leading from Ffordd in this parish by way of Lanygors to Sarnau Road. The two footbridges placed there by the Council some 15 years ago have become rotten and dilapidated and are now dangerous to cross.

March 1918
Purpose – to explain the position in regard to the quotas allocated from ploughing by the Agricultural Sub-Committee.

March 1919
A circular has been received from the Carmarthenshire Agricultural Education Committee stating that they are this year again offering short courses on cheese making in the County. The travelling cheese school, complete with equipment, will visit different districts within county on receipt of an application for a visit.

It was decided to call the attention of the Rural District Council to the bad state of the road leading to Clomendy Farm and the following resolution was unanimously passed that the RDC take over as a road, repairable by the Council, the road from the entrance of Cochybarlys Farm leading through Clomendy to a point adjoining Penyclyn Road.

March 1924
A circular letter was read from the Ministry of Agriculture and Fisheries dated 6 March 1924 which

dealt with the subject of provision of allotments in rural districts. It was unanimously agreed that the 'poster' which invites applications for the scholarship for the sons and daughters of agricultural workmen and others described thereon be exhibited in a conspicuous place in the parish.

June 1924

A letter was read from the Welsh Church Commission with reference to the Transfer of Burial Grounds as referred to in the Welsh Church Act 1914–19.

After having an able and clear explanatory address by the Chairman, the Revd E. Jones BD, the Vicarage, on the subject, it was unanimously resolved by the proposition of Mr Thomas Thomas, School House, seconded by William Thomas, Shop Newydd, that the matter should be left entirely in the possession and control of the church as hitherto, and that no change should take place when the present vicar ceases to the incumbent of the parish.

November 1926

Agreed to make an application to the Agricultural Sub-Committee for lectures in selected agricultural and horticultural subjects, namely, soils – their origin and nature, cultivation and improvement; grass and clover seeds – their names, seeding of land down to grass and the management of newly formed; production of clean milk and laws of breeding.

March 1927

All the members of the parish meeting present desired to express their high appreciation of the efficient manner Mr William Thomas has carried out his duties during the 30 years he has been rate collector for the parish and all regret that through the rearrangement of the collection of the rates he goes out of the office he has held so long to the entire satisfaction of all concerned and a great credit to himself.

April 1927

It was proposed by Mr David Evans, Gilfach, seconded by Mr Thomas Davies, Penycoed, that William Thomas, Shop Newydd, be appointed Clerk of the Parish. Carried unanimously. The salary be £3 per annum.

March 1934

After a very interesting discussion on the advisability of establishing a Parish Council it was unanimously resolved, on the proposition of Mr John Lewis, District Councillor, of Meini Llwydion Farm, seconded by Mr Samuel Rees, School House, schoolmaster, that a strong appeal be sent through the Clerk, David Jones Esq, to the Carmarthenshire County Council, that they allow Llangain to form a Parish Council of their own.

The Parish, as it had been recently proved, could not be conveniently joined with any neighbouring parish, and although the parish meeting had conducted its affairs very efficiently in the past, it was felt that through the councils more could be done and, as Llangain was gaining in importance and population, there was a general feeling that a Parish Council was necessary to deal with the working of the general internal business of the parish, and the meeting earnestly appealed to the County Council to grant powers to form a Parish Council in the immediate future.

January 1935

Congratulation was extended to Mr Samuel Rees, head teacher of Llangain Council School, on his appointment as Chairman of the Carmarthen & District Branch of the National Union of Teachers.

March 1935

The Chairman called for nominations for the Office of Parish Councillor (15 in number) and nomination papers were handed in for the following:

David Davies	Werncorgam Fach	Farmer
Walter Davies	Ystradwalter	Farmer
Johnny Davies	Green Castle	Farmer
Thomas Davies	Penycoed	Farmer
Thomas Davies	Clomendy	Farmer
David Evans	Gilfach	Farmer
Jack Evans	Dderwen	Blacksmith
Clifford Griffiths	Werncorgam Fawr	Farmer
William John	Cwrthir Farm	Farmer
Ernie Jones	Penyclun	Farmer
Arthur Lewis	Lanygor	Farmer
John Lewis	Meinillwydion	Farmer
Samuel Rees	School House	Schoolmaster
Edward Williams	Panyrdderwen	Retired
Tom Williams	Llangain Mills	Miller

The Chairman decided that all nominations to be valid and whose candidatures are not withdrawn, were not more in number that the persons to be elected. The Chairman also declared to be duly elected.

December 1937

It was decided that no application be made for street name plates in as much that we have in the parish of Llangain directing finger posts set up in various parts.

September 1940

After a lengthy discussion regarding parish scrap iron, it was unanimously decided not to appoint an organiser, as they considered that the present arrangements now in operation in the parish in collecting scrap iron was working very smoothly and satisfactorily and that the Council have every confidence in the two blacksmiths who had the knowledge of knowing where to get the scraps and in the opinion of the Council they were carrying out the work efficiently.

March 1946
William Thomas tendered his resignation due to advanced age and defective eyesight. He has served the council as councillor and also as clerk for the past 45 years.

It was passed by the members present to call the attention of the County Council to a few dangerous corners on the roads within the parish, including the two corners by Plasuchaf Cottage.

February 1949
It was unanimously decided to apply for a precept of £12, which exceeded a 4d rate. Therefore a parish meeting would be convened to deal with the matter.

December 1950
Councillor John John, Islwyn, raised the matter of the entrance of the Old Road onto main Llanstephan Road at Shop Newydd. At this point the main road is very narrow and the level of the adjoining field being so high above the Old Road at the corner which practically leaves the sight at all when entering the main road. The clerk was instructed to forward the complaint to the County Council.

August 1958
It was unanimously decided to proceed with the erection of the bus shelter as soon as possible. Materials to be used, concrete blocks as shown at the meeting, with asbestos roofing or concrete. It was also decided that Mr Owen Cartref should be asked to erect the shelter.

September 1959
A bill of £62 was presented by Mr Owen Cartref for the erection of the bus shelter at Smyrna crossroads and was passed for payment after discussion.

February 1960
Councillor Hesford provided a quotation of £3.10s.0d. for painting the word LLANGAIN on the lintel of the bus shelter. Also the state of litter in the new shelter was discussed.

March 1960
After some discussion regarding the introduction of street lighting in the parish and in accordance with the governing procedure to be followed by a council it was agreed to place two lamps, one at Maesyrawel and one at Smyrna crossroads.

February 1963
A precept of £62.4s.0d. was set – 4d. rate for the parish, 2d. rate for general purposes and 2d. for

lighting. This was carried unanimously.

A letter from the tenants of the council houses (Maesyrawel Nos 1–6) was read by Cllr Islwyn Jones asking for an extra street light. As other parts of the parish were first on the list the request would be considered in rotation. The first place to be considered would be Belmont.

July 1964
The chairman asked councillors to be upstanding for a two minutes' silence in memory of the late Cllr Nathan Davies, No. 1 Maesyrawel.

December 1965
A letter from SWEB was regarding the new street-lighting charges as from April 1966.

The new annual charge would be £10.10s.9d. for dusk to 11p.m. lighting. All-year lighting would cost £11.14s.0d.

April 1972
It was decided to write to the GPO requesting them to move the mailbox from Smyrna crossroads to Troon (top of Penycoed hill) since there was one at the new Mini Market and Post Office in Coedmor Avenue.

January 1974
The Council allocated £260 and £150 for the General Account.

March 1974 (Last Parish Council Meeting)
A proposition made by Cllr E.E. Hesford and seconded by Cllr Tom Williams that the records and finances of this present council be transferred to the new Community Council.

January 1978
A letter from the District Secretary in relation to the development of a site at Llangain for general housing purposes was read to the Council. The Clerk to the Community Council stated that he had also been informed that it was proposed to build approximately 90 council houses over a two or three phase and that in time factor it would be over a period of three or four years. The Clerk was informed that the District Council had also reported that there were 15 applications from within the community area for council houses and that there could well be other applications once the project was known. After a full discussion members felt that clarification was required on the following points:
(1) In 1975 the approximate extent of building was given as 60 bungalows, whereas now the number proposed is approximately 90.
(2) One of the conditions of sale of land was that the building was confined to the building of bungalows. Confirmation of this was required from the District Council.

Parish Council dinner at the Boars' Head in the mid-1970s. Left to right, back row: *Cllr Ieuan Hobbs, Cllr Elwyn Davies, Cllr Jack Davies, Mrs Nesta Hobbs, Mrs Sally Davies, Mrs Annie John, Mrs Millie Jones;* middle row: *Cllr Ernie Jones, Mrs Beryl Davies, Mrs Dilys Davies, Mrs Olive Williams, Mrs Margaret Bowen, Mr Johnny Thomas (Chief Executicve Carmarthen District Council);* front row: *Cllr Dave Bowen (Chairman), District Cllr I.J. Williams, Cllr William Evans (Chairman Carmarthen District Council 1973–76 (Carway)), County Cllr Ronnie John, Jack Davies (Clerk).*

(3) It would also help the Council to make a decision if a plan of the proposed development was made available to them by the District Council.

Stress was also made on the rural character of the Community and that to agree to such a project would change this. Furthermore, such a large complex tended to create an unsettled community and experience showed that residents occupied the houses merely as means later to transfer to houses within the town area.

April 1978
District Councillor I.J. Williams reported that effluent was escaping from Penycoed pumping station and this was contaminating the road surface. This was a health hazard and a danger. Water authority to be informed.

July 1978
The Clerk stated that the area manager had agreed to include money in the estimate for the 1979/80 programme in respect of land covered by Coedmor for road improvement. However, the remaining matters would be delayed until the building programme in the adjoining field was underway. [*This scheme (Dôl-y-Dderwen to Coedmor Avenue) was first pursued in September 1975, then again in the 1980s.*]

An outline of the public meeting on 22 June 1978 was given and, after some further observations, it was decided that Llangain should be entered in the Best Kept Village Competition for the first time. Due to the wide scattered nature of the village, the Clerk to ascertain the exact boundary of the area to be judged and to inform all organisations and ask for their support to ensure success of the venture.

November 1978
The Clerk reported that a letter had been received from the District Secretary and this indicated that in the event of further developments at Llangain then the old school building would be brought up to the necessary standard and that about 50 pupils could be housed in the old school.

December 1978
The Chairman stated that the purpose of the special meeting was to consider a planning application for the conversion of a dwelling to a public house at Pantydderwen. Observations were then invited and councillors were reminded that the observations should be directed in relation to planning and not licensing.

Councillor I.J. Williams stated that the curtillage of the dwelling concerned was narrow and an elongated strip and was an undesirable site for a public house. The site as indicated on the plan was insufficient for the parking of cars. Councillor Hesford supported this. Councillor D.L. Davies stated that

Parish Council annual dinner, 1977. Left to right, back row: *Terence Hesford (Clerk), Cllrs Derek Davies, Hugh Thomas, Dewi Evans, Rhoslyn Morris, Vincent Davies, Idwal Williams, Ieuan Hobbs;* front row: *District Cllr Griff Rees, County Cllr J.A.J Harries, Cllr H.H. Gealy (Vice Chairman), Alderman D.H. Davies, Cllr Ellis Davies (Chairman), Cllr Jean Davies, Cllr Emrys Hesford.*

the intention was to provide a village public house and that the land was, in his opinion, sufficient for local need. Councillor Hugh Thomas supported the proposals. Other members also spoke in favour of the conversion.

When the Chairman called for a show of hands it was established that seven members were in favour of the application, whilst two considered the site unsuitable for planning permission.

July 1979
Reference was made to County Cllr J.A.J. Harries having been included in the recent Birthday Honours List, when he was made a Commander of the Order of the British Empire (CBE). It was felt that this was a well-deserved honour and the Council were appreciative of the honour that such recognition had brought to the district by one of its own 'local boys'. The Council endorsed the action of the Chairman in having a letter of congratulations sent to Mr Harries.

July 1981
Land-fill Site at Green Castle – Carmarthen side (Grid reference 394170).
Summary: The Council was unanimous

in objecting to the proposal on grounds of the close proximity to the schools at Johnstown, the prevailing winds towards Pensarn and Pibwrlwyd, flooding of the Tywi at high tide near a large percentage of the proposed site; Unigate Milk Factory serving one of the biggest milk catchment areas in the country only a mile away; dangerous access off the B4312, Pwntan stream into which most of the land drains will be contaminated. Raising the land level on the west side of the river Tywi will aggravate the flooding situation on the east side of the river.

Land-Fill Site at Green Castle – Llangain side (Grid reference 396163).
Summary: Another site meeting was held on 10 July 1981 with Mr B. Rees, Director of Works, CDC, in attendance. Councillors were told that a 10ft pressed wall would be built above the high-water level and a metal road constructed from the B4312 down to the tipping site. Two factors of concern became apparent. Providing water on site could have an effect on the Llangain

Cllr J.A.J. Harries, CBE, Chairman of Dyfed County Council 1978–79.

supply, which at the time was poor due to the lack of pressure. Also the area concerned was designated as a Farm Nature Reserve.

A public meeting was convened on 6 August to give the local community an account of the action to date, to seek views and support from individual electors.

Reference was made to a District Council meeting that day in which that Council agreed to the proposal to create a land-fill site at Hafodwen, even though strong argument had been submitted to establish that the site was unsuitable. It was felt that it would be the thin edge of the wedge and that eventually the site would be extended in the Llangain direction. It was recommended that the Council should consider voicing objection to the Hafodwen site.

In order to strengthen opposition to the proposed site at Green Castle it was suggested that an action committee be formed, the Secretary of State for Wales be contacted with the view to convene a public enquiry and that there should be liaison between Llangain and Johnstown. Support was also sought from neighbouring Community Councils, including Llansteffan/Llanybri, Llangynog, Llandyfaelog and St Ishmael, as well as Carmarthen Town Council.

A special meeting of Llangain Community Council was held during the summer recess. The general opinion was that the replies received from the District Council planning department were vague and in parts noncommittal, which strengthened the Council's views that objection be made to both applications.

Public opinion was strong, with 229 electors out of an electoral register of 285 having signed a petition, and when people living outside the parish supported it the petition exceeded 400 signatures, which was then handed into Carmarthen.

The Community Council reported back at another public meeting on 7 September 1981, when the Rt Hon. Roger Thomas, MP, was present. By this time it had become clear that the owner of Old Castle would not sell part of his land, which was within the tipping area. It was unlikely that the District Council would ask for an enforcement order to purchase.

October 1981
It was reported that the two applications for landfill sites had now been withdrawn.

January 1989
A letter is to be sent to Annie Bath, landlady of Pantydderwen, congratulating her on being included in the *Good Pub Guide 1989*.

March 1991
A summary of what had been happening in the field above the 60 site. Mr Brain had been illegally quarrying soil – mineral operation, and selling it to Llanelli Borough Council. The Clerk, CDC and DCC,

Llangain winning the the Lord Merthyr Award for the Best Kept Village in Dyfed in 1988. Left to right: Cllr Haydn Williams (Chairman Community Council), County Cllr Wilf Davies (Chairman Carmarthen District Council), Cllr Ellis Davies, the Hon. Robin Lewis (Merthyr family).

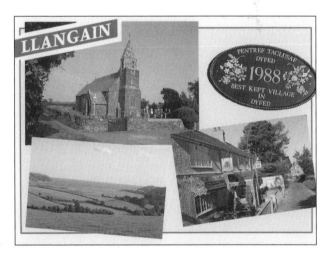

Llangain postcard, 1990, from a project by Haydn Williams, sponsored by Gary Thomas, Bwthyn-Y-Felin (Good News, Carmarthen). (PEMBROKESHIRE EYE POSTCARDS)

along with several officers of both District and County Councils and with support from our councillors serving on both Councils, managed to obtain a Court Injunction on 7 March – seven days after the operation was brought to light. This injunction was not served on Mr Brain until the 10th as he had gone into hiding *[Whether this is absolutely accurate is another matter.]* The operation has now stopped with the field devastated.

It was reported at this point that there may be some surface water entering the sewage system. WWA to be informed.

September 1993
Members were concerned that a number of fairways had been changed on the golf course. It was decided

to write to the CDC raising concern regarding the changes, the number of balls which seem to be going astray and the fact that it now has 11 holes.

Public enquiry for Mr Brain's agricultural building below Green Castle/Waun Llongau. It was agreed that as many councillors as possible attend the Council Chambers on 12 October. It was decided that the Community Council would speak in favour of upholding the refusal.

March 1994

This meeting was convened by the Clerk to discuss an appeal by Mr and Mrs D. Rees, Waun Llongau, Green Castle Corner, Llangain. to the Secretary of State for Wales against the decision of CDC to refuse planning permission for the removal of condition 1 from D4/17091/15. The Clerk read the appellant's statement, which essentially consisted of an appeal to have the agricultural conditions removed from the thatched dwelling at Waun Llongau. Since the agricultural enterprise had failed the appellants were having difficulty in selling the property, in spite of reducing the price from £250,000 to £165,000.

It was unanimously resolved to oppose the removal of condition 1 since the appellant had originally been granted permission for a mobile home. He had then built the dwelling without planning permission, which was later granted retrospectively as long as condition 1 remained in force. Full details of the response to the appellant's statement are given in the planning file.

September 1994

The Clerk reported that there had been a site visit from the Area Surveyor on 4/8/94, with County Cllr Arthur Harries and Cllr Haydn Williams also in

Llangain Community Council Chairman (Cllr John Jones) greeting the (mock) Mayor of Llansteffan (Des Cridland) and the Vicar of Llansteffan (Revd Sian Jones) at Smyrna crossroads on the occasion of the return of the church bells, via Llangain 28 February, 1998.

attendance. He had since received a letter which he had read out and which agreed to most of our requests. The exception was item 7, the request for the removal of the remaining section of hedge bank adjacent to the graveyard and replacing this with wall, railings and footway. The cost, £8000, was too high for such a short length of footway unless the Chapel were prepared to accept a lower standard boundary, i.e. railings.

January 1999

Mr and Mrs Manning of Penycoed had written to CCC to complain about the discharge of effluent from the pumping station. They had given the Clerk copies of the correspondence. The Director of

Presentation of a silver goblet to Cllr J.A.J. Harries, CBE, JP, MRCVS (County Cllr 1974–2001) by Cllr Roland Jeremy (Chairman) at the Council's annual dinner at Pantydderwen, 2002. Mrs Mair Harries received a bouquet of flowers.

Presentation of a gift and a bouquet of flowers to Mrs Elaine Collins, Johnstown (Clerk 1999–2002) by Cllrs Roland Jeremy (Chairman) and Margaret Jenkins (Vice Chairman).

Operations had replied to state that the uprated pumps will not cope in extreme weather conditions. However, he had asked the Consultancy Division to carry out a complete appraisal of the Llangain sewerage system as soon as possible. Clerk to write expressing concern and asking to be kept informed.

February 2000
It was clarified what the Millennium Committee would be providing and that this did not include a weather vane. The Memorial Hall committee are very grateful for the Community Council's offer. The weather vane would be fitted to the roof of the hall at a cost of £438.69 including VAT.

June 2005
A letter had been received from the Carmarthenshire Tourist Association advising that the Community website (www.llangain.org.uk) has been launched and is operating live on the World Wide Web.

Local Government Boundary Commission for Wales: Special Community Review

The Review commenced in 1976 and draft proposals in respect of each community was supplied to communities in 1978. As far as Llangain was concerned, there were two main proposals:
1. the boundary to be extended to include a complex of houses at the Brook, part of lower Llangain or Llangain Isaf, on the Llansteffan side of Fernhill Brook.
2. the number of Councillors be reduced from 15 to 9. The Council agreed with the extension of the boundary but felt that having regard to the rural character of the parish and the distribution of its population, it would be a retrograde step of the service given if the number of Councillors was reduced. The observations were submitted to the Boundary Commission and the representations were supported by Carmarthen District Council.

The 1983 report confirmed the boundary change. However, it also recommended that the community should have a council of seven members. The figure was derived by a nationally agreed scale based on the number of electors on the register:

0–299 Electors	7 Councillors
300–399 Electors	8 Councillors
400–499 Electors	9 Councillors
500–749 Electors	10 Councillors
750–999 Electors	11 Councillors

Elections

Between 1946 and 1970 elections were held every three years. After the initial five years of the Community Council elections have been held every four years since 1979. Due to the Boundary Commission Community Area Review (local government revision), the council was reduced from 15 to seven members in the 1987 election (the Carmarthen Communities Order 1986). The new council was made up of the following councillors: Derek Davies, Ellis Davies, Vincent Davies, Margaret Jenkins, Marilyn John, Rhoslyn Morris and Haydn Williams.

By now, however, due to the additions to the electoral register, the County Council has allocated two new seats to the Community Council, thus increasing the number of councillors from seven to nine. This was brought into effect in the 2004 election.

Council Members 2007

Wendy Beck	Penycoed	Accountant
Terry Griffiths	Brynderi	Businessman
Roland Jeremy	Dôl y Dderwen	Retired Paramedic
Marilyn John	Greenacres	Retired
John Jones	Church Farm	Farmer
Anne-Louise Morgans	The Moorings	Businesswoman
Lloyd Phillips	Hendy	Farmer
Glyn Williams	Broadlands	Retired Bank Manager
Haydn Williams	Glascoed	Education

Chairmen 1894–1974

1894–96	Revd David Evans	Vicarage
1896–97	Charles Bankes Davies	Llwyndu
1897–98	William Williams	Llangain Factory
1898–99	William Morris	Llwyn
1899–1900	James Jones	Penyclun
1900–01	John Lloyd Thomas	Gilfach
1901–02	Revd Evan Jones	Vicarage
1902–03	Revd Evan Jones	Vicarage
1903–04	David Jones	Ystradwalter

1904–05	James Morris	Penhen
1905–06	William Lewis	Meini
1906–07	David Morris	Church House
1907–08	William Williams	Llangain Factory
1908–09	Thomas Thomas	Wauncorgan Fawr
1909–10	J W Harries	Pilroath
1910–11	David Morris	Llangorse
1911–12	J.Ll. Thomas	Gilfach
1912–13	J.Ll. Thomas	Gilfach
1913–14	John Lewis	Clomendy
1914–15	John Lewis	Clomendy
1915–16	Thomas Morgan Jones	Dolaumeinion
1916–17	David Evans	Wauncorgam Fach
1917–18	David Evans	Wauncorgam Fach
1918–19	Charles Bankes Davies	Llwyndu
1919–20	David Evans	Gilfach
1920–21	David Evans	Gilfach
1921–22	Thomas Davies	Forlans
1922–23	William John	Cwrthir
1923–24	William John	Cwrthir
1924–25	Thomas Rees Jones, JP	Plas Cwrthir
1925–26	Alderman T R Jones, JP	Plas Cwrthir
1926–27	Alderman T.R. Jones, JP	Plas Cwrthir
1927–28	David Jones	Dolaumeinion
1928–29	David Jones	Dolaumeinion
1929–30	David Evans	Gilfach
1930–31	David Evans	Gilfach
1931–32	David Evans	Gilfach
1932–33	Thomas Davies	Clomendy
1933–34	Thomas Davies	Clomendy
1934–35	David Davies	Hendy
1935–36	Samuel Rees	School House
1936–37	Samuel Rees	School House
1937–38	John Lewis	Meini
1938–39	John Lewis	Meini
1939–40	John Lewis	Meini
1940–41	John Lewis	Meini
1941–42	John Lewis	Meini
1942–43	John Lewis	Meini
1943–44	John Lewis	Meini
1944–45	John Lewis	Meini
1945–46	John Lewis	Meini
1946–47	William John	Cwrthir
1947–48	William John	Cwrthir
1948–49	Thomas Howells	Tanlan Fach
1949–50	J.C. Griffiths	Wauncorgam Fawr
1950–51	E.E. Jones	Penyclun
1951–52	Thomas Roberts	Penycoed
1952–53	W.H. Howells	Cwrthir
1953–54	Samuel Rees	School House
1954–55	J. John	Islwyn
1955–56	Elwyn Davies	Clunmawr
1956–57	Ieuan Hobbs	Ty Isaf
1957–58	A.V. Key	Plas Cwrthir
1958–59	Willie Jones	Cillefwr
1959–60	Jack Davies	Cwrthir
1960–61	R.L. Yorath	Cochybarlys
1961–62	E. Hesford	Tawelfryn

1962–63	I.J. Williams Cefnglas
1963–64	Colin Lewis Lletyrneuadd
1964–65	D.S. Lewis Vicarage
1965–66	Ieuan Hobbs T_ Isaf
1966–67	Jonny Jones T_'r Ysgol
1967–68	W.T. Evans Glanyrafon
1968–69	Ralph Platt Maesyrawel
1969–70	Dave Bowen Avoca
1970–71	Willie Jones Cillefwr
1971–72	E. Hesford Tawelfryn
1972–73	Goronwy Phillips T_'r Ysgol
1973–74	Elwyn Davies Glennydd

Community Council

1974–75	Ieuan Hobbs T_ Isaf
1975–76	Elwyn Davies Glennydd
1976–77	Ellis Davies Pantrynn
1977–78	H.H. Gealy/Hugh Thomas Banc-yr-Helyg, Heol Smyrna/Clunmawr
1978–79	Margaret Jenkins Coedmor Avenue
1979–80	Vincent Davies Llwyn
1980–81	Haydn Williams Coedmor
1981–82	David Griffiths Brynderi
1982–83	Robert Hunt Forlan
1983–84	Wynford Jones Penyclun
1984–85	Alan Jones Chalfont, Heol Smyrna
1985–86	Ellis Davies Pantrynn
1986–87	Vincent Davies Llwyn
1987–88	Derek Davies Coedmor Avenue
1988–89	Haydn Williams Coedmor
1989–90	Margaret Jenkins Coedmor Avenue

1990–91	Rhoslyn Morris Rhianlyn
1991–92	Margaret Jenkins Coedmor Avenue
1992–93	John Jones Church House
1993–94	Wyn Griffiths Wauncorgam Fawr
1994–95	Brian Rowlands Coedmor Avenue
1995–96	Haydn Williams Glascoed
1996–97	Margaret Jenkins Coedmor Avenue
1997–98	John Jones Church House
1998–99	Terry Griffiths Brynderi
1999–2000	Margaret Jenkins Coedmor Avenue
2000–01	Peris Williams Cnwc-y-Deri
2001–02	Roland Jeremy Dôl-y-Dderwen
2002–03	Margaret Jenkins Coedmor Avenue
2003–04	Glyn Williams Broadlands
2004–05	John Jones Church Farm
2005–06	Haydn Williams Glascoed
2006–07	Wendy Beck Penycoed
2007–08	Roland Jeremy Dôl-y-Dderwen

Clerks

1894–97	Unknown
1897–1927	William Thomas Shop Newydd (Rate Collector)
1927–46	William Thomas Shop Newydd (First Clerk proper)
1946–60	Jack Evans Pantrynn
1960–73	Jack Davies Cwrthir/Bryntywi
1974–77	Terence Hesford Llansteffan
1978–87	E.D. Phillips Carmarthen
1987–88	Ralph Platt Maesyrawel
1988–93	Llinos Lowden Kidwelly
1993–99	Peris Williams Cnwc-y-Deri

1999–2002	Elaine Collins Johnstown	1964–73	I.J. Williams Cefnglas
2002–03	Gill Richards Dôl-y-Dderwen	1974–89	G.T. Rees Llansteffan
2003–04	Gill Thomas Carmarthen	1989–91	John Peake Llansteffan
2004–04	Megan Morgan Belmont	1991–96	Una Davies Llangynog
2004–	Iwan Griffiths Pontargothi		

County Councillors

| | | 1931–53 | T.Ll. Harries Pilroath |

District Councillors

The first reference to a district councillor is in July 1917 – David Thomas, Ystrad Farm, Johnstown, who appears to be holding that position until 1919 when Revd Evan Jones BD of the Vicarage became district councillor.

1931–51	J. Lewis Meini	1954–67	J.H. Davies Llanybri
		1967–71	Ronnie John Llanybri
		1971–74	T.V. Fisher-Hoch Llansteffan
1951–58	A.V. Key Plas Cwrthir	1974–2001	J.A.J. Harries Pilroath
		2001–04	Osi Osmond Llansteffan
1958–63	W.H. Howells Cwrthir	2004–	Daff Davies Maesgwynne

Assembly Member

The Welsh Assembly Elections 2007 saw a 'local girl' gain a seat in the Senedd in Cardiff Bay. Nerys Evans AM, who represents the Mid and West Wales Region, is the daughter of Mr and Mrs Glanmor Davies-Evans, Swn yr Einion, Llangain.

Council Insignia

During the early 1990s it was considered appropriate and timely to have a chairman's insignia in line with the growing trend among Community Councils at the time. Cllr Haydn Williams offered to donate an insignia to the council in memory of his father, Evan John Williams, who had died in 1991. This was done in 1995. The occasion also marked the centenary of the Local Government Act which set up parish meetings and councils in the first place. The dedication was later to include his mother, Rachel Eleanor (Nellie) Williams who died in 2004.

The following are the historical and family notes that accompany the insignia and deed, which are in the possession of both the Council and the Williams family.

Smyrna Chapel

This Independent Nonconformist chapel, probably the most prominent landmark within the parish, is an impressive building standing on a hill at the village centre as the village is known today. Built in 1835 under the patronage of the Revd William James, the area minister until 1862, 'Heol Smyrna' and 'Ger y Capel!' are local names given in recognition of this familiar place of worship.

The minister, the Revd Towyn Jones FRSA, using his artistic skills, made a substantial input into the final design of the insignia manufactured by Thomas Fattorini Ltd of Birmingham. He also chose a suitable quotation by William Morris (1834–96), the poet and writer, to reflect the dedication on the engraving.

The deeds that ye do upon the earth,
It is for fellowship's sake that ye do them.

Green Castle

Green Castle is another well-known local landmark, probably, nowadays, most notorious as a dangerous corner on the B4321. In the past it was sometimes referred to as Tro Pwll Du, named after the pool in the Tywi below, which was said to be haunted by strange phantoms.

Green Castle is also known as Castell Moel (sometimes pronounced mole locally), Moel being the Welsh word for bald, or bare, and it is not unlikely that the eminence was once bereft of vegetation. Such is not now the case. But it is possible there had

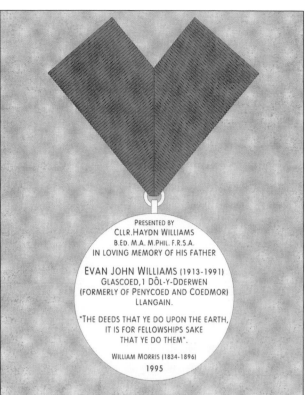

The Council Insignia, manufactured by Thomas Fattorini Ltd, Birmingham, 1994.

Engraving on the reverse of the Chairman's Insignia, 1995.

been some earthen fortification there at one time. Strictly speaking the imposing remnant of Green Castle on a bluff above the Tywi, a mile or so from the village, has nothing to do with a castle but represents a residence of the fifteenth century.

As the surrounding district was amply protected by two powerful stone-built castles, Carmarthen and Llansteffan, the Normans would hardly have found it necessary to fortify this outpost.

The ruins of a large, impressive, late-medieval residence still stands, looking much as it does in Buck's engraving of 1740. This part of the design for the pendant is based on this print and consequently the date 1138 is also copied.

St Cain's Church

The present picturesque church nestling amongst gentle hills and meadows is another parish landmark. Built in 1871, it celebrated its 125th anniversary on 27 July 1996.

The word 'llan' is derived from the Celtic period and originally meant monastic enclosure. Now it means the church. Hence Llangain means the church of St Cain. St Keyne (sixth century) is the best known of Prince Brychan of Brycheiniog's reputed daughters.

The year 1994 saw the centenary of Parish Councils, established when Parliament, under the premiership of Gladstone, passed an Act to reform the system of local government.

The parish, the smallest unit of British local government, began as a unit of church government. In principle, a parish is an area which is served by one church and one clergyman, though now many parishes have extra churches and assistant clergy.

When the old organisation of manors was breaking down after the Reformation, the parish was adopted as the unit of general local government. The people of the parish, meeting in the church vestry, were made responsible for a number of duties, e.g. repairing the roads, looking after the poor, catching the sparrows that ate the corn and providing a village constable. These meetings were open to all house-holders who could speak and vote. Gradually their more important duties were taken over and given to new and more efficient boards and councils as they were established, such as the guardians of the poor.

By the end of the nineteenth century open vestries were almost extinct but under the Local Government Act of 1894 they were reorganised by Parliament as part of a new system of local government. The modern system of civil parish administration is now embodied in the Local Government Act, 1972.

The responsibilities which the old vestry meeting had to the Parish Church are now taken over by the Parochial Church Council, which, together with the vicar and churchwardens, looks after the affairs of the church. The parish today, therefore, is a unit of local government and also the unit for the work of the national Church, as it has been for centuries.

Mrs E.J. Williams placing the insignia on Cllr Brian Rowlands, the first receiving chairman.

Under the 1974 reorganisation all districts in Wales were divided into Communities. Where there was a Parish Council, it became a Community Council and certain former Borough and Urban District Councils became community councils by order of the Secretary of State. Llangain Community Council, therefore, was formed on 1 April 1974.

Oak Tree

The common oak tree, which is a native of Britain, is very much a local deciduous tree. Several place names within the village and parish incorporate the Welsh translation of 'oak' and 'tree' in the form of 'Derw', 'Deri', 'Derwen' and 'Coed'. Dôl-y-Dderwen (meadow of the oak), named by the family, is flanked by the old oak (Church Road) and the new oak (Smyrna crossroads) and is overlooked by Pantydderwen (hollow of the oak). This local tavern naturally has the oak as its symbol, while the local primary school has adopted the oak, along with the Cromlech, or Dolmen, as its logo. The Woodland Trust, which is the country's largest and most successful charity concerned solely with the conservation of Britain's woodland heritage of broad-leaved and native trees, bought Green Castle Woods in 1993, which brings the symbolic design of the pendant right up to present times.

Sheaf of Corn

In 1811, Nicholas Carlisle, in his *Topographical*

Llangain Community Council and guests pose for the centenary and insignia photograph, 1995. Left to right, back row: County Cllr J.A.J Harries, Cllrs John Parry, Margaret Jenkins, Wyn Griffiths, Derek Davies, District Cllr Una Davies; front row: Mrs E.J. Williams, Cllr Haydn Williams (Vice Chairman), Cllr Brian Rowlands (Chairman), Dr Peris Williams (Clerk), Revd J. Towyn Jones (Smyrna Minister).

Llangain Community Council annual dinner at Pantyrathro Mansion Hotel, 2006. Left to right, back row: *Cllrs Glyn Williams, Terry Griffiths, Daf Davies (County), Roland Jeremy, Lloyd Phillips;* front row: *Cllrs John Jones, Mr Iwan Griffiths (Clerk), Haydn Williams (Chariman), Wendy Beck, Anne-Louise Morgans. Cllr Marilyn John not present.*

Dictionary of the Dominion of Wales, stated that the parish contained from 2,500 to 3,000 acres of enclosed and well-cultivated land and 'is peculiarly adapted to the growth of corn, which is not excelled by any part of the principality'.

Samuel Lewis, in his *Topographical Dictionary of Wales*,1838, wrote that 'the soil is extremely favourable to the growth of corn of which great quantities are raised of a quality not surpassed by that of any part of the principality'.

According to Kelly's *Directory of Monmouthshire and South Wales*, 1906, the chief crops in this farming community were wheat, barley and oats.

In this historical light, therefore, the sheaf of corn, perhaps above any other agricultural symbol, is a very apt and fitting one to reflect the backbone of this farming community.

Family Notes
The significance of the pendant design doubles up to link with the late Mr and Mrs E.J. Williams. Both were deacons at Smyrna Chapel, where they worshipped for over 50 and 60 years respectively.

Land adding ample future burial plots to the existing graveyard, from the gate to the row of evergreen trees, was donated by them while farming at Penycoed (a farm below the chapel) between 1955 and 1969.

Heol Smyrna was named in recognition of the chapel when land was sold for residential development (Cefnmeusydd to Cwmnantyreira) by Mr and Mrs E.J. Williams during the 1960s.

From Leland's statement that 'only small tokens' of the edifice remained at Green Castle in 1538, it seems that it had become ruinous. As the owners continued to reside at Green Castle during the sixteenth century, their dwelling was probably the adjacent mansion, which developed into the farmhouse in use today. Mrs E.J. Williams had lived there with her mother, Mrs S.J. Davies (later of Pantydderwen), during the 1930s, before moving to Blaentir. Their forbears had long been tenants of Green Castle. Among surviving cousins to Mrs E.J. Williams are brother and sister Mr Les Davies and Miss Olwen Davies, of Arwel, formerly of nearby Pwntan Bach, now known as Green Acres, whose aunty opened the local Memorial Hall on 3 April 1964.

The Parish Church contains a memorial to Lce-Cpl Willie Davies (Welsh Regiment) of Green Castle, who died in action in France on 23 March 1918, aged 20. He was a brother-in-law to Mrs S.J. Davies, whose daughter is Mrs E.J. Williams and whose grandson is the donor of the insignia. There are continued strong church connections, therefore, with the family.

Llangain Parish information panel ,produced by Llangain Community Council, 1997, with historical text by Haydn Williams. Designed and illustrated by Sarah Lees, Llandybie, it was grant-aided by the Prince's Trust – Bro. and manufactured by Armourseal, Cheshire.

The driving force and architect of the 1978/79 restoration programme, the Revd Canon Victor Jones, BA, often referred to the small team of dedicated churchmen and 'friend' from Smyrna Chapel, who had given freely of their hard labour, skills and time to the huge project throughout the 18 months. The 'friend', of course, referred to the non-member but loyal supporter of the cause, Mr E.J. Williams, Coedmor, whose main contribution had been the hacking away at the plaster, at any height, that covered the once hidden but now wonderfully displayed original stonework.

The main places of abode, locally, for them have been Penycoed and Coedmor. Since Mr Williams had contracted the disease known as 'farmer's lung' and Mrs Williams had been seriously ill in hospital, having developed septicaemia and yellow jaundice as the result of gall bladder surgery in 1967, the couple had had to retire from farming. The family built Coedmor as a semi-retirement bungalow and retained land to accompany it. The adjacent development, when completed during the 1970s, was named Coedmor Avenue, or Coedlan Coedmor, in recognition of the family's local ownership of land and their continuing local connection. Most of the five children and their families live locally.

Dôl-y-Dderwen began to be developed in 1988, and the family decided to make Glascoed, No. 1 Dôl-

y-Dderwen, their new home, on land which was formerly theirs. This name is derived from the two places that Mr and Mrs Williams have farmed within the locality, namely 'Glasfryn' and 'Penycoed'. Also, Mrs E.J. Williams came to Llangain from Blaengors Mansion, Llangynin, and St Clears. Her grandfather renovated the place and called it Glascoed. Having moved from Coedmor to Glascoed at Easter 1990, sadly, E.J. Williams was to have less than a year before his death on 15 January 1991 at the age of 77. Mrs E.J. Williams outlived him until 2004.

The Village Information Panel
(Situated at Smyrna Crossroads)

Produced by Llangain Community Council, 1997.
Historical Text by Cllr Haydn Williams, Llangain.
Grant Aided by The Prince's Trust-Bro.
Designed and illustrated by Sarah Lees, Llandybie.

Council's Insignia
This insignia donated in 1995 is in memory of Evan John Williams (1913–91), Glascoed, No. 1 Dôl-y-Dderwen (formerly of Penycoed and Coedmor). The central symbol, the sheaf of corn, reflects the backbone of this farming community. Surrounding this are three local landmarks, while the oak tree recurs in several place-names in the village.

Prehistory
There are a few cromlechs, or dolmens, the best examples being Meini Llwydion (Greystones) and Merlin's Quoits. They were communal burial places for family groups dating back to the Neolithic period (c.3000BC).

Green Castle
A local landmark at the sharp bend on the B4312. The ruins of the impressive, late-medieval residence still stands. It was never a castle but a residence built for the Reed family in the early-fifteenth century and was in ruin in Elizabethan times. It is possible there had been some earthen fortification there at one time. Some believe this to be at Old Castle. Doubtless this would have been a motte and bailey. Until recent times ships used to lie at anchor below to offload onto lighter vessels for transport to Carmarthen.

Education
In 1846 the only school was a Sunday school. Llangain Board School was built in 1875 and officially opened in 1876 and was in use until superseded by the new school in 1977.

Church
The present church of St Cain was built in 1871. There is a beautiful tiled mural on either side of the altar in memory of the Gwyn family of Pilroath and Plas Cwrthir. An Elizabethan chalice is dated 1576.

Chapel
The Congregational Chapel is a prominent landmark within the parish. Originally built in 1835, it was rebuilt in1865. The present chapel is dated 1915. The white building provided stabling for horses during chapel services. The loft served as the vestry.

Coedmor
Built in 1968 for Mr and Mrs E.J. Williams, retired farmers of Penycoed. Coedmor Avenue was so named in recognition of their ownership of the land and the family's continuing local connection.

Bwthyn-y-Felin
An old woollen mill which employed four full-time workers in its heyday. Llangain Mill/Factory closed in the 1940s.

Plas Cwrthir
The mansion was built as a double-pile house around the mid-nineteenth century. William Edward Bevan Gwyn, Pilroath, was the first resident.

Llwyndu
This residence was built in the first half of the nineteenth century. In 1821–23 Captain Henry Harding lived there and it was afterwards the home of Frederick Philipps, JP. In 1906 the owner was Charles Bankes Davies. It has an upper and lower lodge. The original name for the upper lodge, 'The Beeches', was 'Chweched', meaning 'Sixth', indicating the six lanes.

Pilroath
Pilroath is situated at the southern end of the parish above the confluence of the Rhoth Brook and the Afon Tywi. In 1902 the property was purchased by T.J. Harries, Esq., who built the present mansion. The property was occupied by the Harries family for three generations and owned until 1994 by County Cllr Arthur Harries, CBE, JP, MRCVS.

Fernhill
A manor house dating back to 1723 and listed as a Grade II building for its architectural and historic connection. Famous as a frequent childhood holiday retreat of the world-renowned poet Dylan Thomas (1914–53), it became immortalised in one of his best-known poems.

Fernhill is also known for its association with the notorious county hangman, Robert Rickets Evans, who lived there at the turn of the century. His daughter was heiress to a fortune. He imprisoned her in a cell in the courtyard (which can still be seen today) to gain her fortune, but her lover helped her to escape, according to folklore.

Brynderi
This house was built c.1928 as a retirement home for the Revd Evan Jones, BD, Vicar of Llangain between 1900 and 1934.

The Woodland Trust
The Trust which is Britain's largest charity concerned solely with woodland conservation through acquisition and management, bought Greencastle Woods in 1993. The entire area is now open to the public.

Wildlife
The combination of woodland, meadow, hedge, stream, river edge and quarry face provide a great diversity of habitat, creating an important refuge for all kinds of wildlife. Birds seen frequently include kestrel, sparrow hawk, buzzard, lesser spotted woodpecker and flycatcher. Old hay meadow flowers exist alongside oak, birch, willow and alder.

Pantydderwen
Originally a small cottage which once housed the Post Office and local sweet shop, it became a public house in 1980. The golf course opened in 1993.

Pantyrathro
This mansion was enlarged and restored by James Richards in the early 1800s. It was improved as a direct result of selling local milk products to London with the coming of the railway to Carmarthen. It became the local hotel c.1980.

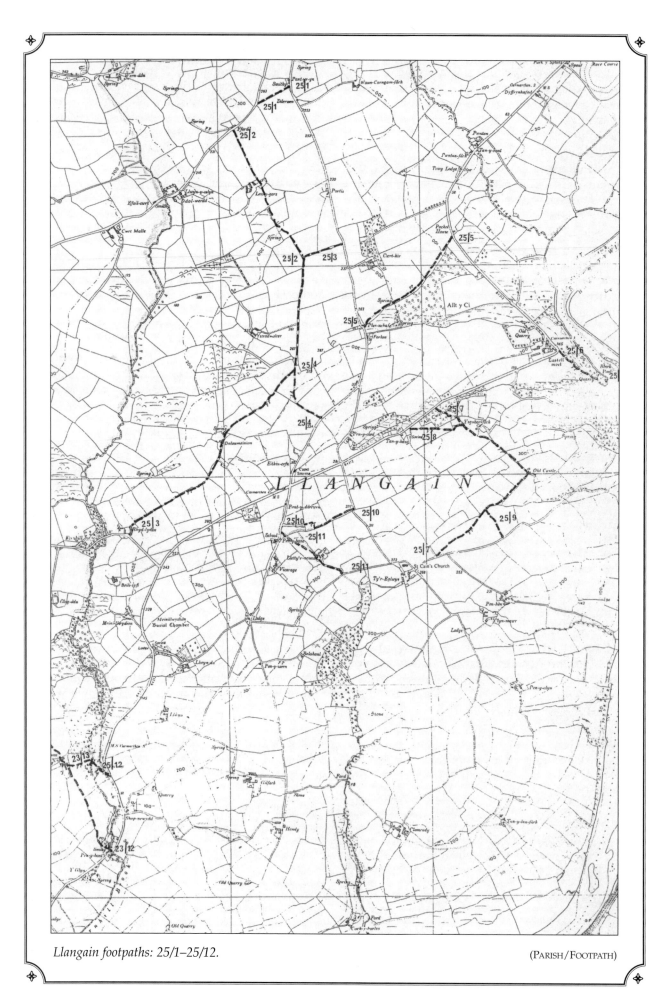

Llangain footpaths: 25/1–25/12.

(PARISH/FOOTPATH)

Parish Footpaths

25/1 Ffordd to Pantyryn. Starts through wicket gate from Alltycnap-Llangynog Road about 170 yards (156m) north-east of Ffordd Farm: north-east through field along north side of hedge and out by wicket gate at Pantyryn (Smithy) on Heol Smyrna.

25/2 Fordd to Ystradwalter Lane. Starts from Alltycnap-Llangynog Road at Ffordd Farm; through fieldgate and along road on east of hedge to Llanygors, passing farm on east side; through fields by two footbridges and wicket gate and out by fieldgate to bend in lane leading to Ystradwalter.

25/3 Heol Smyrna to Rhydlydan. Starts with field gate from Heol Smyrna about 300 yards (277m) south of Portis, west along road to Ystradwalter for 225 yards (208m) to junction with FP25/2, then continuing south to the end of the same road; through gap in hedge and small field diagonally, then south-west through fields by fieldgates to Dolaumenion, passing through farmyard. Continues along short farm road, then through three fields alongside hedges and out by fieldgate to lane; along lane and out by Rhydlydan.

25/4 Heol Smyrna to Ystradwalter. Starts over stile from road about 300 yards (277m) north of Smyrna Chapel; north-west through field along northern side of hedge, over stile and northwards diagonally through field to meet FP25/3 in north corner of field No.305 about 300 yards (277m) south-east of Ystradwalter.

25/5 Cefnglas to Packet House (disappeared). Starts with wicket gate from Heol Smyrna at Cefnglas north-east through fields by wicket gate, along north side of hedge and out by wicket gate to Carmarthen-Llansteffan Road (B4312), nearly half a mile north-west of Green Castle.

25/6 Green Castle to River Tywi (Black Pool). Starts from Carmarthen-Llansteffan Road (B4312) at Green Castle bend; through field along west side of woods to old quarry and down to the River Tywi at Black Pool (Pwll Du).

25/7 Carmarthen-Llansteffan Road to Old Castle and Llangain Church. Starts from Carmarthen-Llansteffan Road about 220 yards (203m) east of Danybanc (disappeared); through fieldgate and south-east through Allt Cware-coch; along east side of field and through fieldgate to pass along west side of second field; fieldgate and along western end of fourth field; through gap in hedge and along private road to Old Castle Farm; through fieldgate and south-west along private road; along south-eastern sides of two fields, through fieldgate and diagonally across last field; out by fieldgate to unclassified road about 170 yards(156m) east of Llangain Church.

25/8 Danybanc to Ysguborfach. Starts from the Carmarthen-Llansteffan Road about 40 yards (37m) east of Danybanc (disappeared); through fieldgate and diagonally eastwards across field; over fence and long hedge in north-east corner of field to join Footpath 25/7 about 80 yards (74m) north-west of Ysguborfach.

25/9 Old Castle to Llangain Church-Allt Morfa Howell Road. Starts from FP25/7 in north-east corner of field OS No.240; southwards along eastern side of field and out by fieldgate to the unclassified road from Llangain Church towards Allt Morfa Howell at a point about 50 yards (46m) west of the private road leading to Penhen (dilapidated farmhouse).

25/10 Neuadd Gain to Coedmor Avenue. Starts from road about 400 yards (370m) north-west of Llangain Church (opposite the old church hall); west along north side of hedge towards Brynteg, then north and west around Brynteg via a stile to Coedmor Avenue.

25/11 Memorial Hall to Lletyrneuadd. Starts from the Memorial Hall car park; south east through field along west side of hedge to Lletyrneuadd farmyard, continuing along the farm lane to the road between Beeches (Chweched/Six Roads) and Llangain Church.

25/12 Bwythyn y Felin to Pentrewyman. Starts from Carmarthen-Llansteffan Road; north-west along road to Bwthyn y Felin (Llangain Mill), entering yard by fieldgate; through field to footbridge across Fernhill Brook and parish boundary. (Foothpath continues to Pentrewyman in Llansteffan Parish.)

Memorial Hall Management Committee at the opening ceremony, 1964. Left to right, back row: Tom Harries, Wynford Jones, Leslie John, David Jones, Eurig Griffiths, Henri Harries, Rhoslyn Morris; middle row: Dick Yorath, Gwyn Walters, Tom Thomas, David Owen, Emrys Hesford, Sam Rees, Ernie Jones, Tom Morris, Brown Jones; front row: Islwyn Jones (Eisteddfod Secretary), Ieuan Hobbs, Sally Bowen (Secretary, Ladies Committee), Idwal Williams (Vice Chairman), T.Ll. Harries (Chairman), Tom Williams (Treasurer), Colin Lewis (Secretary), Milly Jones (Chair, Ladies Committee), William Jones.

LLANGAIN A'R CYLCH

NEUADD GOFFA A CHANOLFAN

GYMDEITHASOL

DROS RYDDID GOLLASANT EU GWAED

1914—1918   1939—1945

Opening
Ceremony

2.30 p.m., FRIDAY, APRIL 3rd, 1964.

Llangain Memorial Hall opening ceremony programme, 3 April 1964.

LLANGAIN MEMORIAL HALL

★ FRIDAY, 3rd APRIL, 1964 ★
at 7.30 p.m.

Celebrity
Concert

to mark the Occasion of the Opening of the Hall

Chairman :
Iorwerth Howells, B.A., LL.B.
Director of Education

PROGRAMME - - - - - - 6d.

(Proceeds towards Hall Fund).

Celebrity Concert to mark the occasion of the opening of the Memorial Hall, 3 April, 1964. Chairman for the evening was Iorwerth Howells, BA, LLB. , Director of Education.

CHAPTER 6

Modern Times

Llangain Memorial Hall

Llangain and District Memorial Hall was built in 1963 on land donated by Mr Tom Roberts, Penycoed, and officially opened on 24 April, 1964. It has since been extended and refurbished to include access for the disabled, thanks to a grant from the National Lotteries Charity Board and other benefactors. In addition, the hall has a sound system grant-aided by NLCB. An extension has been built to store equipment for the Llangain Youth Club, and a new stage-lighting system has been installed, thanks to grant assistance from Carmarthenshire County Council and the Arts Council of Wales respectively.

A typical and successful annual event was the Eisteddfod, held on the Friday before the October half term, which drew competitors from far and wide. It remained popular throughout the '70s and '80s. The traditional Boxing Day fancy dress was well attended, and the Noson Lawen, or annual concert, continued to be a huge success well into the new millennium.

In 2007, activities include the annual horticultural show, which celebrated its silver jubilee in 2003,

children's ballet classes, short-mat bowls and the youth club in the main hall. Many other local organisations use the committee room for their regular committee meetings.

A Welsh drama, *Malwod Mawr*, a comedy dealing with rural life in Carmarthenshire, played to a

The official unveiling, on 3 April 1964, of the memorial plaque to Lce- Cpl Willie Davies by his sister, Mrs M. Davies (formerly of Green Castle and the author's great-aunt).

The Memorial Hall Ladies' Committee, 1964. Left to right, back row: Ida Hobbs, Catherine Williams, Deina Jones, Molly Jones, Eileen Jones, Dorothy Davies, Sally Jones, Eiry Thomas; front row: Irene Walters, Nancy John, Milly Jones (Chair), Sally Bowen, Mattie Jones.

Annual dinner of the Memorial Hall, mid-1960s. Left to right, back row: *Elfed Rees, Ernie Jones, Eileen Jones, Sally Bowen, David Owen, Rhoslyn Morris, ?, Ieuan Jones, Elwyn Thomas;* third row: *Minnie Evans, Bety Rees, Megan Bowen, Mr Evans, Irene Owen, Islwyn Jones, Mrs Collins, Raymond Bowen, Olive Williams, Ronald James, Dai Jones;* second row: *Gwyn Walters, Millie Jones, I.J. Williams, Ieuan Hobbs, Tom Williams, Mr Collins;* front row: *Irene Walters, Betty Thomas, Eiry Jones, Mattie Jones, Rhiannon Morris, Sally Jones.*

Memorial Hall Committee Christmas dinner at the Glanymor Club, Laugharne, 1969. Left to right, back row: *Wynford Jones, Sally Bowen, Eileen Jones, Mollie Thomas, Gwenllian Walters, Milly Jones, Irene Walters, Tom Morris;* middle row: *Willie Bowen, Mrs Lewis, Rhiannon Morris, Norma Smith, May Vowles, Tom Vowles, Mattie Jones, Minnie Evans, Tom Thomas, Ernie Jones, Rhoslyn Morris;* front row: *Tom Vowles, Islwyn Jones, Gwyn Walters, Idwal Williams, Trevor Smith, Willie Evans.*

Members of the original Llangain Horticultural Show Committee admiring some entries, 1960s Left to right:
Tom Thomas, Gwyn Walters, I. J. Williams, Dilwyn Jones, Linda Jones, Milly Jones, Willie Evans, Islwyn Jones.

Produce at the Horticultural Show.

Arts and crafts at the Horticultural Show.

A visit to London by members of the Women's Institute, mid-1950s. Left to right: Eira Davies, Betty Evans
(Hendy), Dilys Davies, Muriel Harries (President), ?, Dorothy Davies, Morffydd Jones, Eiluned Harries, Nellie
Williams, Dilys Jones, Mollie Thomas, Betty Evans (Llwyn).

Members of Llangain WI admiring the ruby anniversary cake (1947–87). **Left to right:** *Lizzie Thomas, Nellie Williams, Dilys Davies, Dianne Davies, Margaret Heath, Olive Williams.*

The golden anniversary cake (inset, right), made by Diane Davies, Y Garreg Lwyd, being cut by Lizzie Thomas and Dilys Davies, to celebrate the 50th anniversary (1947–97) of Llangain WI.

capacity audience in 2004, with music provided by local boy Iwan Evans.

Horticultural Show

The Memorial hall committee was venturesome and soon after 1964 a group was formed to launch an annual Horticultural Show. It was successful for many years and after a lapse of a decade or so it was continued again in 9178. The show has been popular over the last thirty years, with competitors drawn from far and wide.

The Women's Institute

The Women's Institute movement originated in Canada in 1897. In 1915 the National Federation of Women's Institutes (NFWI) was founded in Britain, originally as part of the Agricultural Organisation Society (AOS). The first Institute was in Llanfairpwll, Anglesey. Individual Institutes are self-governing and are grouped into county federations which together make up the NFWI. The WI encourages women to participate in community life, cultural projects and public campaigns. The Anglesey Federation of Women's Institutes was formed in 1930 and has been known as the Gwynedd–Isle of Anglesey Federation since 1974.

The first meeting of the WI in Llangain was held on 21 October 1947 in the school. The President was Mrs Harries of Pilroath. In 1969 a banner was made by Mrs Margaret Bowen of Avoca. For the jubilee celebrations of the county in 1986, Mrs Marilyn Davies and Mrs Jean Davies were asked to design a tablecloth which also celebrated the 40th anniversary of the Institute in Llangain. The beautiful hand-embroidered cloth and the banner are proudly used on special occasions.

On 21 October 1997, the President, Mrs Vina Williams of Cnwc y Deri, welcomed members to the hall to celebrate the 50th anniversary of the Institute. During the evening a wonderful cake, made by Mrs Diane Davies of Garreglwyd, was cut by founder members Mrs Dilys Davies and Mrs Lizzie Thomas. The Institute, under the presidency of Mrs Maureen Roberts of Ael-y-Bryn, continues to play an active part in village activities and celebrated its diamond jubilee in 2007.

Sports and Recreation Association

This association provides and manages recreational facilities in the village. The association was formed in 1977 as a result of the success of Queen Elizabeth's silver jubilee celebrations. It incorporated arrangements for the horticultural show at the time, but a separate committee was formed a year later specifically to arrange the show.

Since the new school had been built on the old

The skate park established in memory of James Preece, 1986–2001.

school field it was necessary to make further arrangements for a new playing-field. This was done in conjunction with the Education Department of the Dyfed County Council and the Sports and Recreation Association on land purchased from Mr and Mrs Rhoslyn Morris of Beilisyfi.

The playing-fields are leased to Llangain Football Club, the tennis courts were leased to Llangain Tennis Club, and play equipment is provided for the use of the young. During the last few years the association has been active in raising funds in order to provide new, and update some of the existing, play equipment. To this end, an application to 'Play Wales' was submitted which successfully resulted in a grant of £2,500.

A skateboard park has been built in memory of James Preece, who tragically lost his life, aged 15, whilst cycling in the village in 2001. The funds were raised due to the generosity of the Queen Elizabeth Maridunum School, the family and friends of James Preece and the residents of Llangain, and with the financial support of Mr Mark James, Chief Executive of Carmarthenshire County Council.

The Committee has representatives from most of the village clubs and associations.

The Evergreen Club
(Originally the Llangain Old Age Pensioners' Welfare Association)

A committee was formed in 1963 and members met at Smyrna Chapel vestry. In 1973 the venue changed to the Church Hall and two years later to the

Llangain Football Club, 1994. Left to right, back row: *Michael Sizer, Geraint Davies, Julian Jones, Jason Thomas, Robert Smith, Philip Mead, Neil Vizard, Keith Owen, Richard Jupp, Keith Lewis (Manager);* front row: *Jamie Jones, Jeffrey Goldsmith, Steve Lee, Gary Bowen (Captain), Nicky Goldsmith, Simon Colvin, Matthew Lewis, Huw Smith.*

Memorial Hall. The club belonged to the National Federation of OAPs and representatives attended their AGMs in various parts of the UK. The Red Cross also subsidise two members each year on a week's holiday at 'The Rest' in Porthcawl. At present the membership remains at 30–40. Three trips are made each summer and members of neighbouring villages support them and there is also an annual Christmas dinner.

The Youth Club

There have been various youth clubs in the community over the years. Following a period of some 15 years when no active youth club existed in the village, the present club was formed in 2000 and is open to all young people of secondary-school age under the supervision of youth leaders provided by the Carmarthenshire County Council. Youngsters currently enjoy a very wide range of sporting and entertainment facilities.

The provision of these facilities has been made possible by the generous support of the community (both individuals and club associations), the Memorial Hall Committee, the Community Council and the National Lottery. Activities include basketball, football, table-tennis, badminton and pool, and there is a computer and a range of musical instruments. Being affiliated to the Welsh Youth Club Association, members have the opportunity to participate in the Duke of Edinburgh Award Scheme and to go to the Cardiff Ice Rink at Christmas for their annual 'Midnite Skate'.

The Football Club

There had been a football team on an informal basis

for a very brief period in the mid 1960s using Penycoed field on Church Road as a playing field, but Llangain Football Club was formed in the season of 1979/80 as a junior side in the Carmarthenshire League, under the guidance of Derek Davies (known as Big D), with Jean, his wife, as secretary. The captain of that side was Geraint (Skiff) Davies, who is still a player.

Senior football started during the 1981/82 season. The club captain, Gary Bowen, remained so until 1995 but was tragically killed in a road accident in 1996.

LLANGAIN FOOTBALL CLUB.

1995 TOUR LIMERICK

MATCH PROGRAMME

SATURDAY 22nd APRIL 1995

PIKE ROVERS v LLANGAIN F.C.

The match programme for Saturday 22 April, Pike Rovers v. Llangain FC, during Llangain Football Club's 1995 tour to Limerick, Ireland.

He had played a major part in the development of Llangain Football Club since the club had won promotion towards the mid-1990s.

The club has been developed over the years, with changing rooms and showers now part of an extension to the Memorial Hall. However, in 2006, due to individual commitments in a modern age, the team decided to disband on a healthy note while in the First Division of the Carmarthenshire League.

Kluids

A discussion group was formed in 1984 with a certain 'genius, philosopher and citizen extraordinary of the British Commonwealth of Nations and the Universe' as Archkluid!

They called themselves Knights of Llangain United In Discussion (Drinking!) Sessions. The group thrived until the new millennium, when Frank Evans, Archkluid, felt that it had run its course and suggested to fellow knights that it was better to finish with a bang rather than a whimper!

The following verse (sung to the tune ' The British Grenadier') is the first in a series of verses on individual members, while the second is about Frank, the Archkluid himself.

Some learned great societies
Academies and such
Have graced this land of ours,
But none have done so much
To lift the human spirit

And lift the human arm
As the noble crowd of people
Of Kluidian wit and charm.

We've Frank a fiddle maker,
Who plays the ivories
And talks of universal
Truths, facts and theories.
He'll paint a pretty picture,
Work wonders with a glass,
But these fade to oblivion
In sweet talk to a lass.

Gwilym Thomas

The Archkluid, Frank Evans – 'genius, philosopher and citizen extraordinary of the British Commonwealth of Nations!', who passed away in 2006, aged 94.

The Knights of Llangain United In Debate (KLUID) and their Shield of Wisdom, with the words 'Gair i'r Call' (A Word to the Wise). Left to right: Brian Evans, Brian Rowlands, Frank Evans (Archkluid), Jorge Pejsak, Nel Rees, Terry Painter, Colin McDonald, Judith Oxborrow, Cled Davies, ?, Mary McDonald, Judith Wright, Tony Wyke.

Tennis court opening, 1989. Left to right: ?, Marilyn Davies, Gaynor Thomas, Gerald Williams (BBC tennis commentator), Gill Thomas, Dot Jones, Gary Thomas.

Short Mat Bowls

Funds were raised in 1988 to buy equipment and a committee set about getting a grant. Over the years the club has had a healthy membership of about 20 and plays twice weekly. The club is affiliated to the Welsh Short Mat Bowls Association (WSMBA) and the Carmarthen and District Short Mat Bowls Association (CDSMBA) league. The members have also represented Wales in tournaments.

The Tennis Club

The tennis club was formed in 1989 after fund-raising and a grant from the Sports Council enabled two courts to be constructed on the recreation ground. The courts were opened on 1 April 1989 by top tennis commentator Gerald Williams. From 1993 to 2003 the club coach was Peris Williams who, working with the primary schoolchildren, introduced them to tennis by teaching them mini tennis in the Memorial Hall.

With the introduction of club nights, membership rose to over 30 juniors and 16 adults. Several juniors became Carmarthenshire Schools' champions and tournaments were held during the annual village Fun Days.

In 2004, when the club disbanded, the courts became the responsibility of the Sports and Recreation Association and were open for anyone in the village to play on.

Gerald Williams, the BBC tennis commentator, proudly showing a Llangain Tennis Club sweater, 1989.

Junior Rugby Football Training Club

The club was established by a few fathers, including Peter Jenkins, Ryan Davies, Fran Burson, Chris Thomas and Alan Jones, who were all keen to teach their sons the basic skills of rugby football. Initially the group met at the Memorial Hall, but the enthusiasm of the adults was soon reflected in the young-

Llangain Players' Cinderella, 2001. Left to right, back row: *Sian Stacey, Fiona Strong, Gethin Robinson, Vanessa Weaver, Judy Baxter, Glenys Altman, Annie Delahunty, Dean Richards, Glyn Robinson, Roger Van Praet, Mell Stacey, Simon Weaver, Dai Stacey, Patrick Thomas, Dawn Robinson, Kai Baxter, Roger Altman, Karen Richards, Becky Evans, Ian Richards, Alex Thomas, Gwyneth Evans;* middle row: *Bethan Delahunty, Gill Richards (director), Sian Van Praet, Linda Weaver;* front row: *Gwyn Stacey, Laura Evans, Andrew Richards, Carys Van Praet, Bethan Richards, Aron Altman, Rachel Baxter, Tomos Van Praet.*

Llangain Players millennium pantomime, Little Red Riding Hood, 2000. Left to right: *Sian Stacey, Andrew Richards, Bethan Richards, Tomos Van Praet, Gill Richards (director), Ethan Altman, Carys Van Praet, Gwyn Stacey.*

sters, who brought their friends to the weekly sessions, and resulted in a larger venue being found – the village soccer pitch in summer and the local leisure centre Astroturf in winter. The club now regularly meets throughout the year, with the adults funding the cost of hiring the Astroturf. Children of all ages are welcome. A formal committee was formed in 1994 with Dr Chris John, a local GP, as chairman, and Peter Jenkins as coach.

The club has held an annual event – the 'Fun Day' – since 1993, the objective being to give local families a day of entertainment. Various activities are held, including cricket, rugby and soccer matches, a tennis tournament and other events aimed principally at the youngsters. The day normally culminates in a sing-song around a bonfire.

Llangain Players

Following the success of *Red Riding Hood*, the millennium pantomime, a local amateur dramatic group was formed originally under the directorship of Mrs Gill Richards. Since then it has gone from strength to strength, with annual productions such as *Jack and the Beansatalk* and *Peter Pan* involving not only local people but those of neighbouring villages.

The Gardening Club

The Club caters for all types of gardeners, from beginners to specialists, all enjoying the varied programme, from in-house speakers to guest speakers and demonstrations. Throughout the year the members enjoy outings, social evenings and a village garden walk.

The Falklands

Carmarthen Journal, 13 August, 1982

Villagers turned out to give Mike Bowen, the 22-year-old son of Dave and Margaret Bowen of Avoca, Heol Smyrna, a hero's welcome return on Friday evening, 23 July. Michael had survived on HMS Broadsword *during the Battle of the Falklands. An informal gathering was held in the Pantydderwen. On Tuesday evening, 27 July, a formal sherry reception was given in the Memorial Hall in his honour. Mr Tom Vowles (himself an ex-Navy man) presided and referred to the kind of experiences that Michael had undergone over the past few months. Mr David Jones, Pantyddderwen, made the presentation of a silver engraved plaque and platinum fountain pens. Michael then proceeded to cut the highly decorated cake made by Mrs May Vowles of Glanygolau. A good night was enjoyed by all.*

The Woodlands Trust

The Woodland Trust, established in 1972, is the UK's leading woodland conservation charity. It has over 1,000 sites in its care, amounting to around 20,000 hectares (50,000 acres), and aims to conserve, restore and re-establish woodlands.

The Trust bought Green Castle Woods from Mr and Mrs Robinson in 1993. The target for the local public appeal was £20,000 and funding was also obtained from local authorities and various bodies while the trust committed the balance required from its other national fund-raising.

Green Castle Woods includes three separate semi-natural ancient woodlands and the meadows and areas of recently planted native woodland which separate them. Two of the woodlands are principally oak, the third is very variable, containing stands dominated by birch or ash, or alder and willow. The B4312 Carmarthen to Llansteffan road bisects the site. The Afon Tywi forms part of the northern boundary and is part of the Carmarthen Bay and Estuaries Site of Special Scientific Interest (it is now also designated a Special Area of Conservation and a European Marine Site).

Mike Bowen with proud and relieved parents, Dave and Margaret Bowen and sister Andrea at the Memorial Hall 'Welcome Home' reception.

Green Castle Woods information board in the Woodland Trust car park.

Fun Times

Scooter Time! The early 1960s, with Glanmor Davies-Evans (left) and Alcwyn Rogers (right), proud of their scooters, parked either side of the smart Ford Popular. The boy is little Chris, from neighbouring Danyrhiw.

The Bluebirds, 1963, Llangain's answer to the X factor! Playing at the Church Hall (now Neuadd Gain) are, left to right: *Gareth Williams (author's brother), Gwynfor Davies (Nathan the poet's son), Keith Soper, John Evans, Bernard Comey.*

Fun Times

New Years Fancy Dress, 1966. Left to right: Elwyn Thomas, Betty Thomas, Ann Jones, Eiry Thomas with a lamb and Corra the sheepdog, Eileen Jones, Mattie Jones, Newspaper Man, Huw Bowen.

New Years Fancy Dress, 1967. Left to right, back row: Haydn Williams, Aneurin Bowen, Gwenllian Walters, ?, Wendy Vowles, Anthony Harries; middle row: Jill Thomas, Gillian Davies, Eleri Jones (?), Rhoslyn Morris, Hefin Morris, Eleri Morris, Iona Morris; front row: ?, Clive Bignell, Wendy Bignell, Alan Davies, Michael Davies, Dorian Bowen, Colin Davies, David Davies, Tom Rogers. Minyrafon can be seen sitting by the back wall.

Fun Times

The carnival held to celebrate the investiture of HRH The Prince of Wales, July 1969. Left to right, foreground: Mattie Jones, Vernon Bignell, Barbara Gould, Dewi Evans, Eddie John, Marina Bignell.

At the investiture carnival, July 1969. Left to right: Wendy Bignell, Margaret James, Nigel Bowen.

Fun Times

The Punk Rockers' Float at the 1981 carnival. Left to right, back row: Geraint Davies, Hayley Evans, Robert Jones (baby), Gemma Jones, Julie Evans, Stuart Berry, Richard Thomas, Jayne Griffiths, Simon Evans, Ian Rowlands, Richard Griffiths; front row: Melaine Evans, Wendy Jones, Peter Evans, Geraint Davies (Brynderwen), Nicky Berry, Andrew Rowlands, Margaret Rowlands, Hazel Berry, Gareth Davies, Margaret Thomas.

Heave Ho! Carnival, 1981. Left to right: David 'shamby' Jones, Derek Thomas, Ian Brewer, Warren Berry, Gary Bowen, Ryan Davies.

Fun Times

Carnival Queen, 1981. **Left to right:** *Kay John (attendant), Donna Jones (Rose Queen), Eirwen Clement (attendant), Gail Thomas (Queen).*

Above: 'Off to the Royal Welsh Show', 1983 carnival. Left to right: *Jack Davies, Gillian Davies and Eiri Davies (in cow), Philip Morgan, Beryl Davies, Gwyneth Morgan.*

The donkey derby in the 1980s, with some dodgy men! Local characters include, **left to right:** *Derek Davies (Big D), Alan Waters, Ian Bowen, Gwyn Davies (Gwyn Fat).*

A dual in the Wild West! Wynford Jones and Ryan Davies fighting it out on the greasy pole in the silver jubilee carnival, 1977.

Left: *Carnival time, Summer 1981, in the presence of HRHs The Prince and Princess of Wales (Philip Williams and Alison Davies).*

Fun Times

A Christmas party in the Memorial Hall, 1989.

An impromptu summer's evening street party in the early 1990s, enjoyed by the residents of Maesyrawel, with music by Frank Evans on the piano through his open lounge window! Left to right: Marjorie Broadbent, Edwin Jones, Edith Davies, Val Beynon, Stephen Evans, Joyce Williams, Gwyneth Evans, Ken Bowen, Colin McDonald, ?, Alan Broadbent, Phyllis John.

Seeing double! It could have been the real 'Coronation Street' at Llangain Carnival when these 'regulars' of the Rovers Return rolled up for the day, 1970s. Left to right: Eleri Marks, Phyllis Morgan, Enor Davies, Ellis Davies, Beryl Davies, Lynwen Morgan, Glenys Jones, Gillian Davies, John Morgan.

Smyrna Sunday-school outing to Tenby, Summer 1982.

Left: Kevin Davies as Robin Hood and Lynne Davies as Gipsy Rose, Christmas 1979.

People of Llangain

Philip Williams (Getta's nephew), Margaretta Williams, Edward Jones (nephew), c.1942.

Mr & Mrs Henry Jones, Minyrafon and their grandsons. Left to right: Mrs Sarah Jones, Alcwyn Rogers, Peter Rogers, Henry Jones.

Margaretta Williams, Pantydderwen, 1950.

Left: 'Fred the Sticks' proudly displaying his craftsmanship, 2000.

Sporting Achievement

Rhys Gruffydd, Brandreth, British U16 Track Sprint Champion 1998, Welsh Junior Road Champion 1999 and Member of Great Britain Junior Cycling World Championship Squad 2000.

Below: *David Jones, Llys-yr-Haul, No. 3 Ger-y-Capel, running for Carmarthen Harriers in the Welsh 2000 Championship at Cwmbran Stadium and winning the U17 3,000m event. He was also Welsh Champion at U15, U17, U20 at cross country, road, track and indoor events 1999–2002, with international representation with the Great Britain and Northern Ireland Athletics Team and at the 95th World Junior Cross Country Championships in Dublin (2002). David was also Young Sportsman of the Year (Carmarthenshire, 2002).*

Modern Warfare

Above: *Sapper Simon Jenkins in Iraq, 2003.*

Left: *Warrant Officers Daniel Heath (Royal Signals) and Christopher Heath (REME) have seen active service in the Gulf War, Bosnia and Afghanistan.*

Postscript
Reflections on My Country Upbringing

As I write this final part of *The Book of Llangain* and tell my own story, I am intrinsically aware of how fortunate I have been having had such loving and conscientious parents who were always there for me. This coupled with a rural upbringing on a farm in such a beautiful part of the lower Tywi valley in the predominantly Welsh speaking county of Sir Gar in this little corner of Wales made it all the more idyllic.

Although both my parents were deeply rooted in agriculture within the county, my father was actually born in Ynyshir near Porth in the Rhondda (Fach) since the family had gone in search of employment at the beginning of the last century. After leaving school at 14 he returned to Carmarthenshire and entered service on farms in the Myddfai and Gwynfe area at the foot of the Mynydd Du (Black Mountain). The rest of his family returned soon after to farm Gelliglud in Whitemill, Carmarthen.

To be born into a community gives a sense of belonging from the moment one can first meet people and converse. I am the youngest of five children with some years between me and my four siblings - consisting of my brother and three sisters. They spent their early years in Glastryn but since the family then moved to Penycoed, I grew up there. I was one month premature and on arrival in this world the first thing that my mother did was to count and check I had all my fingers and toes.

Mairwen started her prenursing training at Ammanford and would catch the early bus to Carmarthen and another to her destination. (Convenient public transport was one of the reasons why my parents were keen to buy Penycoed.) In due course she gained her State Registered Nurse status and was awarded first prize in both Surgery and Medicine.

Einir went into Banking and worked at Barclays in Carmarthen and Gareth joined the Bancyfelin branch of R.S.Bird Ltd and was the company's top salesman a few times with holidays abroad as a reward. Hilda went into administration and performed secretarial and accounts duties initially at Kingsburys in Carmarthen.

So they were all allowed to follow their own vocations and interests without any pressure to take over the farm. My father was once asked if I had any interest in farming. He smiled gently and replied emphatically that I was in the world of books - 'yn byd y llyfrau ma'hwn!' and didn't expect me to become a farmer.

Penycoed in its beautiful setting in a small valley and perched 'above the woods' with its long, meandering and clear stream did provide an idyllic location for a happy and carefree childhood. It was an average sized dairy farm for those days consisting of around 60 acres spread over eight fields with simple but effective meanings, mostly indicating the geographical location of the fields in relation to the farmhouse. 'Cae tu ol ty' (behind the house), for example, was the field leading up and away from the house parallel to Penycoed hill with another field beyond giving a panoramic view of Carmarthen and the upper Tywi valley. These now belong to Hafodwen farm on the outskirts of Johnstown. 'Cae dan ty' (below the house) was the meadow by the corner and leading to the junction at Church Road. The field with Smyrna perched at the top was known as 'cae dan capel'!

When my parents bought the farm for around £4,000 some fifty years ago, it needed a huge amount of work done to it as a whole. Many potential buyers walked away. I often overheard Mam telling visitors that Dad having cut the hedges and cleared certain areas of the farm by hand, burnt the mountains of trash for a fortnight and that was no exaggeration! The large field the other side of the main road between the two crossroads (now Coedmor and Dol-y-Dderwen) was originally three small meadows as was the field behind the present Coedmor Avenue, Brynteg and the land beyond. The six fields were rearranged into two workable fields. In the process, a huge prehistoric stone known as a Cromlech or Dolmen was discovered in some undergrowth and is now located inside the garden gate at Coedmor. Later, it was to serve as an ideal milk stand for our daily delivery to the future home. No ordinary farmer would have relished such pain staking work!

The outbuildings were spruced up with whitewash and all windows and doors painted in regency green as opposed to the usual bright red. This work was always team work with Mam throwing herself into the project whole heartedly and when it came to painting the top windows of the farmhouse she was up there and getting on with it. Many a motorist driving along the main road nearby, narrowly avoided an accident when spotting a woman on top of the ladder - a rare sight!

The farm was one huge adventure land with the outbuildings providing numerous places to explore and play games such as 'hide and seek' and 'cowboys and indians' when my friends visited. The stream below the farmyard comprises of several springs that run down from the land across the main road and into Penycoed lane and is a proper stream before entering the woods. This provided me with another but completely different dimension to playtime.

Watching and observing the wildlife was fascinating. Catching tadpoles in jam jars became an annual event for several years and witnessing the gradual metamorphosis from tiny tadpoles into frogs in large preserving jars was a perfect nature lesson at first hand experience. Identifying wild flowers and pressing them into an exercise book was another pastime. The hedges around the farm had wild flowers in abundance with the well known fox gloves being a popular and an easy species to recognise.

The 1960s was the decade when the Beatles made a revolutionary impact on the pop world and I remember having Beatle haircuts and impersonating them by pretending to play the guitar. I was having piano lessons with Mrs Gilbody in Carmarthen but I'm afraid that eventually practicing the piano became too much like donkey work. Another pastime was to 'dress up' as various personalities such as a vicar and play church or chapel, which amused the family.

My parents were adventurous and took the risk of arranging a herd of Ayrshire cows to be brought down from Scotland without seeing them beforehand. Ayrshire cows are beautiful creatures with a fine bone structure and are good milkers and this turned out to be very true of the ones that arrived on the farmyard. Another cowshed had been built for the purpose and called 'Beudy Mawr' since 'Beudy Bach' was alongside giving a 'Little and Large' set up! Mr Bird from St Clears erected the new building. Incidentally, we miraculously escaped the nightmare of the Foot and Mouth epidemic of 1967 which crossed over the farm twice and affected neighbouring farms.

We had a new large wooden poultry shed built and it housed dozens of healthy chickens that laid beautiful free range eggs as a result of roaming free in the open air. (The redundant mobile henhouse, by the way, soon became my den!) Mam loved her chickens and had a good knowledge of the various breeds. But I remember her saying how upset she was once when she woke up one morning in Glasfryn to discover the small shed in the meadow behind the farmhouse containing newly born chicks had been burnt completely overnight when an oil incubator went on fire and she could only find the tiny skeletons left amongst the ashes - a harrowing sight.

A frequent, natural and essential sight at the other end of the life cycle of course, would be to see Mam killing a hen for Sunday lunch. This was done by placing a knife to the rear of the mouth and slitting its throat, completely bleeding it by holding it upside down for a while and then plucking it naked.

People would create their own fun in those days

and not least children who knew how to amuse and entertain themselves. Dad built me a wooden go-cart with proper sides and a raised plank as a seat. It even had battery operated indicators. I use to load empty cardboard packets of groceries such as Daz washing powder and similar items and imagined I had consumers on my grocery round which was from the farm to the junction, up the main road, along Heol Smyrna and back down the hill with stops at convenient field gates. Far less traffic existed in the Sixties!

One of my favourite memories of my childhood days was the social gathering on Saturday nights when friends from neighbouring farms would gather to see films. In particular I remember my sisters' and my brother's friends such as Victor and Gerald Davies of Dolaumeinion and the Hesford children from Tawelfryn and the boys of Plas Isaf (Cefnglas).

Hired films would be shown on a screen above the settle hung on the back wall between the kitchen and the pantry. On one occasion I remember how Victor tied my mother's apron strings to the Aga rail in the corner just inside the back door. When it came to half time and Mam was about to fetch the refreshments, her apron strings remained tied to the rail as she went forward. Roars of laughter of course as she reacted to the prank.

Those evenings became television nights when we were the first to buy a black and white set in the immediate vicinity. They were great nights too since the whole phenomenon of watching programmes such as the London Palladium and Coronation Street 'on the box' was fascinating. But as more families acquired a set, the numbers dwindled and viewing became family based.

A raised storage space along a length of a barn wall provided an ideal platform for our little and informal childrens' concerts. The individual items which included songs, recitations and poems along with short sketches and jokes would be performed by a small group of us consisting of old friends as well as some 'new kids on the block' such as Andrea and Michael Bowen, Gillian and Raymond Smith and Roger Thomas.

Our regular audiences would be small but included some VIPs - none other than the future Dean of St David's Cathedral, namely, the Very Revd Dr Gordon MacWilliam. He became affectionately known as 'Dr Mac.' in the locality. The MacWilliams were new residents living at the top of 'Cae pen ty' in Heol Smyrna. On moving day to their new home called Pen Parc in 1964, their son, Andrew was far more concerned with getting to my birthday party than helping his parents to unpack. Having jumped over the new boundary, he was down in the farmhouse within seconds.

My parents started selling building plots in the early 1960s and it was very pleasant to meet all the new people who came to the farmhouse especially the ones that brought me chewy toffees! Having completed business, my father would ask them whether they were church or chapel since almost everyone were affiliated to a place of worship in those days. The same social question would be irrelevant today. Nevertheless I reckon asking newcomers whether they are mere residents or active villagers would be a secular equivalent nowadays!!

Mr Evans of Cefnmeusydd was a mobile grocer and I remember going on some of his daily rounds both within and outside the county. Our area grocer, however, was Mr Howells from Llanybri who called on Tuesdays and announced his arrival by knocking on the back door, opened the door slightly and shouted 'grocer' in his own distinctive way. Monday evenings were reserved for Mr Tom Rogers from the Post Office at Minyrafon who was an egg and butter merchant. There had been a little shop at Brynmor in Morfa Bach before my time which was kept by a Myfanwy Thomas (Eirian Hesford's aunt).

The tuck shop I remember well was at Haulfryn near Smyrna crossroads. Bess Stewart who had a disabled arm sold sweets, cigarettes and Sunday papers. She was born in the now disappeared cottage called Danybanc (below Penycoed double bend). I remember being told of another cottage called Porth y Cliniau that once existed along Ystradwalter lane.

As I became older I had to earn my pocket money. Little tasks on a Saturday morning earned me 2/6d (12 1/2 new pence) which involved cleaning the small goose pen and the 'lloc lloi '(calfpen) along with one or two other duties. The geese lived alongside the pig sty which was south facing and therefore allowing the pigs to bask in the afternoon sun and where they wallowed in the mud and the 'lloc lloi' (calf pen) which was at the pine end of the barn and stable block.

I was afraid of the geese since they would chase me up the yard with their outstretched necks and noise on an all out attack on the intruder. I used to have the last laugh, however, when I would reach the path which led up to the house and close the small gate behind me. After their ritual attack or threat in defence of their territory and a settling period of a few minutes I was able to retrace my steps and get on with the job in hand which was to remove the stale and soiled straw.

A similar job awaited me in the calf pen but the reception was a complete contrast. The cute calves were friendly and sometimes over welcoming especially when they would drivel all over my clothes but it was fun. I remember making a certain mix with milk for them as food. It smelt inviting and I was often tempted to drink some of it but common sense prevailed. But curiosity, however, got the better of me once, when I ate some cattle cake but it was soon spat out!

Along with cows, pigs, geese, chickens, cats and dogs we had a horse and a donkey. I remember one mid winter's night when it had been snowing and I was most concerned about a recently born foal which I called 'Prince'. Obviously they were not in any danger from the snow storm or my father would have fetched them in and they were seeking natural shelter up on the field overlooking the town. I was not satisfied and pestered Dad until we both went up to bring mother and foal into the stable for the night. Our donkey provided hilarious times and even Carlo, the sheepdog was placed on its back to enjoy a ride.

The annual 'Casglu Celennig' is an old custom whereby those who visit homes to wish people a Happy New Year by singing an appropriate verse are duly given a monetary reward if you called before midday.

Blwyddyn Newydd Dda i chi
Ac i bawb sydd yn y ty
Codwch yn fore, cynnwch y tan
Ewch i'r ffynnon i ol dwr glan.

My round would take me from the farm, calling firstly with Mamgu at Pantydderwen then onto Maesyrawel, the Vicarage, Chweched, Llwyn, down the back road to Danyrhiw, Islwyn, Belmont and Ty Isaf. Then on to the Post Office at Minyrafon and Y Glyn, Ty Canol and the Morfa Bach area. I would then make my return journey via the main road and call with Miss Myra and her father at Llwyndu. (Years later the visits would be singing carols and drinking a glass of port or two!). Then the last stretch towards Smyrna and if before noon would involve calling at Brynderi, Cartref and Haulfryn for good measure!

The farm in general always seemed to be bustling with various activities between everybody, with many friends calling with us not least some of my siblings' partners. I remember some of the older lads like Ieuan Hesford scrambling on bikes through the woods below the farmhouse on a few occasions. Seeing some of my sisters and others learning to drive in an old car in the field below the bungalows was another sight to behold.

My driving aim was modest in comparison which was to learn to ride a full sized bike. Wendy of the Forlan taught me. Practice runs were from the gentle hill above the cottage and as far as Cefnglas. After perseverance on my part and patience on hers I succeeded. I borrowed her bike to ride home for supper. On arriving home, Mam asked how I appeared as if out of nowhere since only seconds later she had looked up Penycoed hill and hadn't seen me walking down. Of course, I had taken no time to do the run.

Haymaking was great fun especially when the round bales gave us the props for den making. Then we would ride high on top of the cart back to the 'rhydlan' where the elevator would take the bales high towards the shed roof. There was some help from family friends and the suppers afterwards were real social events and the occasional glass of cider was challenging.

But soon Dad developed an allergic disease called 'Farmer's Lung' where the dust from moldy hay affects the lungs. It's similar to pneumoconiosis in mining. He was advised to switch to silage to alleviate the severity of the condition. This he did and soon we had silos built alongside the hay barns.

Silage making brought similar fun for me and friends in the form of larking around in the carts as the grass was blown in to a certain level before climbing out and hanging on the back with feet on a bar below the main carriage. They were care free days!

Farmers are very tied to their work and are unable to have proper holidays. But we had a caravan in Kiln Park near Tenby and Mam would take some of us down there when circumstances allowed a short break. Otherwise any leisure would have to be be in the form of day visits.

Besides day visits to beaches like Pendine or Saundersfoot, I was lucky enough to be taken to see different castles, churches and chapels throughout the three counties which became Dyfed. Then there was a trip to see the newly opened Severn Bridge in the autumn of 1966. But above all, I fondly remember visits to North Wales to attractions like Beddgelert to pursue the well known legend of Llywelyn the Great, Prince of Gwynedd and Gelert his faithful hound. On another occasion I was taken to see Caernarfon soon after the investiture of the Prince of Wales in 1969 and remember the splendour and the enormity of such a castle. Having had our picnic before arriving, only a mere soft ice cream each was needed to set us homeward on a journey which had taken us from coast to coast, the length of Wales and all between two milkings - what a tremendous effort!

My other 'holidays' would be short stays withy my Mamgu and great aunt Getta at Pantydderwen - all quarter a mile away! Every other day, so I'm told, I would pop home to check that Dad and Mam were alright. Concern settled, I would return.

There was a long, neat vegetable and flower garden with an old pig sty under the sycamore tree at the highest point on the hill. I would pick some flowers from there on my way to school when it was my turn to take flowers for the small classroom. Below the cottage was some grass area, a clothes line and a path surfaced with burnt ashes from the open fires providing a solid surface under foot leading to a garden shed made of zinc sheeting.

We would walk some lanes nearby including the one to the crossroads which had a hedge either side with plenty of elder flower. She was good at making home made wine. I now realise how potent it must have been and not surprised that I was only given one glass! Pantydderwen was a watering hole even in those days!

Aunt Getta was crippled with rheumatoid arthritis and suffered greatly and after some years was confined to the front parlour before having to be admitted to Argel residential home in Johnstown. My bedroom was the small room whose window is above the porch. Then after Getta's passing I use to sleep in her bedroom which was to the left as one looks at the cottage.

Mamgu would reminisce about the old days as we sat by the open fire. It was there I was to record some of her memories when I became a student. A good evening would involve playing 'snakes and ladders' and 'draughts' which she was too good at playing for my liking!

Despite my busy childhood, I did attend the local school! A Miss Davies from Llandysul taught me followed by Miss Evans (later Mrs Williams) in the small classroom. I escaped the stern reign of Sam Rees and was taught by Islwyn Jones. I thoroughly enjoyed school with him as schoolmaster. He was encouraging, innovative and pleasant with it. He once told my parents during a visit to the farm that he was amused with the speed I wrote with my left hand in class times were changing which allowed the child to learn to write using either hand. Life was pleasant for us pupils. The location was perfect on a hill overlooking the parish with a school field alongside - a rare commodity in the 1960s. The field was well used particularly at play times in the summer as well as the weekly game of rounders and the annual sports day.

I was fascinated with the large map of Wales that Mr Jones had painted to scale one summer holiday on the boys' yard at the back of the school. It was something different, unique and very special. Pity that it's no longer there!

Mr Jones introduced lessons which involved the use of the school radio set. The BBC was beginning to broadcast programmes for all ages and covering a range of topics and they were exciting. He also introduced basketry which went down a treat and I still have certain handmade items I produced such as a small bin and a round plate size container to place something on. He arranged library shelves along the back of the classroom for extra reading.

It's funny how one remembers certain school furniture or artefacts. There was a large school clock above the door leading to the cloakroom inside the girls' yard. I believe that the hand bell used in the new school at present is the very one used when I was there. There was also a big globe of the world that whirled around with a dry screech if given a fly spin in the passing!

Dinners supplied in containers delivered from County Hall terminated when the new Memorial Hall opened. Mrs Thomas of Ty Canol was able to excel herself now by cooking everything on site in the purpose built kitchen at the hall. Orderly lines of pupils could be seen going from school after midday, across the road to the front of I Maesyrawel and proceed towards the back door of the hall. Everyone would wipe their feet on the sunken coconut mat, hang their coats and went to sit down by the tables in the back stage area. Dinner monitors would then give out the cutlery, water jugs and beakers before settling down to enjoy the cook's special dinner and pudding.

Milk was delivered from the Gilfach Farm and it was Jersey cow's milk which I found far too rich and unpalatable. I often felt nausea and would end up retching - an unsavoury school memory!

There were annual visits from a blind piano tuner from Abergwili and we would in turn meet him off the bus at the crossroads. Such experiences while conducting our duties were a sober reminder of how lucky we were to be able to see all around us every second of every minute of every hour each day. He was a quiet, pleasant man who was grateful for every gesture of help and respect.

The 11+ came round and exams were taken in the small classroom over two whole days. A11 visual aids and facts displayed on the walls were hidden by large sheets of white paper. Eventually on learning that I had passed to the Boys Grammar School, I decided I didn't want to go. The couple of years previously had seen some girls going to the 'Girls' Gram' and others to its neighbour, Ystrad Tywi secondary school but no boys had passed to the school in town.

I stuck to my guns overnight but on learning from the cook the following morning that Anthony Harries of Y Glyn had passed I changed my mind immediately. Anthony had gone to a local private school in Quay Street for a while and I had lost touch with him temporarily. Things were fine again and Mr Jones, the head was appropriately proud and relieved that a place at the 'Gram' was not wasted.

The journey to the new school was on a double decker bus. There were clear views of the countryside including Mr Wyke's neat garden on a slight slope at Green Castle and going through the natural tunnel of overhanging trees after the corner was fun but also scary because of the noise of some light branches scratching the bus roof.

Further on there was a dip in the road and a narrow bridge over Nant Pwntan with Danybont below. Some years later, the school bus was in collision with a cement lorry which caused both vehicles to lean over slightly. No one was hurt and soon after a road improvement scheme took place which is the way it is today.

There were some fantastic characters teaching at the Queen Elizabeth Boys Grammar School. Teachers like D.J. Evans, the Deputy Head, Matthew Rees and Wyn Jenkins who left an indelible impression but not least my R.I. teacher, namely the Revd Glyndwr Walker who had such an influence on me and as a result I pursued the subject to degree level and later as an undergraduate, my mentor was Dr MacWilliam or Dr Mac.as he was best known.

Besides the usual daily chores both within the farmhouse and helping on the farm such as milking time there were designated days when housewives did certain tasks. Mam did the washing for the seven of us on Mondays and the ironing was done on Tuesdays. Wednesdays were market days while Thursdays and Fridays were spent cleaning the farmhouse and doing other chores. Saturday mornings were spent shopping while the afternoons involved preparing vegetables for Sundays.

Sundays revolved around the church and chapeL My brother and sisters had attended Smyrna along with our parents for several years and I can recall attending special occasions and Sunday school Christmas parties when a small boy. But my siblings were friendly with the Wyke children, for example who happened to be church going and so they started going along with them. Anyway, Mamgu was a faithful church member and along with the encouragement by Mrs Thomas, wife of 'Ficer bach', they were confirmed.

It was only natural for me, therefore, to follow suit and when the time came for my rite of passage, I was confirmed along with some contemporaries at St Peter's Church, Carmarthen. There were many families within the community that did a 'mix and match' when it came to religion in those days. But I am very conscious of my church and chapel background and will always respect both denominations.

As I grew up I became more involved with the church. Initially this was by attending Sunday School which had two or three classes and the occasional Matins or Evensong. During the hardest weeks of winter, D.S Lewis, the vicar would hold the classes at the vicarage. Not even the enormous snow drifts of 1963 stopped me though from knocking at the vicarage door and asking if there was Sunday School. I received a welcoming smile and a reassuring answer that there would be the following week.

Then as I went through my teenage years I started taking part in services by reading the lessons and serving at the altar. The vicar at this time was A.J Jones, Llangynog since both parishes had amalgamated - a sign of changing times! The Revd.Albert John Jones was a real country pastor with fishing and shooting as pastimes. He was an interesting character with an amazingly strong voice and on one occasion his singing in Russian resounded through the farmhouse and was captured on my small cassette recorder, the ipod of the day.

Weddings were great social occasions and the community turned out to see the bride making her way to join her lover in holy matrimony. It was a custom to hold a rope across the lane in Church Road to stop the wedding entourage and coins had to be thrown out of the vehicles to assure easy passage.

My sisters experienced such customary delays in the 1960s.

Alongside those work hard, play hard family days, came sad and anxious times. The switching from haymaking to silage harvesting was not doing the trick. Dad's 'Farmer's Lung' condition worsened during winters. But things were to get worse.

Mam was admitted to Priory Street hospital in 1967 for a routine gall bladder removal. As it turned out, the procedure should have been much sooner because she had suffered for some time. She developed yellow jaundice and when the wound burst open on a Sunday she was rushed down to theatre. Septicemia set in and her condition worsened. The following day, the family were called in and I was fetched from school.

I remember it all vividly. It was the final week of term after the end of year exams. Gareth came to fetch me in the Vauxhall 101, the family car and Miss Tew, the school secretary brought him along to the music room where I was in class with Gerwyn Thomas. I was dismissed and we went to Mam's bedside.

As I made my way along the corridor it became increasingly clear that there was something dreadfully wrong since all three of my sisters were upset outside the ward. Mam was surrounded with tubes and other surgical apparatus. Dad asked if I had any results and I replied that I had had 87% in French with Ken Davies. He told me to tell her. I went nearer, held her hand and softly relayed my result. Mam was obviously weak and very ill but conjured up enough strength to tap my hand with a finger to indicate that she had understood and was aware of my presence. I sometimes think whether that exchange was a turning point in her dreadful ordeal.

Over the coming weeks Mam agonisingly slowly but most surely pulled back from the brink of death and made a good recovery and came home towards the end of that summer holiday. The sitting room at the front of the house became a bedsit for a while while she gained enough strength to climb the stairs. There was no welcome home in the whole world like that homecoming that summer.

During the following winter it appeared that switching to silage making had not improved Dad's health because he had become a weak and gaunt figure. My parents had no choice but to give up farming, sell the farm and semi retire to a purpose built bungalow on our own land opposite Pantydderwen in 196X. They retained some acreage in the form of two fields by Coedmor. Dad went to work in the Farmer's Co-op alongside the Quay at Carmarthen and then as porter at Trinity College.

Coedmor began a brand new chapter in our lives.

The large plot of about a third of an acre had sumptuous views up the Tywi valley and offered plenty of scope for landscaping. All three of us had our own responsibilities when it came to maintaining the grounds. Generally speaking, our Friday evenings in the summer involved Dad seeing to the vegetable garden while Mam looked after all the flower borders including the endless weeding while I took on mowing duties.

As I advanced through my teen years towards young adulthood, I became more involved in village life and with the church in particular. The vicar encouraged my interest in ecclesiastical matters and taught me and other potential choir members to chant the most prominent parts of the Liturgy. The Easter service, 1971 was unique in as much that Llangain Church saw a robed choir processing to the stalls in the chancel for the first time in its history. Two pews had been removed at the back of the nave to accommodate a choir vestry.

Mrs Jones had taken measurements of us to have robes but due to the lapse of time in making final arrangements, we had grown and the robes were significantly shorter on some choristers, blatantly displaying their bell bottom trousers. Although a bit of a shame, it was very funny.

When the Revd Victor Jones followed his brother, 'AJ' as Parish Vicar, I was given responsibility to oversee the choir and I introduced the Festival of Nine Lessons and Carols at Christmas. This progressed to taking services including addresses.

A major church restoration programme took place over a period of eighteen months between 1978-79 during which weekly services took place in the Church Hall. I vividly remember the moving reopening and dedication service just under thirty years ago where the church was full to capacity in the presence of the Bishop. The driving force behind the entire work was 'Vic' the Vicar and parishioners were delighted when he was suitably rewarded by being made a Canon of St. David's Cathedral soon after. They were wonderful times.

The Memorial Hall was still in its infancy and various committees were sprouting up and along with the two places of worship and the school, fund raising seemed endless in the growing community which was gradually taking the shape of a village. But my bike proved useful to cycle throughout the parish selling raffle tickets in pursuing such goals.

Leisure and play times centred a great deal around the Harries family in the Glyn. Anthony and his brothers, Timothy, Robert and Huw would arrange disco nights for friends in an outside shed.

Bibliography

Lloyd, J.E., *History of Carmarthenshire* (Vols I & II, 1935, 1939)

Lewis, Samuel, *Topographical Dictionary of Wales 1838*

Nicholas, T., *The Annals and Antiquities of the Counties and County Families of Wales*, 1872

Kelly's Directory of Monmouthshire and South Wales, 1906

Jones, Francis, *Annals of an Old Manor House: Green Castle* (The Carmarthenshire Antiquary)

James, Terrence, *Shipping and the River Towy: Problems of Navigation* (The Carmarthenshire Antiquary)

Maps of the Estate of Fred Bludworth, 1779

Churchwardens' Presentments, 1684, 1790

Church Records

Carmarthen Journal

The Welshman

Evans, Hopkin, *Eglwysi Cylch Llansteffan* (Llawllyfr Undeb Caerfyrddin a'r Cylch)

School Log-books

Jones, Francis, *Historic Carmarthenshire Homes and their Families* (1987)

Various Property Sale Catalogues

Parish Council Records

Subscribers

Roger and Glenys Altman

Mairwen and Carl Atkins, Llangain, Carmarthen

Bethan, Cwmllyfri, Llanybri

John Bevan, Llangain, Carmarthen

Ian, Val and Poppy Bowen, Beeches, Llangain

Michael A. Cox, Llangain

Mr Geraint L. Davies

Mr Arwyn Davies

Mr and Mrs Brian Davis and family, Blaencwm,
    Llangain

Mrs Wendy Day, Pencader

Ann Delahunty, Llangain

Gillian M. Edwards, Rhydargaeau, Carmarthen

Lynda England, Penarth, Cardiff

Ellis and Barbara Evans, Llangain

Gareth and Anne Evans, Fferm Cwrthir

Griffith Evans, Llantrisant

Mr Myrddin Ford, Meidrim

Rhys Ieuan Freeman, Llangain

Olivia Angharad Freeman, Llangain

Catherine George, Ger y Capel, Llangain

Miss Maggie Howells, Llangain

Megan John, Coedmor, Llangain

Mrs Phylis M. John

Mr Stephen W. John, Llangynnog

Dr Chris John, Pengelli Isaf, Llangain

Jonathan Jones, Llangain

Dr Dilwyn Jones, Aberystwyth

Roger A. Jones, Llangain, Carmarthen

David Jones, Llangain

Euros Jones, Waterloo Terrace, Carmarthen

Elvira Jones, Furnace Road, Carmarthen

Iona E. Jones (née Morris), Carmarthen

Mrs Anne Jones and Mr Howard Jones, Llangain

Ysgol Llangain

Llety'r Neuadd, Llangain

Llyfrgell Genedlaethol Cymru, Aberystwyth

Mrs Dilys Longden, Llanllwch, Carmarthen

The Very Rev. Dr G. MacWilliam, Llangain

Alice L. Mellows, Port Talbot

Mr R. and Mrs A.L. Morgans, Llangain

Rhiannon M. Morris (née Davies), Llangain

Edward S. Page, Llangain, Carmarthen

Miss Eiluned Rees, Llansteffan

Eddie and Maureen Roberts

Hazel Speller, Dinas Powys, Cardiff

Ceridwen Stringer, Kidwelly, Carms

Barry T. Taylor, Llangain, Carmarthen

Gwilym Thomas, Brynteg, Llangain

Beryl Thomas, 1 Isfryn, Llangynog

Lloyd and Eunice Thomas, Johnstown, Carmarthen

Trinity College, Carmarthen

Nesta K. Vizard, Llangain, Carmarthen

John F.W. Walling, Newton Abbot, Devon

G. Lilian Ward, Llangain, Carmarthen

R. Eleri Waters (née Morris), Llangynog

Peris and Vina Williams, Cnwc Y Deri, Llangain

Allan Wynne Jones, Hengwrt, Machynlleth, Powys